The Last Stuart Queen: Louise, Countess Of Albany: Her Life & Letters...

Herbert Millingchamp Vaughan

THE LAST STUART QUEEN

THE LAST STUART QUEEN: LOUISE COUNTESS OF ALBANY: HER LIFE & LETTERS BY HERBERT M. VAUGHAN, F.S.A.

NEW YORK
BRENTANO'S
1911

PRINTED IN GREAT BRITAIN
BY BALLANTYNE & COMPANY LTD
LONDON

AD MEMORIAM
F. E.
AMICI AMICORUM

Florentiae MDCCCCX

CONTENTS

CONTENTS

CONTENTS

CONTENTS

Contents

CHAPTER XIV. "QUEEN OF FLORENCE."
(1803–1823)

CHAPTER XV. UGO FOSCOLO.
(1812–1816)

CHAPTER XVI. DEATH OF THE LAST STUART QUEEN.
(1824)

xi

ILLUSTRATIONS

xiii

INTRODUCTION

THE life of Louise, Princess of Stolberg-Gedern, wife of
Prince Charles-Edward Stuart, but commonly known as
the Countess of Albany, may conveniently be divided
into three well-defined periods. First, the years extending from the date of her marriage in 1772 with the British
Pretender until her legal separation from him in 1784;
and covering the whole of her relations with Charles and
Henry Stuart, as well as the early phases of her celebrated
romance with the poet Vittorio Alfieri. Second, her close
companionship with Count Vittorio Alfieri from her legal
separation until the poet's death in 1803; a period in her
life wherewith the generality of people is not so familiar
as with the earlier portion dealing with the Stuarts.
Third, her twenty years' residence in Florence as the
mistress of a *salon* which had an European notoriety,
constituting the last and least interesting part of her
career. The following work makes the attempt to give a
brief but succinct account of all three periods, whilst carefully refusing to stray from the central figure of the
Countess of Albany into diverging paths or into extraneous
episodes that are only remotely connected with the chosen
subject of this biography—an error into which one at
least of her leading biographers has most certainly fallen.

The earliest published biography of the Countess of
Albany is *Die Gräfin von Albany*—a work that will always
retain its foremost place—by Baron Alfred von Reumont,
a Prussian diplomatist at the Grand-Ducal Court of
Florence and the leading Continental authority on the
exiled Royal Stuarts in Italy. This book, together with
a most [valuable] Appendix of original documents in

English, French, and Italian, drawn from the most varied sources, was published at Berlin in 1860, and it has never been translated into English. Reumont's biography, which in spite of its undoubted merits is somewhat too digressive in its scope and character, was followed by three studies of the Countess from the pen of Monsieur St. Réné Taillandier in the *Revue des Deux Mondes* (1861), which taken together form a tolerable monograph, although Reumont, on whose work these studies were admittedly based, complains in his essay, *Gli Ultimi Stuardi*, of the Frenchman's plagiarism ; whilst the sympathetic pages on the Countess contained in the *Nouveaux Lundis* by Monsieur de Sainte-Beuve were again mere literary comments on Taillandier's biography. The first English writer to introduce the personality of the Countess of Albany to English readers was " Vernon Lee," whose brilliant study published in 1884 aims little at originality, although her discovery of the curious love-letters at Siena and their partial quotation give an additional value to her work. No other biography of the Countess has succeeded " Vernon Lee's " book, issued a quarter of a century ago, unless we choose to accept as such the interesting and sympathetic, perhaps over-sympathetic, account afforded us by Marchesa Vitelleschi in the second volume of her delightful work, *A Court in Exile*, published in 1903, the year of the Alfieri centenary.

This centenary naturally gave birth to a numerous progeny of books, great and small, on the famous Italian poet and patriot, and it was inevitable on such an occasion that his " Egeria," his " Donna Amata," should come in for her share of public attention, and also of an ample criticism, which, generally speaking, was anything but favourable, as the many allusions contained in this volume will demonstrate. There exists of course, a vast number of articles and studies in the Italian learned reviews concerning the Countess of Albany, especially in regard to her relations with Alfieri, but so far no important biography has been published in Italian, although von Reu-

xvi

mont's work was translated soon after its appearance by
Signore Cossilla.

The private letters of the Countess, who was an
indefatigable correspondent, have been edited in certain
cases by French and Italian writers, notably in recent
years by Monsieur Pélissier. I have purposely included a
considerable number of these letters in the present volume,
and in particular a selection from her correspondence with
Signora Teresa Mocenni of Siena and with Ugo Foscolo
the poet, since they in particular serve to throw a clear,
and in some instances a new light upon the personality
of the writer. In spite, however, of the valuable efforts
in this direction undertaken by Monsieur Pélissier,
Professor Calligaris, Signor Antona-Traversi and many
others, whole *carteggi* or masses of correspondence of the
Countess still remain unpublished, although they have
been perused and utilised by various authors. This pile
of known but unpublished manuscript includes eighty
letters to the Arch-priest Ansano Luti of Siena, sent
between the date of Teresa Mocenni's death in 1802 and
that of the Arch-priest in 1807 ; fifty-two letters to the
Cavaliere Alessandro Cerretani of Siena, written between
1807 and 1815 ; and about forty letters included amongst
the Stuart MSS. in the British Museum, which, though
unpublished *in toto*, have been largely drawn upon by
Reumont and by various English writers. The earliest
of her private letters extant and published are those
directed to Carl-Victor Bonstetten in 1774–5, included
by Monsieur Pélissier in his *Lettres et Ecrits divers de la
Comtesse d'Albany* (Paris, Émile Paul, 1902), wherein the
defective education of the lady at this period is very
fully exhibited.

The letters addressed to Henry Stuart, Cardinal of
York, between 1780 and 1784 show a considerable advance
and improvement both in grammar and style, due perhaps
to Alfieri's early literary influence. The five remarkable
love-letters directed to Francesco Gori, Alfieri's chosen
friend, date from the autumn of 1783, and are couched in

b   xvii

tolerable Italian, whereas almost the whole of her correspondence was usually conducted in French. Of her innumerable letters to Alfieri himself scarcely a line remains, all of them having been purposely destroyed either by Alfieri, by the Countess, by Fabre, or by Fabre's executor. By far the most important of the various published *carteggi* is that addressed jointly to Madame Teresa Mocenni and the Arch-priest Luti at Siena between 1797 and 1802, which has been most ably edited and published by Monsieur Léon-G. Pélissier (Paris, A. Fontemoing, 1904). Next perhaps in interest ranks the shorter correspondence with Ugo Foscolo, edited by Signore Antona-Traversi so long ago as 1887. From both these volumes we have drawn freely in this present work. Although, perhaps, quantities of unpublished letters of the Countess are still in existence, it is pretty certain that what remains wholly unknown cannot equal in interest or value these two sets of letters to Teresa Mocenni and to Ugo Foscolo.

Letters addressed to the Countess of Albany by her many friends previous to the death of Alfieri are rare, a circumstance which may, perhaps, be explained by the loss of her library and effects during the Reign of Terror in Paris. From the opening years of the nineteenth century, however, we have a vast mass of correspondence, consisting largely of letters preserved in the Musée Fabre at Montpellier. So early as 1863, Monsieur St. Réné Taillandier edited the letters of Sismondi to the Countess between 1807 and 1823, including in the same volume a selection of letters, much mutilated by their editor, to the Countess from Madame de Souza, Madame de Stael, and others. The numerous letters at the Musée Fabre were, however, not thoroughly or properly arranged, edited and printed until recent years, when Monsieur Pélissier undertook this task. His bulky *Portefeuille de la Comtesse d'Albany* (Paris, Fontemoing 1902), which is intended to afford " materials for the life of a woman and for a society," contains no fewer than 359 letters, in addition to a large number of stray notes and fragments,

xviii

from a most heterogeneous set of friends and acquaintances of almost every nationality. This most valuable work has been extensively perused and consulted by me ; yet, frankly speaking, it cannot be said that the contents of the *Portefeuille* are very absorbing, if taken as a whole ; since letters of genuine interest or of literary charm, such as those of Madame de Souza and Carlo Poerio, form the exception rather than the rule in this voluminous collection. Having given this signal proof of his industry and interest in this subject, we venture to hope that in course of time Monsieur Pélissier will edit for us (as, indeed, he seems in one place to promise), the whole mass of the letters of the Countess to her friends at Siena, numbers of which still remain in manuscript in the libraries of Siena, Milan, and Florence.

Again, what has become of the many letters of the Countess addressed to Sismondi ? We have a great many of Sismondi's letters to her, and there can be no reason to doubt that the historian carefully preserved the replies which this great lady, " his sole source of pride," deigned to write to himself. The Countess' letters to so public and distinguished a personage as the novelist Madame Adèle de Souza must also remain in safe if hidden keeping. Undoubtedly, there still exists plenty of material to be sought and found in connection with the life-story of Louise Countess of Albany, and the present volume aims rather at giving a picture of her personality from the numerous sources at present available than of presenting the reader with a number of new facts concerning the chequered career of the Last Stuart Queen.

BIBLIOGRAPHY

AMONGST the printed books dealing with the life and times of the Countess of Albany, I have found the following list of especial use and value during the progress of this work :

Baron Alfred von Reumont. *Die Gräfin von Albany.* (Berlin, 1860.) Quoted as Reumont.

Saint-René Taillandier. *La Comtesse d'Albany.* Included in vol. xxxi. of *La Révue des Deux Mondes.* (Paris, 1861.) Quoted as Taillandier.

"Vernon Lee." *The Countess of Albany.* "Eminent Women Series." (London : Allen and Co., 1884.) Quoted as Vernon Lee.

Léon-G. Pélissier. *Le Portefeuille de la Comtesse d'Albany.* (Paris : Fontemoing, 1902.)

Lettres Inédites de la Comtesse d'Albany à ses Amis de Sienne. (Paris : Fontemoing, 1904.)

C. Antona-Traversi. *Lettere Inedite di Luigia di Stolberg, Comtessa d'Albany à Ugo Foscolo.* (Roma, 1887.)

E. Del Cerro. *Vittorio Alfieri e la Comtessa d'Albany. Storia di una Grande Passione.* (Torino : Roma, 1905.)

E. Bertana. *V. Alfieri studiato nella Vita, nel Pensiero e nell' Arte* (Torino, 1902.) Quoted as Bertana.

Léon-G. Pélissier. *Lettres et Écrits divers de la Comtesse d'Albany.* (Paris, 1901.)

G. Mazzatinti. *Lettere Edite ed Inedite di V. Alfieri.* (Torino, 1890.)

Le Carte Alfieriane di Montpellier. (*Giornale Storico della Letteratura Italiana.* Vols. iii., iv., and ix.)

E. Teza. *Vita, Giornale e Lettere di V. Alfieri.* (Firenze, 1861.)

R. de Bourdellès. *Études Italiennes. V. Alfieri.* (Paris, 1907.)

C. Milanesi. *V. Alfieri in Siena.* (No date or place.)

C. Milanesi e J. Bernardi. *Lettere Inedite di V. Alfieri.* (Firenze, 1864.)

BIBLIOGRAPHY

Baron A. von Reumont. *V. Alfieri in Alsazia.* (*Archivio Storico Italiano.* Serie iv., vol. x.)

Gli Ultimi Stuardi. (*Archivio Storico Italiano.* Serie iv., vol. viii.)

D. Silvagni. *La Corte e la Società Romana nei Secoli XVIII. e XIX.* Firenze, 1881.) Quoted as Silvagni.

Count Vittorio Alfieri. *Vita di V. Alfieri scritta da Esso.* (Londra, 1807.) Quoted as Vita.

Opere. (Italia, 1822.)

Poesie Amorose. (Forming vol. xv. of the *Opere di V. Alfieri,* published at Piacenza in 1810.)

The Tragedies of V. Alfieri. Translated by E. A. Bowring, C.B. (London, 1876.)

Massimo d'Azeglio. *I Miei Ricordi.* (Firenze, 1867.)

C. A. Fabris. *Studii Alfieriani.* (Firenze, 1895.)

G. Biagi. *Aneddotti Letterari.* (Milano, 1896.)

G. Calligaris. *Un Carteggio della Comtessa d'Albany.* (Reale Instituto Lombardo, Rendiconti. Vol. xxxiii., serie ii., Milano, 1900.)

R. Tomei-Finamore. *La Comtessa d'Albany e il suo Carteggio Senese* (Rivista Abruzzese, 1892.)

A. Sassi. *Il Degno Amore di V. Alfieri.* (Nuova Antologia, vol. cxci.)

La Vedovanza dell' Amica di. V. Alfieri. (Nuova Antologia, vol. cxcii.)

E. Grimaldi. *V. Alfieri e il suo Degno Amore.* (Matera, 1906.)

" Jarro." *V. Alfieri in Firenze.* (Firenze, 1896.)

G. Sforza. *Dodieci Storici Aneddotti. La Vedova di un Pretendente e Napoleone I. in 1804.* (Modena, 1895.)

G. Conti. *Firenze Vecchia.* (Firenze, 1899.)

Léon-G. Pélissier. *Canova, la Comtesse d'Albany et le Tombeau de Alfierii à Sta. Croce.* (*Nuovo Archivio Veneto.* 1902.)

E. Del Cerro. *Epistolario . . . di Ugo Foscolo e di Quirina Mocenni Magiotti.* (Firenze, 1904.)

A. D'Ancona. *Un Segretario dell' Alfieri.* (*Varietà Storiche e Letterarie,* serie i. Milano, 1883.)

C. A. Ste. Beuve. *Nouveaux Lundis.* Vols. v., vi. (Paris, 1866.)

St. René Taillandier. *Lettres Inédites de J. C. L. Sismondi, etc., à Madame la Comtesse d'Albany.* (Paris, 1862.)

E. J. De Lécluze. *Souvenirs de Soixante Années.* (Paris, 1862.)

L. Dutens. *Memoires d'un Voyageur qui se repose.* (Londres, 1806.)

BIBLIOGRAPHY

Historical MSS. Commission Reports. Appendix, Part vi. of Tenth Report. (London, 1887.)

Edinburgh Review. (*The Countess of Albany, the Last Stuarts, and Alfieri*, vol. cxiv., pp. 145–182, 1861.)

Marchesa Vitelleschi. *A Court in Exile.* (London: Hutchinson and Co., 1903.)

H. M. Vaughan. *The Last of the Royal Stuarts.* (London: Methuen and Co., 1906.)

J. H. Jesse. *Memoirs of the Pretenders.* (London, 1845.)

Earl Stanhope. *Decline of the Last Stuarts.* (Roxburgh Club's Publications, 1845.)

A. C. Ewald. *Life of Prince Charles Stuart.* (London, 1904.)

J. Doran. *Mann and Manners at the Court of Florence.* (London, 1876.)

J. Siebermacher. *Hohe adel Deutschland. Wappenbuch.* (Nürnberg, 1878.)

De la Chenaye-Dubois et Badier. *La Dictionnaire de la Noblesse.* (Paris 1866.)

J. Hubner. *Genealogiche Tabellen.* (Leipzig, 1737.)

G. E. C. [ockayne]. *Complete Peerage.* (London, 1887.)

CHAPTER I

YOUTH AND MARRIAGE

"As for myself, I have experienced misfortune from my earliest years. I was born the eldest of the children of my mother, who wanted a son and consequently received me ill and treated me with intense harshness all my youth up, placing me in a nunnery, where I learned nothing, in order to save herself expense and have more money for her own amusements; for my mother has never thought of aught else than to play, to enjoy life and to wear pretty dresses up to her present age of sixty-five. She wedded me, so as to get rid of me, to the most odious man that ever existed; a man who united in his own person every imaginable failing and prejudice, in addition to the lacquey's special vice of drunkenness."—*Letter of the Countess of Albany to Teresa Mocenni*, July 9, 1798.

THE marriage of Gustave-Adolphe, second son of the Prince of Stolberg-Gedern, with Elisabeth-Philippine-Claudia, Princesse de Hornes, proved the means of uniting a large number of noble and semi-regal houses in Germany and Flanders, and even in lands more remote. The family of the bridegroom, one of the oldest and most distinguished in the Empire, actually claimed kinship with the proud Italian feudal stock of Colonna, for the court heralds were wont to speak of a common ancestor of the two families in a certain Otho de Columnâ, a friend of the Emperor Justinian. Through his mother, the Prince was closely connected with the Counts of Nassau-Saarbrücken and the Princes of Hohenlohe-Langenburg, and through his paternal grandmother with the ducal House of Mecklenburg-Güstrow. On the bride's part, the Princes of Hornes ranked amongst the first of Flemish houses and were nearly related to the de

A 1

Lignes and the Counts of Esseneux ; whilst through her
mother, Lady Charlotte Bruce, the youthful Princess of
Stolberg-Gedern could claim alliance with the British
earldoms of Elgin and Stamford. From a rapid glance
at the genealogy given in this book,* it will be at once
perceived how varied but interesting an admixture of
German, French, Flemish, British and even Spanish
blood was destined to flow in the veins of any descendants
of this illustrious pair.

In course of time, the young wife, who was Princesse
de Hornes and Comtesse de Baucignies in her own right,
as the younger daughter and co-heiress of Prince
Maximilien-Emmanuele de Hornes,† became the mother
of four children, all daughters. Three months after the
birth of Gustavine, the youngest, in the summer of 1757,
Prince Gustave-Adolphe himself met with a soldier's
death on the battle-field of Leuthen, fighting in behalf
of his sovereign, the Empress-Queen Maria-Teresa,
against the victorious forces of Frederick the Great of
Prussia. Thus at the early age of twenty-four did the
Princess of Stolberg-Gedern find herself left a widow with
four infant daughters, with scanty means at her disposal,
and without any prospect of future wealth, for it was upon
the chances of her late husband's military career and
expected appointments that the youthful pair had built
their hopes for an assured position in the future, worthy
of their exalted birth and connections. The bereaved
lady was, therefore, only too glad to avail herself in her
undeserved and unforeseen distress of the help promptly
and generously offered her by the Empress-Queen, who
was always ready to reward past services, and whose warm
sympathy was especially aroused by the premature close
of this young prince's career.

The eldest of the four daughters of this match,
Louise, whose life-story forms the subject matter of this

* *See* Genealogical Table on p. xxiv. Also Reumont, vol. ii., pp. 135, 138,
and *Appendix*, p. 281.

† Together with her elder sister, the wife of Prince Salm-Kyrburg.

2

biography, was born and baptised in the old cathedral city of Mons in Hainault on September 20, 1752, the registry of her baptism being couched in the following explicit terms.

"On the twentieth day of September 1752 was baptised Louise-Maximilienne-Caroline-Emmanuele, legitimate daughter of his Highness Prince Gustave-Adolphe of Stolberg, Colonel, and of her Highness the Princess Elisabeth of Hornes, husband and wife. Her god-fathers were his Highness Prince Maximilien-Emanuel of Hornes, knight of the Golden Fleece of the first class, and his Highness Prince Frederic Charles, Prince of Stolberg. Her god-mothers were the very illustrious and noble dame, Alexandrine, Princesse de Croy, canoness of Saint Wandru, acting on the part of her Highness the Princess Louise of Stolberg née Princesse de Nassau (whose Christian name was evidently bestowed specially on her infant god-daughter), and her Highness the Princess Albertine of Hornes, née Princesse de Gavre." *

Left fatherless, as we have already explained, at the tender age of five, the prospects of the little Louise at once became the particular care of the good-natured Empress. In her seventh year the child was sent to be educated in the school attached to the chapter of St. Wandru in Mons, perhaps the most wealthy and exclusive of the various noble chapters in the Austrian Netherlands, that were specially reserved for the convenience of impoverished members of the great houses of the Empire. The widowed Princess of Stolberg, always devoted to society and amusement to the day of her death, felt only too thankful to be rid of one of her children, whose existence was ever a source of trouble and expense to herself, so that in the quiet cloisters of Mons the child was brought up and given such instruction as the spirit of the eighteenth century demanded in the case of a young princess. In after years, when embittered by matrimonial and financial troubles, Louise of Stolberg was wont to

* Reumont, *Appendix*, p 282.

3

speak with intense bitterness of the alleged grievances of her youth at Mons, accusing her mother of parsimony and indifference, and declaring she had received no education worthy of the name; but it is easy to perceive that these belated complaints were greatly exaggerated. Neither mother nor daughter certainly were ever imbued with mutual affection; but it is reasonable to suppose that Louise of Stolberg must have been tolerably happy and fairly well instructed at Mons according to the low standard of a frivolous age. As the child grew towards womanhood, the kindness and interest of the Empress were again manifested in a notification of her coming election to the first vacant prebend in the chapter, which was ruled by no less a personage than the Princess Anne-Charlotte of Lorraine, sister-in-law of the Empress herself.

The registers of the Chapter of St. Wandru give brief official particulars of the reception both of Louise and of her next sister Caroline-Augusta into the body of *les dames chanoinenesses* in the summer of 1767.

"On the 20th of June 1767 Mademoiselle Louise-Maximilienne-Caroline-Emmanuele, legitimate daughter of the noble and illustrious Gustave-Adolphe, Prince of Stolberg and of the Holy Roman Empire, late lieutenant-general of the forces of Her Imperial Majesty the Apostolic Queen, and of the noble and illustrious Lady, Elisabeth-Philippine-Claudia, Princess of Hornes and of the Empire, who was baptised on September 20, 1752, has been put in possession of the prebend of St. Wandru, become vacant through the marriage of Princess Marie-Anne-Victoire of Salm with the Duke of Lerma, in accordance with the Letters Patent of Her Imperial Majesty the Queen-Apostolic given at Vienna on December 21, 1761. The usual ceremonies were performed; the usual office in the morning was said; the Count of Mastaing took the required oath in her name; and she herself made the customary offering of a piece of gold in the presence of the officials." *

* Reumont, *Appendix*, p. 283.

As in the case of her predecessor, the fortunate Princess Marie of Salm, the acceptance of one of these well-endowed and convenient semi-ecclesiastical posts was hoped to form merely the stepping-stone to a brilliant match, failing which expectation the revenues of the prebend of St. Wandru would manage to keep their owner comfortably in single-blessedness, for Louise of Stolberg, apart from her prebendal stall, was absolutely destitute.

The easy-going practice of the day allowed Louise and Caroline-Augusta frequently to leave the cloister of St. Wandru and to attend the assemblies of Brussels, which formed the especial delight of their worldly-minded mother. In society the two sisters speedily attracted attention, for both were pretty and agreeable, whilst the elder was already becoming noticed for a piquant conversation and a thirst for learning, which were far from usual in a young woman of her birth and breeding. Strange to say, the first definite offer of marriage that commended itself to the Princess of Stolberg was directed to Caroline-Augusta, then barely sixteen years of age. This proposal was made on behalf of the young Marquis of Jamaica, son and heir of the Duke of Berwick, head of the important House of Fitz-James, that was sprung from the famous Duke of Berwick, the natural son of King James II. of England and the frail Arabella Churchill, whose shame had done so much to raise the fortunes of her unscrupulous brother, John Churchill, Duke of Marlborough. As the heir of a great and wealthy nobleman who was thrice a duke—of] Berwick in Britain, of Liria in Spain, and of Veragua in Portugal—* as well as a Spanish grandee and prince of the Empire, such a match was naturally welcomed by the Princess of Stolberg, whose sole aim seems to have been the mating of her daughters with persons of wealth and position. In all probability the one drawback to this union in the eyes of the Princess-Mother was the circumstance that it was Caroline-

* *Dictionnaire de la Noblesse.* Tome viii., pp. 66-73.

5

Augusta and not Louise that had been selected, for she herself and her eldest daughter owned little or no affection for one another. But the forthcoming marriage with the heir of the Duke of Berwick was destined to lead quite unexpectedly to a second and a yet more brilliant alliance, concerning which, however, political complications made it prudent for the delighted woman to keep absolute silence for the time being. The betrothal of the young Marquis de la Jamaïque with Caroline-Augusta of Stolberg-Gedern had moved the elderly Duc de Fitz-James, his uncle, to treat with the Princess of Stolberg on behalf of a very exalted personage, who was graciously wont to acknowledge a relationship between himself and the illegitimate House of Fitz-James. This was none other than the Chevalier Charles-Edward Stuart—the Charles III. of the Jacobites and the Young Pretender of the Hanoverians—who was now fifty years of age, a wanderer of damaged health and reputation, but still of some slight value to the cause of French policy as the representative of an exiled royal line; although, as Sir Nathaniel Wraxall aptly remarks, " the French court may, indeed, be censured in the eye of policy for not having earlier negociated and concluded the Pretender's marriage, if it was desired to perpetuate the Stuart line of claimants to the English crown." *

At this precise moment, however, the French Government, always willing to wound, though half afraid to strike at British prestige and prosperity, had suggested the advisability of marriage to the unhappy and discredited Pretender, who thereupon eagerly hastened to Paris, only too ready to allow himself to be dragged forth once more from ignominious obscurity to be made a pawn on the great chess-board of European politics. Charles was treated with scant ceremony in Paris, where he was not even permitted access to the King, and was finally requested to quit the city altogether on the demand of the

* H. B. Wheatley, *Memoirs of Sir N. W. Wraxall*, vol. i., p. 213. (London 1884.)

6

English ambassador, although the matrimonial scheme was still pursued by the French ministers, who covered themselves with lying protestations that no such affair was afoot. Under the direction of the old Duc de Fitz-James, who was now upholding the interests of the head of the House of Stuart, these intrigues were proceeding with the greatest secrecy throughout the autumn months of 1771 ; amongst other princesses, Marie-Louise of Salm-Kyrburg and Isabella of Mansfeld being approached in the matter without success. What ultimately decided on the choice of Louise of Stolberg-Gedern for this particular purpose was no doubt, the actual marriage of her younger sister with the Marquis of Jamaica in the October of this very year. The splendour of a so-called royal alliance, the substantial dowry offered by the French court, and also perhaps the golden chance of getting rid of a satirical and rebellious daughter were sufficiently strong inducements to make the Princess-Mother over-look certain very real dangers involved in this match Her main fear was, of course, the inevitable wrath of the Empress-Queen, the patroness and almoner of the whole family of the deceased Gustave-Adolphe, but this grave risk the determined lady boldly decided to run. Ignoring political complications therefore, the Princess of Stolberg-Gedern promptly gave her own consent to the proposed match, and easily obtained that of her daughter of nine-teen, who was far too young and inexperienced to realise the true nature of this royal alliance with a man of fifty that was being judiciously dangled before her eyes. With great secrecy the young Louise was taken to Paris, and there wedded by proxy to Prince Charles-Edward Stuart, who was himself impatiently awaiting the arrival of his consort in Rome, the place of his birth and his residence since his father's death in 1766.* Nor from

* *Hist. MSS. Commission. Tenth Report. Appendix.* Part vi., pp. 222, 223. The whole story of the marriage negociations and financial arrange-ments between Charles Stuart and Louise of Stolberg can be traced in this volume from pp. 222-233.

7

what was reported to him by Lord Caryll, Colonel Ryan, the Duc de Fitz-James and other devoted adherents who were in the secret, had he any reason to feel uneasy about the unseen bride that the half-contemptuous bounty of the French court had thus enabled him to marry and maintain. Although he had failed in the days of his buoyant youth and bright hopes to ally himself, as his father had warmly recommended, with one of " the first princesses in Europe," yet Louise of Stolberg-Gedern, albeit only the penniless daughter of a German princeling, was from the point of birth fit to mate with the highest sovereign in Europe, and was, indeed, as highly connected as the Princess Clementina Sobieska, bride of the titular King James III. Her youth, her charm, her health, her wit were all that could be desired by a middle-aged monarch and by such of the old Jacobite party left in Britain who still turned with feelings of hope and affection to the lonely and dissolute exile in the Roman palace of the Santi Apostoli. " What think you of this affair ? " writes a Scottish adherent to Bishop Forbes. " She is pretty and young, he strong and vigorous. They may produce a race of pretenders that never will finish, which the French will be always playing upon every quarrel. *Crescant laete.* May they increase fruitfully. *Honi soit qui mal y pense.*" * Certainly, the auspices were not for the moment altogether unfavourable, for both bride and bridegroom, though they had never seen one another, were at least openly set upon the union. Marriages of political convenience between persons of disproportionate ages have not necessarily proved unhappy or disastrous ; so perhaps the cheerful prognostications of this Scottish Jacobite were not wholly unjustified at the moment. As for the crafty Princess of Stolberg, she had counted correctly on the ultimate success of her plan ; to complete the match first and to bear the brunt of Maria-Teresa's wrath after it was an accomplished fact. The exiled Stuarts and their

* *Lion in Mourning,* p. 265.

8

pretensions for some time past had been unfavourably regarded at the Imperial Court; whilst from the political obligations that Austria-Hungary owed to Britain and the House of Hanover the Empress-Queen was deeply incensed at the news, as the Princess-Mother had clearly foreseen. Furious at this act of deceit on the part of one she had consistently befriended and honoured, the Empress at once sent word to the offending Princess of Stolberg, through her minister Kaunitz, never to appear again in her presence, and even threatened to deprive her of the allowance on which the Stolberg family relied for its very existence. But the final result of all this disturbance was as the clever but unscrupulous woman had anticipated. After living in retirement for a decent interval, until such time as the Empress' first outburst of indignation had spent itself, the Princess carefully drew up a most humble and pathetic apology to her sovereign,[*] which eventually had the desired effect of winning for her the return of the Imperial favour, for Maria-Teresa had apparently too much personal liking for her suppliant to wish to punish with continued severity her late treacherous action, or to notice the obvious insincerity of her letter of repentance. In due time the Princess of Stolberg was restored to her former post at court, and the episode was apparently forgiven or forgotten.

After the marriage by proxy, which took place in Paris on March 28, 1772, the young bride hastened southward, escorted by her mother and Colonel Ryan to Venice, whence she took ship for Ancona. Charles himself meanwhile, all anxiety to see his chosen mate, made his way, together with the Jacobite peer Lord Caryll, from Rome, so as to intercept Louise at the little town of Macerata, not far from the shrine of Loreto in the March of Ancona. Here arrangements had been made, through the kindness of Cardinal Marefoschi, Charles' chief champion in the Sacred College, for the forthcoming ceremony to be carried out with an amount of display suitable to the union

[*] Reumont, *Appendix*, pp. 284, 285.

9

of two such distinguished persons. On the afternoon of Good Friday, April 14, the expected bride at last alighted at the Marefoschi mansion in the little hill-set town; whereupon the impatient bridegroom, delighted with her youthful charm and prettiness, which far exceeded his most sanguine hopes, at once demanded the performance of the rite in the private chapel of the palace, wherein there still exists a tablet to record the nuptials of " Charles the Third, King of Great Britain, France, and Ireland," with the Princess Louise of Stolberg-Gedern.* The ominous circumstance that the wedding took place on Good Friday seems to have in no wise affected the husband, although in after years Louise was wont to observe that only misery could have resulted from an union celebrated on " The Lamentation Day of Christendom." The marriage itself was followed by banquets and receptions, causing an unusual amount of stir in quiet Macerata, and on Easter Sunday the pair departed for Rome.

It must not be supposed by the reader for a moment that there was aught else than mutual satisfaction at the beginning of this match, or that the nineteen-year-old bride conceived immediately a loathing unutterable for a spouse who was over thirty years her senior, and in whom she discovered later a drunkard and a man of ungovernable temper. From the bridegroom's point of view, of course, Louise was everything that could be desired, and Charles Stuart openly expressed his sincere admiration for the pretty doll-like wife with her slender figure enveloped in stiff brocades, with her flaxen hair rolled and contorted in the extreme of fashion, and with two prominent and most unnecessary daubs of rouge on her fresh young cheeks. So delighted was he with her sweet smiling face, her graceful form, and even with her queer and unexpected taste for literature and art, that he immediately decided to show his royal approval in the most practical manner by expressing his intention of increasing this charming young creature's pin-money by

* Vitelleschi, vol. ii., pp. 387–392.

MEDALS OF LOUISE AND CHARLES STUART IN 1772
MEDALLION OF LOUISE

an additional 3000 *livres*; an action that must have appealed strongly to the worldly Princess-Mother. On the bride's part, we have no hesitation in saying she was supremely happy. Her husband's royal rank appealed to her sense of pride; his marked attention to her sense of gratitude; she was leaving a mother whom she cordially disliked and about to settle in a country which she ardently longed to behold. In spite of her lord's blotched and puffy face, in spite even of an odour of brandy which was perceptible notwithstanding all the mitigating perfume, it does not appear that Louise was seized with any immediate feeling of repulsion; on the contrary she rather liked this splendidly dressed middle-aged Prince with his broad blue ribband and his agreeable stories of past adventure. An intense thrill of personal importance must also have possessed her, as she, Louise of Stolberg, had been bidden to inscribe her name in the marriage register as "Queen of Great Britain, France, and Ireland"; whilst she gathered from her attentive husband's remarks that she might expect to be received with regal honours in Rome. Even if Charles did appear, to her youthful eyes, elderly and broken-down, she had her compensation in the novel feeling of worldly grandeur, as well as in a sense of escape from the dull cloister of St. Wandru and the irksome tutelage of her mother. Heaven considerately hides the book of inevitable fate from all its creatures, so that Louise was only engrossed in the fleeting moment, which seemed to open before her a vista of royal honours, of an adoring spouse, of a palace, of jewels, and of liberty in the most delightful city of Europe. Dis-illusion and discontent were bound to arise later; but for the time being the Stuart Queen probably fancied herself far happier and more fortunate than the sister who had made a less important match.

As the bridal pair approached the Eternal City, they found in waiting for them at the Ponte Molle various carriages of state, including those of Henry Stuart, Car-dinal-Duke of York, the younger brother of Charles Stuart,

who had sent his chamberlain Marchese Angelelli ahead
to welcome his sister-in-law. With out-riders in the
royal British liveries of scarlet and with white cockades,
the gala coaches rattled through the Porta del Popolo
and up the narrow Corso amidst a goodly number of
persons attracted partly out of goodwill towards the
exiled reigning House of Britain, but mostly out of idle
curiosity. At the palace in the Piazza Santi Apostoli the
Stuart King's household was drawn up in readiness to
receive its new mistress, who now entered the house
wherein the pious Queen Clementina Stuart had lan-
guished, a prey to fever and jealousy, and where the old
Stuart King had moped for years as a dejected invalid
deserted by his elder son and sunk into a mere phantom
of despised royalty. Nevertheless, the aspect of the
palace, so gloomy and so ill-omened, did not daunt the
cheerful disposition of the young Princess, who ascended
its staircase amid the profound obeisance of a throng of
well-trained servants. Perhaps, however, on dismount-
ing from her coach, she may have been momentarily
disappointed and perplexed at not seeing the promised
guard of papal troopers before the portals that her
garrulous husband had led her to expect. Charles had,
indeed, demanded beforehand that this special guard of
honour, which had been removed after his father's death,
should be restored to him on the grand occasion of the
arrival in Rome of a new Stuart Queen; but his request
had been firmly refused by the Pope.

On the following morning, the Cardinal-Duke of York
came to visit his sister-in-law, and to bring her his bridal
gifts, which included a magnificent court dress stiff with
gold thread and rich with the finest lace, and a gold box
encrusted with diamonds and set with his own portrait
on the lid; whilst within the costly trinket contained an
order on his Roman banker for the sum of £10,000 sterling. Although the kindly but pompous ecclesiastic had
been somewhat inclined to resent his brother's high-
handed conduct with regard to this marriage, of which the

Cardinal had been merely advised at the last moment, after having been kept in complete ignorance throughout all the preliminary negotiations; yet the pretty face, the graceful manners, and the deference shown to himself by the bride at once captivated him, whilst he was led to hope that in matrimony with so charming and innocent a creature might be found the best means of inducing his erring brother to abandon certain evil habits which were causing deep concern to those around him. The Cardinal stayed to dine at the palace of Santi Apostoli, and on the following day Henry Stuart's secretary inserted his master's favourable impressions concerning his first interview with Louise of Stolberg in the bulky *Diary*, wherein all matters connected with the private or official life of the Cardinal-Duke were always enrolled : * " He was delighted to perceive in the youthful Princess all those good qualities wherewith rumour had endowed her, and particularly was he pleased with her great charm of manner and her intellectual attainments, for which the excellent education given her by her parents was responsible. She treated him on an equal footing, and with every mark of respect and affection." Certainly, Louise had contrived to make a complete conquest of the first personage of consequence she encountered in her capacity of wife to a *de jure* sovereign.

The approval and friendship of the Cardinal were to prove ere long of the first consequence to Louise, for she speedily found herself in a centre of hot political intrigue, of which she formed herself an innocent and unsuspecting cause. The position of Charles in Rome was anomalous and undefined. His parents had always been acknowledged as reigning King and Queen by the papal court, whilst Charles himself half a century before had been solemnly recognised as Prince of Wales by the whole

* *Diario del Cardinale Duca di York*—" A Diary of the Sacred Functions and the Illustrious Acts of H.R.H. and Eminence the Lord Cardinal Duke of York "—now preserved in thirty-six volumes in the MS. Department of the British Museum.

of the College of Cardinals, who had come in state to kiss his infant hand. To admit his father's kingship and his own sacred heritage in the title of Prince of Wales was, of course, strong presumption that the treatment should be carried to its natural conclusion on the death of the former. From a logical standpoint, therefore, the Prince had the best of the present argument with the Holy See ; but seeing how changed were circumstances and how impracticable it had become at this juncture for the Roman Court to acknowledge the British Pretender, instead of pressing his claim, Charles should have been content to wait incognito for happier auspices under which to present his petition to the Pope. This was the attitude assumed by the Cardinal-Duke of York, and that it was both a sensible and a dignified one cannot be denied ; whilst it was deeply to be regretted that the elder Prince had not followed his brother's good example in this matter. But Charles never stopped to consider whether his conduct was impolitic or ungenerous towards a court which, though far from unwilling, was practically unable to grant his repeated requests for a royal recognition. Into this perennial grievance he had now dragged his helpless bride, forcing her on every occasion to insist on the honours due to a queen-consort, much to Louise's embarrassment. It was true that at her husband's request she had signed the marriage register at Macerata as Queen of Britain, and had been delighted later to see her childish profile on the medal struck to commemorate the event ; but some private conversation with the Cardinal-Duke soon roused her quick intelligence to perceive the combined folly and uselessness of her husband's pretensions, however logical in a sense they might appear. Even Sir Horace Mann, the British Minister at Florence, who never fails to take every opportunity of sneering at Henry Stuart, admits the wisdom of the Cardinal's attitude on this point ; and he also adds that Louise's " taking the stile of Queen was contrary to her own and the Cardinal's entreaty " ; for it was to Henry

Stuart that the young bride constantly looked for advice
in the midst of the increasing difficulties of her position as
the wife of a disowned monarch, who persisted in declaring that " the Queen is entitled to the same ceremonies
as the King, and the Prince of Wales also when there shall
be one."

Yet another reason may, however, be adduced to
account for Louise's reluctance to follow her husband's
lead in this matter. Such an assumption of majesty had
the effect of considerably lessening their social circle,
for it was explicitly forbidden to the Roman nobility to
treat as a reigning monarch the man who had once
everywhere been acknowledged as Prince of Wales. As a
queen also Louise was not permitted by her husband
to return the visits of the great Roman ladies, whilst all
who entered the Stuart palace were expected by the
inexorable sovereign of that tiny court to make use of
those very marks of etiquette that the papal government out of political prudence strictly forbade. It was
wellnigh an untenable position, and one which could only
be rendered feasible and agreeable by the Pretender's
frank abnegation for the nonce of all these rejected
claims. But though this dilemma was a constant thorn
in her side, the young bride found much to delight her
during her first year in Rome. The churches, the
gardens, the galleries, the theatres, the public assemblies
were all visited by the newly-wed pair, who were received
on all sides with a respectful sympathy that was in reality
far better than a curt and grudging recognition of their
unprofitable claims to mock majesty. Although debarred
by the Chevalier's pretensions from the balls and receptions in the Roman palaces, yet the Princess was able to
receive in her house many persons of every nationality, so
that she obtained constant opportunities of cultivating her
natural social talents and of indulging her decided taste for
the arts, science, and literature. However violent and
waspish he might show himself to his adherents, and
even to his most devoted friends, the Chevalier at this

15

stage was never anything but gentle and indulgent towards his wife, who had still to learn by future experience the depths of fury and sottishness to which the erstwhile hero of Scotland could occasionally sink. The stories of his youthful adventures were told and re-told repeatedly, and the bride was still able to laugh heartily at the tale of her husband's disguise in female dress, or to sympathise with the evil fate of many a loyal Highlander that he recalled with tears. Louise was, in short, regarded and treated by Charles as a mere child, whose every whim must be gratified if possible; and thus between her husband's flattering attentions and the novel scenes of the theatre of life as seen upon so lovely a stage as the wonderful city of Rome, the young Princess found existence on the whole fairly smooth and pleasant, although she was perhaps slowly awaking to the fact that events might arise to render her husband unkind and her own life miserable. Nevertheless, as we said before, she could not be regarded as unhappy, for she had already found many compensations for a loveless marriage of political convenience.

Thus, amidst such society as her husband's palace afforded her, and in the enjoyment of the many delights the Eternal City was able to present, Louise was far from being discontented with her lot during her first year of wedded life. The young bride had at once conceived for Rome an undying affection, and but for adverse circumstances in the course of her stormy life, she would gladly have made her permanent abode in this artistic and intellectual capital, which was then attracting educated persons of every condition of life and of every land as to a centre of the arts, of music, of antiquarian study, and of congenial company. The Rome of the Clements and the Benedicts in the spacious days of the eighteenth century was, indeed, a fascinating place with its liberal-minded government, its air of stately repose, its marvellous galleries of sculpture and paintings, its gardens, its villas and palaces, its magnificent churches, and its picturesque ruins veiled in wreaths of ivy and eglantine that a more prosaic age has swept away in the interest of scientific excavation. Thus Louise, during her first visit as the inexperienced child-wife of a querulous would-be sovereign, found Rome a pleasant place to dwell in; and quarter of a century later she could still look back with regret on the fascinating city;—" Women are well off in Rome," so she writes in after years to her friend Teresa Mocenni on June 6, 1801; " the town is beautiful, and there is good society there. It is my favourite of all the places in this world, and how I should love to inhabit it, for the sake of its charming surroundings especially ! "

The wearisome and never-ending controversy between Charles and the Papal Court had, however, its lighter side, for many of the Romans were disinclined to take the irate and insistent Chevalier altogether seriously. The statue of Pasquino, which always mouthed the topics of the day in Rome from the gravest to the frothiest, found a way of solving the difficulty by calling the new Stuart bride " Regina Apostolorum," in obvious allusion to her place of residence close to the great basilica of the Santi Apostoli; and Pasquino's suggestion was taken up and improved upon by one of the many witty foreigners who felt no scruple in partaking of the hospitality of the Stuart palace; and this new title," Regina dei Cuori " (Queen of Hearts), was at least no more treasonable than that contained in the pasquinade already published. The author of this second complimentary name was a Swiss man of letters, Carl-Victor Bonstetten of Bern, a young gentleman with a handsome face and of merry, agreeable manners, destined to play some part in the life of this Queen of Hearts of his own adoption, whose beauty and intellectual tastes he most unaffectedly and openly admired, and of whose person he has left us a flattering picture. " She was of medium height ; " so he writes in his Memoirs; " fair with deep blue eyes ; nose tip-tilted ; and a lovely white English complexion. Her expression was gay and *espiègle ;* and not wholly devoid of raillery, more French than German in its nature. She was enough to turn all our heads in no small degree "; and certainly she succeeded in turning Bonstetten's, as we shall have occasion to describe in the next chapter.

There was in addition yet another reason for the Chevalier's continual fuming and discontent, with which his wife was even more closely concerned than with the everlasting futile intrigues carried on by means of Lord Caryll and Cardinal Marefoschi at the Papal Court. The late match had been arranged by the French ministers with the sole object of perpetuating the Royal House of Stuart in order to have a Pretender to the British throne in continual reserve; so that the timely appearance of a Jacobite Prince of Wales would undoubtedly have served to raise the political status of the exile in Rome. The marriage itself had had the effect of momentarily fanning into a flame the dying embers of Jacobitism in Britain, where for a year or so past the little band of faithful adherents had been looking forward to the appearance of an announcement of " the officially negociated infant." Indeed, less than a twelvemonth after the ceremony at Macerata, a report was actually being spread abroad in England by interested persons that the Princess Louise was pregnant and the Cardinal of York (that constant stumbling-block to the scruples of the Protestant Jacobites) was dead; and this rumour the vigilant Sir Horace Mann, the British Minister in Florence, eventually found sufficiently important to deny formally to his Government. For, as a matter of fact, there was not an atom of truth in this statement, which had been circulated solely with the idea of still further animating the moribund cause. A whole year passed, yet there was no sign of the pretty German bride becoming a mother, and the French agents began in consequence to feel somewhat foolish; whilst the Chevalier grew disappointed and annoyed with the consort that had been selected for him with such care and mystery. From having at first shown himself indulgent and kind, he now began to appear cold and

18

cross in her presence, though at this time there is no reason to suppose he ever ill-treated the wife, who had thus failed to carry out the expectations formed of her. But as time went on, and yet another year passed without any sign of the desired infant, the prince's sense of anger and disappointment increased; more than ever he resorted to drown his chagrin in the fumes of wine, and gradually alienated even his staunchest and oldest friends by his violence and perversity. To add to his troubles, this very moment was regarded as opportune by his cast-off mistress, the unhappy and ill-treated Clementina Walkenshaw, and her daughter Charlotte to appear in Rome in order to obtain some degree of recognition and a better allowance from the prince.* It is, therefore, possible that during this earlier period of her married life Louise may have set eyes on Charlotte Stuart, her husband's natural daughter, who was only a year younger than herself, having been christened at Liège in the name of Charlotte Johnson during the autumn of 1753. In spite of every effort, this pair of suppliants obtained little notice from the hard-hearted prince, who ignored all their tears, arguments and entreaties, and finally allowed both mother and daughter to be coerced into returning to their French convent with a very slender allowance from the purse of the Cardinal-Duke, to whom his elder brother habitually turned as his almoner for whatever money was required. Finally, after the two defenceless women had been obliged to quit Rome, other half-forgotten scandals concerning the roving life led by Charles-Edward between the date of his expulsion from France and the death of his father in 1766 were circulated by those who were anxious to sow further discord between the papal authorities and the court in exile. Old rumours of the prince's unorthodox conduct, not to say actual apostacy, for political convenience were

---

* For this incident, *see* the curious account, sometimes attributed to Charlotte Stuart herself, contained in St. Simon's *Œuvres Complettes.* Tome xii., pp. 206-208. (Strasburg, 1791.)

once more being bruited about, to the intense disgust of the pious Cardinal, with whom his elder brother was again inclined to quarrel. Indeed, Charles had never really forgiven Henry for what he considered his treachery to the Jacobite cause by accepting a scarlet hat a quarter of a century before; and the remembrance of this long-past grievance, combined with their present disagreement over the question of the royal recognition by the Pope, tended again to embitter the two brothers, and all the more so because Louise herself refused to break with the Cardinal, whose sensible advice she was inclined to follow. Yet in the midst of all these worries, both political and domestic, the obstinate Chevalier, more determined than ever to demand of the Pope that which it was most impolitic and, indeed, almost impossible for him to bestow, made a final petition to Clement XIV. for the obtaining of a royal tribune for the expected Jubilee ceremonies in the coming year 1775. Already harassed and goaded by the troubles due to his recent suppression of the Society of Jesus, and far too deeply engaged to interest himself in so trivial a question as to whether the Stuart prince should or should not be styled King in Rome, the Pontiff rejected this new request in polite but plain terms; whereupon the indignant Chevalier determined to betake himself and his wrongs out of the Papal States; a decision that in some vague way he imagined would prove hurtful to the credit of the Papacy. Shaking, as it were, the Roman dust from his feet, and filled with intense bitterness against the Pope, the Roman court, and his own brother the Cardinal of York, the would-be monarch suddenly abandoned the city in high dudgeon, taking with him his consort and such few members of his household as either from secret motives of self-interest or from an unquenchable sense of loyalty still clung to him. And thus to her deep regret was Louise of Stolberg compelled to leave Rome with her determined husband after two years of married life.

CHAPTER II

THREE YEARS IN FLORENCE

" Je commence à m'ennuyer beaucoup à Florence. Dans ce moment nous n'avons que des Italiens, et vous savez comme je les aime ! Je lis tous les contes imaginables pour me faire rire. J'ai épuisé toute une bibliothèque bleu. . . . Tous nos plaisirs se bornent à écouter un opéra pendant quatre heures ; la musique en est assez bonne. Mais quatre heures sont bien long et pouroit être bien mieux employé. Mais c'est toujours le sort des pauvres femmes de faire la volonté des autres."—*Letter of the Countess of Albany to Carl-Victor Bonstetten*, June 9, 1775, dated " Florence *temps d'oublie.*"

ON quitting Rome in the spring of 1774, the Chevalier and his young wife spent a few months in the neighbourhood of Pisa. After two years of a childless marriage, the chances of the appearance of a Jacobite Prince of Wales seemed very remote ; nevertheless, this brief period of wandering during the summer of 1774 was in much later days declared the occasion of the Princess' secret confinement in a villa near the Baths of Lucca. According to the fanciful tale of the Jacobite " Dr. Beaton," a son and heir was born at this spot to the Chevalier, who for safety's sake placed the precious infant at once under the care of a certain Admiral Allen, who in his turn carried off the last hope of the Jacobites to England, where the child was bred as his own son and ultimately came to be recognised as the " Iolair Dhearg," or Red Eagle, the mysterious parent of the two self-styled Sobieski-Stuart brothers, that many persons still living can recall. This mendacious tale of old Dr. Beaton's, which was only revealed to the two children of the alleged heir of the Royal Stuarts after the death of Louise herself, half a

21

century later, is perhaps scarcely worthy of mention in the biography of a woman, who all her life was ignorant of this clumsy posthumous lie concerning herself, and who frequently in her private letters mentions with satisfaction her failure to become a mother, so that a bare and passing allusion only has been made to it in this place. *

Setting aside this mischievous tale, it is enough to state that before the close of 1774, the childless pair, whose relations were gradually growing less harmonious, found themselves in Florence, where Prince Corsini, the head of a great Florentine Papal family that had always shown itself markedly friendly towards the exiled Stuarts, placed at their disposal his villa and garden near the Prato Gate, known as the Casino Corsini. Here Charles decided to settle for the present, and as Leopold I., Grand-Duke of Tuscany, and his Spanish consort absolutely ignored all claims of a British Pretender, he very wisely gave out his wish that he himself and his wife should henceforth be regarded as " the Count and Countess of Albany "; a step that saved them from a repetition of certain disagreeable incidents and slights that had recently occurred in Rome. Royal etiquette was, however, always strictly observed within the walls of the palace ; whilst even in the theatre and at public assemblies the prince, especially when under the influence of wine, was wont occasionally to make scenes owing to the mania for royal recognition which ever exercised his mind. His wife was permitted to receive, but not to return, the visits of the Florentine ladies, who soon ceased to attend at the Casa Stuart on realising this attitude of aloofness, so that the visitors of the pair were chiefly confined to the male sex; a circumstance that was not perhaps deeply deplored by the Comtesse d'Albanie, who, to use a homely but expressive phrase, had always shown herself to be essentially " a man's woman." In the Florentine galleries and churches, the young wife found some

* The Stuart-Sobieski myth has already been analysed by myself in *The Last of the Royal Stuarts*, pp. 275–280.

compensation for her regret in leaving her beloved Rome; yet it is evident from her letters of this period that she did not relish her late enforced change of residence.

"You want to hear the life I lead ?" so she writes in December, 1774, to her Swiss friend, Carl-Victor Bonstetten, to whom she had perhaps lost a small part, a very small part indeed, of her youthful heart. "It would be dismal for anybody but myself. I spend the whole morning in reading. Then I dress quickly and go for a walk. I have always people to dinner, and if there is no opera in the evening, I go to the Casino dei Nobili * and withdraw thence at nine o'clock. Then I write to my friends, to whom I consecrate the closing hours of the day. I like to occupy myself with writing to you, for you are one of my most cherished friends; perhaps you even reign with too much authority in my heart. Would that we were in the Desired Island ! I do not mean England, for really I do not want to be a queen; but I should like to cross the Alps, for Italian society bores me. The Florentines are unsympathetic and provincial, and scandal is their sole topic of conversation." †

This extract, from the first of the letters of her correspondence with Bonstetten which have been preserved, hints certainly at a mild intimacy, almost at an innocent flirtation, between the writer and the gay young Switzer then about twenty-eight years of age. The letters, which are in execrable school-girl French, must obviously have been dispatched without her husband's knowledge or consent, whereby we may infer that he did not closely pry into her private affairs. The same letter also contains the curious phrase, which has sometimes been very unfairly quoted to prove that the young bride of the Chevalier even so early as this was guilty of amorous intrigue, before ever the irresistible Alfieri himself had appeared upon the scene.

"You are the most delightful of men, and the only one

* The fashionable place of assembly for Florentine society.
† L. G. Pélissier, *Lettres et Écrits divers de la Comtesse d'Albany.*

made to capture my heart, my mind and my soul. How lively our friendship would be, if we could but cover the five hundred leagues that separate us ! The tender Maltzam often tells me : 'Monsieur de Bonstetten was the only man who would have been dangerous to you !' and I quite believe it, for you are gay, captivating and intellectual by turns. That is the type of lover I desire ; one who will play the lover only when we two are alone." *

This is, of course, mere badinage, but it certainly sounds neither seemly nor discreet in a young wife of only two year's standing. The allusion to "the tender Maltzam," contained in the passage quoted above, gives us, however, a key to the early life and ideas of the Countess of Albany, as we shall call her henceforward. This person was her lady-in-waiting (and therefore presumably regarded as the pink of propriety by a jealous husband), Catherine, baronne de Maltzam, or Malzen,† a member of a noble Suabian family, who plays an important but hitherto almost unnoticed part in the life of the Countess, for she is only once mentioned by name in Sir Horace Mann's letters to Horace Walpole, and once only by Alfieri in his correspondence. Born in 1735, as she tells us in a letter written many, many years after to her beloved Countess,‡ Madame de Maltzam, who had once been a canoness of Mijet, was the constant friend and companion of Louise from the time of her marriage, apparently, until the death of Charles Stuart in 1788. "The tender Maltzam's" views on matrimonial propriety were undoubtedly lax, but she was evidently well aware of the necessity of keeping within certain prescribed bounds, and it appears obvious that these curious letters to the lively and susceptible Bonstetten were written under the supervision of Madame de Maltzam herself, who probably arranged for their due postage to Bern. In this early correspondence, of which five letters only remain, the Countess rallies Bon-

---

* *Lettres et Ecrits divers*, p. 7.
† The name is spelt in a variety of ways.
‡ *Le Portefeuille de la Comtesse d'Albany*, p. 61.

stetten on his expected marriage with " une belle Suis-
seuse "—" How funny to see you the father of a family !
You are cut out for that part." Again, she frequently
expatiates on the advantages of friendship over love,
declaring that her love for Bonstetten is perfectly safe
owing to the barrier of the intervening Alps, but she adds :
" Let us stick to friendship, love is too dangerous ! "
" If I found a man who was wholly original," so she
writes again, " I should adore him for ever, but I have
not yet discovered one to my taste or one who merited a
constant devotion. You alone have succeeded in touching this heart of stone. I felt and feared it, but the
vast mountains between us serve as my rampart, and I
needed nothing less for my protection ! " This is, of
course, mere fooling ; still it is not very decorous nor in
very good taste. Mingled with her own mock passion
for the fascinating Bonstetten are some obscure allusions,
real or imaginary, to a love affair of Madame de Maltzam's
with a Monsieur Scherer. " She loves him to distraction, and weeps whenever we mention him. But then we
women have the gift of tears ! " So moralises this young
married woman of her more mature companion and
watch-dog, who is seventeen years older than herself.

These few surviving letters contain only one allusion to
her husband. " We are perishing of the heat," she writes
on July 13, 1775. " We are positively roasting. We go
out walking and get bored, and that is no relief. Ah,
if we could but dwell in your mountains, how nice it would
be ! Almost, yes, almost two days ago I saw the moment
when I was to become mistress of my own fate. Death
and disease, the foes of mortals, danced over the head of
my lord and master ; but thank God, his hour was not
yet come ! "

This reference to the Chevalier's illness and recovery
does not betray any deep affection ; but on the other
hand, Louise expresses herself as genuinely pleased at his
late escape from danger, so that we feel justified in concluding that the pair were on tolerable if distant terms

25

of amity in the summer of 1775; although it is known that the Countess used to complain greatly of the long walks in the heat which the Chevalier compelled her to take with him. Sir Horace Mann, who was accurately informed on all matters touching the Stuart household, never mentions actual discord as existing between husband and wife, though he frequently speaks of the Count's ill-health and of his jealous and selfish nature. His letters to Horace Walpole, as well as his despatches to the British foreign office, tell of the drunken extravagances in which the poor Chevalier indulged often at this period, so that we can easily imagine the humiliation her husband's behaviour in public must sometimes have brought to the young and sensitive wife, who was obliged to sit night after night at the theatre, whilst her lord lay fuddled on a sofa in the box beside her.* Drunkenness was itself absent from the lengthy list of fashionable vices to be found and tolerated in Italian society, and for this cause alone the unhappy Countess was pitied by the Florentine ladies she affected to despise. Gaming, pilfering, infidelity, dishonour, scandal;—all were overlooked or excused; but this particular vice made the pair objects of mingled commiseration and contempt in the most tattling and frivolous capital of Europe. From excess in eating and drinking, the Pretender's health, which had long been failing, grew much worse; whilst, as may be easily be imagined in the case of a man with a perpetual grievance against fate, his temper waxed unbearable. Nevertheless, it is evident that Louise put a brave face on her many domestic troubles and outwardly bore herself with calm and dignity, solacing her anxious mind with a severe and continuous course of study. Although the jealousy of her husband, who was still vainly hoping for an heir, made her very existence at times a burden, yet at certain hours the Stuart palace was not without its share of social entertainment and of agreeable conversation or of music. Many persons, chiefly of the

* A. C. Ewald, *Prince Charles Stuart*, pp. 394-396.

male sex, attended the dinner that was daily spread for all who cared to partake of the self-styled monarch's hospitality; and, moreover, Louise was encouraged to pay court in a special degree to any young Englishmen of quality making the grand tour on the Continent, such as Coke of Norfolk or Danby of Yorkshire, to each of whom, it would appear, she gave her miniature. Strangely enough, certain writers have actually sought to make scandalous insinuations against the poor lady for her attentions to these rich young Britons, although it had always formed part of the regular policy of the exiled court to flatter and cajole such individuals both in Rome and Florence. Danby has been credited with a deep and romantic attachment for the Jacobite Queen of Hearts; but as Sir Horace Mann clearly states that this intimacy had the full approval of the jealous husband, there remains no more to be said on the subject. Mann also remarks at this time that, in spite of the Pretender's bad health and worse temper, " his young and amiable wife behaves to him with all the attention, nay tenderness, that is possible "; and we are convinced of the truth of the British envoy's statement, which is re-echoed by Dr. Moore, who describes the Countess of Albany as " a beautiful woman, much beloved by those who know her, who universally describe her as lively, intelligent and agreeable "; or by the Abbé Dutens,* who speaks of her as " the most interesting personality in Florence, thanks to her face, her charm of manner and her hard lot." Dutens also proceeds to describe her as being " of medium height, well-formed, and with a lovely white skin, most beautiful eyes, perfect teeth, a noble and courteous air, and manners that were at once easy, graceful, and modest."

After two years of residence in Florence as guests of the Corsini, the Count of Albany, who had long been seeking to buy a palace of his own, was able to purchase a fine house with a large garden belonging to the Guadagni family.

* *Mémoires d'un Voyageur qui se repose*, vol. ii., p. 247.

This building, remaining to-day almost in its original state, stands a little to the east of the famous church of the Santissima Annunziata in a quiet part of the town, which in those distant days was largely covered by monastic houses with groves and gardens. It is a massive, irregular pile, picturesque but somewhat gloomy and forbidding with its lower windows heavily barred, after the usual manner of Florentine *palazzi*. The garden adjoining is well-shaded with rows of ilex trees that surround an open space set with curious moss-grown statues of peasants, animals and satyrs. The palace, which is now the property of the ducal family of San Clemente, has long been closed to the public, and few of the many thousands of British and American visitors who annually flock to Florence, are aware that in going to visit Fiesole they pass within a few feet of the house which witnessed so many domestic tragedies of the Royal Stuarts. The Palazzo San Clemente, as it is usually called, nowadays looks deserted, and its unkempt garden in springtime is a tangled mass of tall buttercups and the gay purple salvia ; but from the modern street known as the Via Micheli the stranger can still observe at the highest pinnacle of the roof a small iron vane with the royal cipher of " C.R." and the date 1777,* marking the year in which the unhappy Stuart prince acquired this palace, which has the distinction of being the only residence ever actually owned by the exiled family during its century and more of existence on the Continent. Outside his new mansion Charles had placed the great escutcheon with the royal arms of Britain and France and with the date of his succession to the nebulous realms of his father in 1766 ; a circumstance that aroused the interest of the Swedish Baron d'Adlerberth a few years later, who alludes to the then Palazzo Stuart and its royal occupant in a letter, now preserved in the archives of Stockholm.

* A charming but little-known poem on this subject was written by the late Eugene Lee-Hamilton, half-brother of the Countess of Albany's English biographer, the talented writer with the pseudonym of " Vernon Lee."

FORMER STUART PALACE IN FLORENCE
Now Palazzo San Clemente

"The Count of Albany . . . is decrepit and bent; he walks with great difficulty, and so impaired is his memory that he repeats himself every quarter of an hour. On his sombre clothes of daily use he never fails to wear the blue ribband of the Garter, and when he is dressed for any ceremony he dons the mantle of the Order with the ribband at the knee. The portal of his palace bears the shield of England with a royal crown. He speaks with enthusiasm of the exploits of his youth, and with resignation of his misfortunes." *

One of the royal shields, if not the identical one here alluded to by the Swedish courtier, is still to be seen in the entrance hall of the Palazzo San Clemente, and the ill-starred house is said to possess a small chamber frescoed in the gaudy colours of the royal Stuart tartan, left intact by the present owners of the palace, whose ancestor acquired it directly, in 1789, from Charlotte Stuart, Duchess of Albany, the natural daughter of the Chevalier.

As mistress of the newly purchased Palazzo Stuart, the Countess of Albany had undoubtedly reaped certain worldly advantages from her loveless marriage. But as the wife of a royal claimant to one of the first thrones in Europe, her position, even at the best, was decidedly an anomalous one, for she hovered, as Mr. Ewald aptly remarks, between two social worlds, one of which she had voluntarily quitted, whilst a superior order firmly refused her admittance on the footing of a queen-consort. It would be idle, however, to speculate on what might or might not have happened, had Charles chosen to act reasonably and unselfishly, for his conduct was obviously growing more violent and inconsiderate in proportion as his health declined and his old drinking habits gained upon him. Jealous he always was, but till 1777 we confidently hold he had no just cause for suspicion in his youthful wife, for the silly boy-and-girl flirtation on paper with the far-away Bonstetten cannot in fairness be regarded as incriminating. Perhaps her lively sallies of wit

* Le Bourdellès, *Études Italiennes. Appendix*, pp. 260, 261.

or her frequent display of learning or literary attainment among the guests of Palazza Stuart may sometimes have aroused the sulky displeasure of her lord; but there exists plenty of evidence to show that for the three years succeeding their retirement from Rome, Louise of Stolberg-Gedern proved herself a fairly good and attentive wife to a singularly unkind and unpleasant husband. With the year 1777, however, that year which by a tragical coincidence was commemorated by Charles himself on the iron vane of the Florentine palace he had bought for a permanent home, a distinct change in the relations of the pair has to be recorded. Hitherto Louise seems to have obeyed her spouse's arrogant commands with meekness, whilst her habitual good spirits and keen interest in her studies had helped her to endure if not to condone the many undeserved scoldings and indignities she constantly suffered at a drunkard's caprice. The cause of this changed attitude and of her new determination to defend herself from a life of domestic tyranny is naturally to be sought and found in the appearance on the scene of a lover—a distinguished, ardent, and determined lover— in the person of the great Piedmontese poet, Count Vittorio Alfieri of Asti, whose advent in Florence was destined to bring about the turning-point in the life of this beautiful woman mated with a brutal prince, who had long ceased trying to win the gratitude or esteem of his young wife, so as to find in her an ideal companion for his old age. How far the unkind treatment and the sottish habits of Charles Stuart operated in favour of Alfieri's suit must be judged from the following chapters.

CHAPTER III

THE POET AND THE LADY

" . . . It is my intention to become a great Poet, or to die in that attempt whither all my thoughts now lead. The Lady whom I adore is all the more worthy of my love, in that she in no wise hinders me, but ever urges me on to the task. Beyond this I know nothing ; and you will only see me again at Turin, when I am old and crowned with laurels."—*Letter of Vittorio Alfieri, in 1779, written to his friend the Abbé di Caluso* (?).

VITTORIO ALFIERI, son of the Count Antonio Alfieri of Cortemilia, head of one of the oldest and wealthiest families in Piedmont, was born at Asti in January 1749, and was, therefore, nearly four years older than the princess who was fated in due course to become his lady-love, his " Donna Amata." Losing his father whilst still an infant, the little Vittorio had been educated under the well-meant but not judicious guidance of a devoted mother, the Countess Monica Alfieri, and of a kindly step-father, Giacinto Alfieri di Magliano, a cousin of his own. From his earliest years the child showed symptoms of a highly-strung, almost hysterical nature ; fanciful, wayward and mischievous by turns he proved an endless source of trouble to his family at home and later to the tutors of the Academy at Turin, whither at the age of nine he was sent as the only place fit for the proper education of a young Piedmontese nobleman. As soon as he had attained the requisite age, the young Vittorio, as master of his own considerable fortune, began to indulge his strongly pronounced tastes for horseflesh and for travel, (which were his distinguishing passions at this

31

early period of his life) ; for the prospect of a frivolous and aimless existence in Turin at the court of his sovereign the King of Sardinia always seemed most repugnant to the wilful and erratic youth. In accordance with the decadent fashion of the day, Alfieri in speech and method of thought had grown up more French than Italian ; he could barely speak correct Italian, and when not expressing himself in the elegant French of Versailles was reduced to using the unpleasing dialect of his native Piedmont. Of all Italian poetry, literature and history he was woefully ignorant ; and though as a youth he undertook frequent visits to the chief cities of his native land, the sight of the ruins of Rome, of the gorgeous palaces of Venice, of the artistic treasures of Florence seemed to have left but small impression on a mind that had already grown weary of aught save the amorous intrigue, which often constituted the sole aim and object of so many young men of his own position. Journeys further afield to France, England, Germany, even Russia, did little to remove his apathy and indifference ; although the prosperous appearance of England and the devotion of its aristocracy to horses seem to have given the traveller a preference for that state over the other lands visited. Here and there the wanderer found solace for his persistent melancholy in intrigue, and his principal adventures of this type are recorded by the future poet at full length and with artless comment in his curious *Vita*, or Autobiography,* which he composed in after years. At the Hague, the first glimmerings of a high-minded purpose in life were made to dawn upon him through the action of the Portuguese minister there, the Comte d'Acunha, who presented him with a copy of the works of that great prophet of Italian unity, Niccolò Machiavelli, which Alfieri kept and valued to his life's end and always accounted the first and best beloved book in all his library.† But for the present the wise words of the

* *Vita di Vittorio Alfieri, Scritta da Esso.* (Londra, 1807.)
† *" Il decano di miei libri."*

great Florentine thinker brought little satisfaction to the youth, who continued his restless tour of the principal towns of Europe, until he found himself once more in England, where he was free to indulge his taste for horses to satiety. Here, however, he discovered something even more engrossing than the company of racing men and horse-dealers, in the dangerous society of a lady of fashion (and Alfieri never sought such adventures outside his own class), namely, in Penelope, Lady Ligonier, the wife of an Irish baron and the daughter of George Pitt, Lord Rivers. The future poet's attachment was warmly returned, so that many a secret meeting between the pair took place, partly in London and partly at the Ligonier country-place of Ripley in Surrey, whither the ardent Count was wont to ride through the summer gloaming, tying up his horse to a certain oak-tree in the park, that was long pointed out to the curious as the trysting-place of the lovers. Reports of this intimacy, however, ere long reached the husband, who promptly challenged Alfieri to a duel in the Green Park one evening during an interval at the opera. The Italian, who was handicapped by a broken wrist incurred during one of his nocturnal visits to his reigning mistress, was speedily vanquished by his skilled adversary, Lord Ligonier contenting himself with bestowing a mere scratch for form's sake on the stranger who had robbed him of his wife's honour : all of which squalid affair is fully set forth in a pamphlet of the day entitled " *The Generous Husband, or Lord Loelius and the Fair Emilia.*" * Perhaps the peer was willing to show himself magnanimous towards his opponent, for the simple reason that Lady Ligonier was evidently a woman of light reputation; whilst the absurd climax of this romance was reached when the discomfited Italian count learned that the dame for whom he had risked life and limb, and was even now contemplating to make his wife after the conclusion of the divorce action

* *See also The Gentleman's Magazine*, 1771, p. 567. Also under " Ligonier " (*Dictionary of National Biography*, vol. xxxiii.).

then pending,* was also guilty of prior attachment to one of her own grooms; indeed, she seems to have frankly preferred the attractions of the latter to those of her Piedmontese champion. Madame de Maltzam after Alfieri's death cannot help rallying the Countess of Albany on her famous lover's early misadventure in the English lists of love, when she heard the story, apparently for the first time, through the pages of the recently published autobiography of Vittorio Alfieri—"The incident of his third passion," so she writes to the Countess on August 1, 1809, "made me laugh till I cried. I pictured to myself his handsome face filled with amazement at the news of her liking for her husband's jockey! The whole incident seems so inconsistent with the traditional English prudery, that I had to read the passage twice through, to see that I was not mistaken in it. English ladies, I know, are obliging enough in their chamber or in a discreet corner of the parlour; but I had no idea their complaisance extended to the saddle-room." †

This unedifying episode with Lady Ligonier is mentioned here at some length for two reasons; first, because the unhappy lady who preferred her groom to an Italian nobleman, unexpectedly re-appears some twenty years later to her former lover when he is in the company of the Countess of Albany; and second, because the whole incident throws considerable light on the moral obliquity of Alfieri as a professional lady-killer and would-be victor of his neighbours' wives, a pose which he candidly avows in an early sonnet, wherein he jestingly alludes to his conquests among the wives of careless or unsuspecting husbands of his acquaintance. Where, he asks, is that marvellous fountain, in which the luckless Actaeon saw his brow sprouting with the branching horns that are the time-honoured badge of cuckolds?

* The writ of the Sheriff of Surrey against Alfieri in this affair is preserved among the Alfieri MSS. in the Laurentian Library in Florence.

† *Le Portefeuille*, p. 63.

34

Dov'è, dov'è quella mirabil' fonte,
(Grida il piu dei mariti) in cui l'aspetto
Vide Atteon cangiarsi, e a suo dispetto
Palpò l'onor della ramosa fronte ? *

We next find Alfieri pursuing his usual aimless wanderings through Europe, and finally we behold him at
Lisbon, where happily he met with the person who perhaps above all others was really responsible for his original
inspiration with high ideals of literature and patriotism.
This was the Abbé Tommaso Valperga di Caluso, an
excellent specimen of the intellectual, liberal-minded,
well-bred ecclesiastic of the eighteenth century, whose
friendship and sympathy were at once valued at their
true worth by the inconsequent wanderer, still smarting
under his late experiences in London; still bored and
dissatisfied with himself and his surroundings ; and yet
vaguely yearning after better things which seemed wholly
out of his reach. The Abbé di Caluso, whose brother
the Marchese di Valperga was Piedmontese envoy at the
Portuguese court, seems to have taken a strong liking to
his eccentric and extravagant fellow-countryman, and
for many weeks the learned but modest Abbé, " a veritable
re-incarnation of Montaigne," never ceased to encourage,
to instruct, and to restrain the young nobleman who was
still struggling to exchange a life of shallow amusement
for a career of literary energy.

Filled with the noble exhortations of the Abbé di Caluso,
Alfieri now returned to Piedmont in May 1772, a few
weeks after the marriage of Charles-Edward Stuart with
his own as yet unseen " Donna Amata." Here in Turin,
despite another intrigue with the Marchesa di Priè, a
lady several years his senior, the young aspirant began to
carry out the recommendations of his good friend at
Lisbon. Literally chaining himself to his desk, Alfieri
now forced himself to write the draft of his first tragedy,
Cleopatra, the idea of which was suggested to him by the
tapestries hanging in the chambers of his then siren and

* Bertana, p. 184.

35

mistress, the Marchesa di Priè, already mentioned. The drama, which in reality was feeble enough, was finally played by amateur actors at Turin in the summer of 1775, and the applause gained thereby on this occasion had the effect of spurring on the poet to further efforts in the field of tragedy, for he was now seized with the violent desire of rescuing, as he considered, the classic drama of Italy from the languid and exotic form which had been recently bestowed upon it by the plays of Metastasio, for whom he had conceived a boundless contempt as the representative in literature of Italian servility to courtly and foreign influence. But to carry out successfully so great an aim required, as Alfieri well knew, many years of preliminary toil and training. For the ambitious poet had, as we said, delved little if at all in that mine of literary wealth which is perhaps the richest and most inexhaustible of all Italian treasures; he had forgotten his Latin, learned with tears and under protest at the Turin Academy; of Greek he was wholly ignorant; and his acquaintance with classical Italian itself was far from sufficient for the purpose he henceforward held steadfastly in view. To improve his style, to learn a pure idiomatic Italian, to study the great writers of Italy (notably Dante, Petrarch, Ariosto and Tasso), the determined poet now decided to quit Turin with its many temptations to idleness and dissipation, and to seek both the culture and inspiration necessary in the towns of Tuscany. Accordingly, in April 1776, he set out for Pisa, and thence in the summer he removed to Florence, where according to a popular but somewhat improbable tradition, he was first aroused to the singular charm and attraction of the young Countess of Albany by over-hearing her one day in the great gallery of the Uffizi admire the character and appearance of Charles XII. of Sweden, as she stood before the portrait of that chivalrous monarch. From that hour, so the story goes, the poet became her slave; and in order to show his passion at once obtained and clothed himself in garments identical

36

with those wherein Charles of Sweden had been portrayed by the artist. Thus clad, he was wont to pass before the windows of the Stuart palace in order to attract the notice of the Countess within. The tale is highly imaginative, and as Alfieri himself makes no allusion to such an incident in the pages of the *Vita*, it may be dismissed as apocryphal, though it is accepted by Lécluze * and some other writers. "During the summer of 1776," so he writes in his Autobiography, "which I had passed wholly at Florence, I had often observed a very noble and lovely woman, a foreigner of most exalted birth by all accounts. It was impossible not to remark her on meeting her, and still more impossible was it, on once remarking her, for anybody to find her aught but charming. Although a large number of the Florentine gentlemen and nearly all the foreign residents of quality had been received at her house, I myself, always dreamy and morose by nature and ever ready to avoid such women as seemed agreeable and attractive, never went thither, and merely contented myself by frequent glimpses of her at the theatre or when out walking. The first impression she left on my mind was one of infinite charm. Dark eyes with a sparkle in them,† and the sweetest of expressions, in addition (that which one rarely sees in combination) to a very fair skin and light-coloured hair, gave a lustre to her beauty, which was well-nigh irresistible. She was in her twenty-fifth year, and had a sincere taste for all art and literature ; she possessed a disposition that was pure gold ; yet despite her abundant gifts she was rendered miserable by the most distressing troubles at home. How could I ever face such a tower of virtue ? " ‡

Such is Alfieri's own account of his first acquaintance with the Countess of Albany in the summer of 1776, and from it we can gather that he purposely declined to attend

* *Souvenirs de Soixante Années*, p. 168.
† Which in his first sonnet to the Countess are called " *Negri, vivaci, in dolce fuoco ardenti.*"
‡ *Vita*, vol. ii. pp. 57, 58.

at the Stuart palace, for fear of falling a victim to her charms and thereby wrecking his intention of carrying out the great literary scheme wherewith his mind was now obsessed. Hitherto, women had proved a distinct hindrance to him in his self-set career of intellectual glory, so that he was determined studiously to avoid for the future the society of any lady, whose influence might endanger or delay the completion of the project he had in view, for, indeed, it was all too true, as the chosen " Donna Amata " herself remarked in after years, that the Italian women were never willing to share the lover with his Muse. Perhaps it was with the ever-present fear of succumbing against his will and better judgment to this new temptation, that Alfieri now hurriedly departed from Florence and took up his residence at Siena with the object of severe study and preparation for his forthcoming tragedies, which were to revolutionise the Italian drama itself and thereby to put new strength and patriotism into the effete and corrupt minds of the descendants of the ancient Romans.

The decision to settle at mountain-girt Siena, that beautiful and still unspoiled specimen of an Italian mediæval free city, was fraught with important consequences for Alfieri himself, and indirectly for the lady whose entrancing charms he was apparently bent on avoiding in Florence. In the quiet old town, perched aloft among the tawny volcanic hills, Alfieri found the peaceful life tempered with congenial society that his soul craved. Here he quickly became intimate with a small band of cultured people, consisting chiefly of a few liberal-minded priests and some members of the middle and professional classes, amongst whom the rich and handsome young noble with his pale, haughty, clear-cut face, his masses of auburn hair, his ungovernable temper but generous disposition, and his varied experiences of the great world, soon came to be regarded as a sort of Prince Charming of genius and fashion dropped by a lucky chance in this quiet provincial city. With his remarkable appearance, with his string of horses (without which the poet rarely moved), with the romantic and perhaps exaggerated reports of his wealth, literary ambition and eccentric habits, Count Vittorio Alfieri at once became the cynosure of all Siena, and the absolute idol of the little set of persons whom he deigned to honour with his friendship ; and as the Sienese friends of Alfieri will be mentioned frequently during the course of the love-idyll of the poet and the Countess of Albany, a brief account of them will not be found amiss here.[*]

First and foremost of the members of this small intellectual clique, *il crocchietto saporito*, as Alfieri sometimes names his chosen body of Sienese friends, was Francesco Gori-Gandellini, whom ere long he was wont to allude to as "the friend of his heart," and also as "Checco," a nickname that often appears in the poet's letters to another member of this group, the Chevalier Mario Bianchi, of the villa Montechiaro outside Siena. Gori was some ten years older than Alfieri, and his influence over his younger companion was extreme, whilst Alfieri repaid his unselfish devotion with interest, dedicating to him more than one of the early tragedies, which he was now composing. Mario Bianchi, whose name is well known in Italian literature owing to the interesting and curious series of letters directed to him by Alfieri, was, on the other hand, some seven years junior to the poet. A member of an ancient Sienese family and a knight of the Tuscan Order of San Stefano, this young man was resolutely set against the idea of marriage, not so much on account of his hereditary tendency to consumption as because of his deep attachment to a certain married woman of Siena, Teresa Regoli, the young wife of a cross and covetous middle-aged merchant called Ansano Mocenni. Teresa Mocenni, whose name will appear frequently in this work, had been wedded at an early age to her present unsympathetic master, a widower, to whom she had

---

[*] For a full account of Alfieri and his Sienese friends, the reader is referred to C. Milanesi's interesting study, *Alfieri in Siena*.

already borne several children. Owing to her literary proclivities, which sometimes found their vent in tolerable Latin and Italian verses, Madame Teresa Mocenni had contrived to draw to her small *salon* many persons of culture and liberal views in Siena ; whilst the aristocratic Mario Bianchi was openly acknowledged, according to the custom of polite Italian society of the day, as her *cavaliere servente*, or *cicisbeo*, or *patito*, a being for whom our English tongue possesses (perhaps to its credit) no accurate equivalent, but who is thus described in a contemporary sonnet as

> *lo strano, indefinite ente,*
> *Quell' anfibio animale ch' oggi si chiama*
> *Per tutta l'Italia " cavalier' servente."*

Mario Bianchi was, in other words, the cavalier that fashion and custom permitted, and even expected, every Italian lady of quality or influence to attract to herself and to utilise as she thought proper. The homely expression " tame cat " is, perhaps, our nearest English approach to this type of carpet-knight, who was not necessarily, even if he were usually, the ardent lover of the fortunate lady who made full and frequent use of his services.

One other member of this set of Sienese citizens dabbling in poetry, philosophy and political science, must be mentioned here ; namely, the Abbé Ansano Luti, the last surviving member of a respected local family, who was Arch-priest, or Dean of the glorious old cathedral-church of Siena, that tiger-striped black and yellow Gothic pile with its tall arcaded belfry that dominates the ancient city. Luti, who " passed for a man of liberal and unprejudiced mind " and doubtless possessed both wit and erudition, fully shared in the peculiar and immoral, or rather *un-moral*, tenets held by most of the members of this *crocchietto saporito*, the story of which forms quite a chapter to itself in the development of the intellectual and familiar life of Italy in the eighteenth century.

Amongst this pleasant and cultivated little clique, the

fine nobleman and literary lion from Piedmont found ample time both for work and relaxation. There were long walks and talks with Gori in the beautiful countryside that surrounds the tall red mediæval walls of Siena; long discourses of an evening in the *salon* of Casa Mocenni with the pretty and talented mistress of the house, "la Teresina," with her handsome cavalier Mario Bianchi, with the clever but self-indulgent Luti, and with a dozen or so of favoured acquaintances who were admitted to the circle. Here passages from the plays under construction were recited and commented on in the freest spirit; the works of Rousseau, Montesquieu or Voltaire were discussed; and the decadent and enslaved position of Italy, both intellectual and political, was openly lamented. In so congenial an atmosphere, it is not surprising to find how deep an affection Alfieri soon conceived for the hospitable old city, its environs and its people. In a sonnet belonging to this period of his life, the poet sets forth the natural charms of Siena and the names of his favourite companions there, telling the reader how he loves the fresh breeze on the ramparts of the Lizza, and even the clouds of fine white dust that to this day the traveller usually encounters outside the northern gate called Porta Camollìa.

> *A Camollìa mi godo il polverone,*
> *E in sulla Lizza il fresco ventolino.*

In the following year Alfieri, who had meanwhile returned to his native Piedmont, once more continued his studies in Tuscany. After spending some months, much to his satisfaction, in his beloved Siena, he decided to move in the autumn to Florence where he was destined to meet again with the lady of his fate, as he records in the fifth chapter of his Autobiography under the expressve heading: "*Degno amore mi allaccia finalmente per sempre*" (Pure love, enchains me for the last time and for ever). He had, as we have already remarked, avoided a presentation to the Countess of Albany of set purpose during his previous visit to Florence; but on this occasion, deeming

41

himself, so he tells us truthfully or untruthfully, strong enough to approach the desired flame without burning his wings, he allowed a friend to introduce him at the new palace which had been recently purchased by the Stuart king in exile. Here he speedily found his already lofty estimate of its lovely mistress all too low. Her outward beauty, he soon perceived, was but the least of her charms, for the Countess of Albany was sincerely devoted to the attractions of an intellectual existence, and the poet also realised that extraordinary passion of hers for self-improvement and self-culture, which was certainly one of her ruling characteristics. Deeply disturbed at thus finding himself an unwilling victim once again to the power of love, not by reason of any moral scruple but for fear of the ensuing disturbance in his pre-arranged plans for a literary career, the poet suddenly quitted Florence on horseback for Rome, travelling by way of Siena, where he laid the whole story of his difficulties before the ever-sympathetic Gori, the chosen friend of his heart. The latter he now begged to visit Florence, to judge for himself whether this paragon of a married woman were worthy of winning; whether her love would hasten or retard his cherished desire for fame; whether she were, indeed, the one woman in the world who could play the part of Aspasia to his Pericles. The ready Gori assented to this rather peculiar request; he came to Florence; he saw, watched, approved, and reported his approval to the anxious lover *in petto*, who hastened again to Florence with the avowed if secret intention of winning the lady. That the Countess was at this moment of his decision unconscious of the overwhelming effect her beauty, her attainments and her miseries had wrought both in Alfieri's mind and heart is quite possible; but it is absolutely certain that the poet, who was far from unskilled in the art of husband-robbing, had now girt himself to the deliberate task of depriving the wretched Charles Stuart of the bride that the bounty of France had bestowed upon him only five years before.

42

CHARLES-EDWARD STUART
From the portrait by Ozias Humphry, R.A.

That severe critic, Signor Bertana, both of Alfieri and of his " Donna Amata," sums up the strange situation thus in his valuable but caustic study of the great poet of Asti.

"Did Alfieri enter the Stuart palace with a ready formed design ? He *did* enter it with an impression, a very seductive one, which the Countess had left in his mind ever since their first meeting. Thither he turned with the thousand temptations that the charm, the wit, the freshness of the young princess could inspire into his easily inflammable soul. His kindly reception by Charles-Edward, whose favour he well knew how to gain, invited him to redouble his attentions ; any complaint that the Countess allowed to escape her lips concerning her hard position as slave to 'a querulous, exacting and ever-tipsy old husband' ; the shock he felt at beholding this sweet flower of youth tied to a horrid old stick ; the delight that the lady took in books and her pretty prattle of philosophy and letters, which gave her the aspect of a *donna intelletuale*, served to fan the flame. . . .

"It is certain that a woman who could understand, or affect to understand the fury for fame wherewith Alfieri was beset ; a woman who was capable of realising the poet's ambition and not merely of demanding the degrading attentions of the *cavaliere servente*, wherein he had on other occasions unprofitably wasted his time ; a woman who urged him to work, and gave him leisure to undertake it and obtained pleasure in criticising it, must truly have appeared to Alfieri the lady of his destiny." [*]

It was, if we are to believe the poet's own words, this unique quality of literary sympathy and understanding that engendered his resolution to enter the open portals of the Stuart palace, and to seek a victory over the captive bride of the royal dragon dwelling therein. The moment for an enterprise requiring at once caution and skill had arrived ; it was a dangerous but a fascinating game, and to Alfieri the game seemed well worth the candle. An additional zest was, indeed, gained by the acompanying

[*] Bertana, p. 173.

43

fact that the keeper of this priceless jewel was also a king by right of birth : a chance circumstance that weighed not a little in the poet's ill-balanced mind, which was now stocked with fierce republican opinions and ideals drawn from the works of Plutarch and other classical writers that he had recently been studying.

" This fourth and final fever of the heart presented me with totally different symptoms from those accompanying my former adventures. In my three earlier intrigues I had not been moved by any passion of the intellect, whilst in this last case the passions of the mind and of the heart were commingled and equalised, producing thus a feeling less fiery and impetuous, but deeper, profounder and more lasting. Such was the love that ever since has gradually enveloped every thought and affection of mine, and will only cease with my life itself. In two months' space I confessed to myself that she was the (ideal) woman I had been seeking, since instead of finding in her an obstacle to my literary career, a source of impediment to my work, and a cause of starvation, so to speak, to my intellect, I recognised in her a spur, a support and an incentive to every noble effort. Once I had admitted my full appreciation of so rare a treasure, I gave myself up absolutely to my passion. Nor have I been deceived in my judgment made twelve years ago, for at the very moment I pen these words at the present mature and melancholy age that knows no illusions, I feel that I love her more and more every day, in proportion as time destroys the only charm that is not wholly her own, the lustre of her perishable beauty." *

But this account with its generous tribute to the imperishable virtues of the " Donna Amata " was written in after years, and cannot, therefore, be adjudged as altogether applicable to the situation wherein the Countess and Alfieri were placed after the latter's return to Florence in the autumn of 1777. It was indeed, as Signore Bertana declares, with the undoubted intention of sowing

* *Vita,* vol. ii. pp. 59, 60.

the seeds of discontent and discord that Alfieri then entered the Palazzo Stuart and partook of the hospitality,
warmly and unsuspectingly offered, of its luckless master.
For the newly accepted guest was prepared to make full
use of every weapon in his preconceived plot for separat-
ing husband and wife. He was quite willing for this end
to show a fair face towards the husband he was seeking to
wrong; he was endeavouring for his own gain to widen
the breach, already sufficiently broad, between the ill-
matched pair; he was also straining every nerve and
using all his gifts of eloquence and fascination to inspire
the mistress of the house that received him with a feeling
warmer and more tender than the natural liking, with
which she was certain from the first to regard so agreeable
and distinguished a visitor. It is an ugly and an odious
story, but one which Italian writers, with the solitary
exception apparently of Signore Bertana, treat in the
calmest manner, so diverse are the British and Italian
temperaments, and so wide apart are both their national
views and their legislation on domestic morality. We
can feel nothing save disgust and anger against the
deliberate wrecker of a home, even of an unhappy home;
but from the Italian stand-point, such conduct as Alfieri's
seems to be regarded with amusement, if not with
applause.

CHAPTER IV

A FLORENTINE LOVE TRAGEDY

" . . . O despicable race,
Yea, thou wilt one day see thine end.   O thou
Last off-shoot of it, will the sword destroy thee ?
No, not a hand is vile enough to deign
To soil itself with blood like thine ; thy life
Will pass in one long slothful sleep, while he
Who'll hold thy throne will not thy foeman be.
The battle field will be the table ; thou
In drunken revels wilt the memory drown
Of thy unmerited, untasted reign."

(Passage inserted in the MS. but omitted in the published edition of the tragedy of *Maria Stuarda*, by Count Vittorio Alfieri, who states in the margin of the manuscript : " To be omitted as I had the misfortune of knowing this person (Charles-Edward Stuart) and do not wish to incur the stigma of malignity.")

In the malice propense of Alfieri therefore, we have no hesitation in declaring our belief; but is it a very different question to decide upon the exact degree of guilt or innocence in the case of the unhappy wife of Charles Stuart. Exactly when and under what particular circumstance she fell wholly under the insidious spell of her husband's guest we have no means of knowing. That she was hopelessly in love with the poet from the beginning seems improbable—we believe it took some months of seductive arts and cunning innuendo, as well as many a brief passion-scene sought in an unguarded moment, before the firm link of mutual attachment was finally forged between the lover and the lady. When and how Charles made the discovery (if ever he did so) of the intrigue is also unknown to us ; and although Alfieri himself again

46

declares in the *Vita* that he himself was never suspected, but that the husband's jealousy was extended in equal parts to every male visitor at his house, we have good reason to doubt so very convenient but unlikely a statement. The whole course of this strange and treacherous wooing, which occupied in all three years, is still shrouded in almost impenetrable mystery; and it is remarkable that during this period—that is to say, from Alfieri's first reception at the Palazzo Stuart in the autumn of 1777 to the flight of the Countess in December 1780—none in Florence seem to have been aware of the domestic tragedy that was silently developing within the walls of the Chevalier's palace. Sir Horace Mann, who had sure means of learning every detail concerning the daily life in the Pretender's household, never once in his letters makes mention of Alfieri; nor does he seem to be aware of any active intrigue of this kind. He does indeed, in the spring of 1779, give a most lurid account of the miserable Chevalier and alludes to the change in the Countess' appearance, due, presumably, to her lord's bad health and worse conduct. "The Pretender . . . . is in a deplorable state of health. He has a declared fistula, great sores on his legs, and is insupportable in stench and temper, neither of which he takes the least pains to disguise to his wife, whose beauty is vastly faded of late. She has paid dear for the dregs of Royalty." *

Now, if we are to believe the ingenious theory of Signor Bertana, this change for the worse in the Count of Albany was due to the continual anxiety he was enduring at the discovery (a discovery that he was perhaps too proud to reveal) he had made of the guilty relations between his wife and his guest. But we are wholly without clear evidence on the point. Our own opinion is that Charles, always jealous and quarrelsome, perhaps disliked and distrusted Alfieri more than any other of his visitors, but was unable, owing to the poet's astute conduct and apparent friendliness, ever to detect him in the

* *Mann and Manners*, vol. ii. p. 351,

47

smallest actual indiscretion. What does seem evident, however, is that Louise was beginning to resent with more spirit the cruel treatment she had hitherto endured in silence, and that the ill-mated pair, a sprightly and intellectual May linked with a drunken and repulsive December, were leading a cat-and-dog existence which was certainly common talk, though for some reason Sir Horace Mann rarely alludes to their domestic jars in his letters home. There is one place however, and one place only, where some genuine information can be gleaned concerning this tragedy in the bosom of the Stuart family. This source is no other than the poetry of the lover himself, who has, fortunately for those who are still interested in the course of these events, preserved some very enlightening sentences amongst his sonnets and lyrical verses composed during this period of awaiting and aiding the final rupture whereon he had set his heart. From the century of sonnets, which in later years Alfieri published with the object of glorifying his " Donna Amata," much as the high-souled Petrarch had immortalised his Laura de Noves, various allusions can be detected in the verses that were drawn from the love-lorn poet in this early phase of his infatuation for the wife of the Stuart prince. Amongst a great deal of matter that is purely descriptive or vaguely amatory, we occasionally find passages that hint at the proceedings in Palazzo Stuart which led ultimately to the flight and escape of Louise towards the close of the year 1780.

The poet himself endeavours in a sonnet to describe the exact moment wherein his passion was for the first time returned by the object of his persistent siege and of his constant but silent adoration. We cannot of course name the date of Alfieri's conquest of his beautiful hostess (whom elsewhere he describes as driving from her hitherto undisputed throne of beauty the Venus de' Medici in the Florentine Gallery) ; * but this sonnet probably dates from the earlier part of 1778, not long

* In the Sonnet, *O di Tirreno fabbro opra divina !* (*Poesie Amorose*, p. 127).

48

after his return from those hurried rides to Rome and Siena which we have already mentioned.

> Thou lovest me ! O joy, thy radiant glances
> Fall on my face with pleading innocence.
> Mine own consuming fire towards thee advances
> To burn thy feeble arrows of defence.
> Ah, how the love-light in those soft orbs dances !
> How Cupid's jesting face is peering thence !
> The thought of victory my soul entrances ;
> But why so coy, so full of diffidence ?
> Oft have I marked thy trembling eyes of sable
> Moist with the nectar of love's silent spell,
> Full of a new-found joy incalculable,
> As their mysterious depths did plainly tell.
> Oh, speak the word that will my tongue enable
> To bless the day I came, I saw, I fell ! *

Again, the following sonnet is equally illuminating, both as to the condition of misery to which the Countess was reduced and as to her lover's evident intention to rescue her therefrom—

> O Lady, is my fear for thee displeasing,
> When my warm love is half compact of fear ?
> Since I behold thee forced with grief unceasing
> The harsh yoke of an agèd spouse to bear,
> Like some trapped dove in vain for mercy pleading.
> *From hands so impious and from home so drear*
> *I mean to snatch thee*, my alarm increasing
> With each foul act, with every falling tear.
> Thou art a damask rose, pure, fresh and blooming,
> Crushed in the fingers of a filthy clown ;
> And yet (such strange disguise is Love assuming !)
> I needs must curb mine ire and smooth my frown,
> To greet with smiling face thy tyrant's coming,
> Abhorred and dreaded, of ill-starred renown.†

This sonnet, which dates from the year 1778, tells us plainly three things. First, that the lady had long since made the poet her confidant of the miseries of her married life ; second, that he was entreating her to escape with his assistance from a hateful thraldom ; and third, that

* *Ibidem*, p. 122. *Tu m'ami ? oh gioja ! i tuoi raggianti sguardi.*

† *Il mio temer per te, Donna, a ti spiace ?* The italics in the translation given are our own to give emphasis to Alfieri's expressed intentions. *Poesie Amorose*, p. 153.

though doing all that was possible in secret to persuade the wife to elope, Alfieri was yet ready to exhibit an assumed friendship with the husband for the sake of prudence. It might also be added, that the writer speaks in no uncertain terms of her husband's brutality, for the truth of which statement we can turn again to Sir Horace Mann's remarks already mentioned.

Alfieri is thus seen to be on the most intimate terms of affection with the bewildered and ill-treated woman, who must evidently have been struggling at this time between her new-born passion for this brilliant and ardent lover and her own scruples with regard to breaking her marriage vows, or her more mundane dread of the future fate of a run-away wife, that creature which the Italian has always regarded with special abhorrence down to the present day, no matter how great may have been her provocation to desert a husband's roof. There is no hint, certainly, in the sonnets themselves of common-place gallantry between the poet and the Countess of Albany, for, as we said before, these were especially selected and polished at a much later date to tend to the glorification of his latter-day Laura ; but in one of the lyrics we obtain a glimpse, and a very lucid one too, of the amorous interchanges that must have taken place between the lovers, when circumstances proved favourable ; as for example when the royal Cerberus of the Palazzo Stuart was enjoying a nap in the presence of his wife and of the handsome poet, who was wont occasionally to read aloud passages from his new tragedy of *Maria Stuarda* or to discuss politics and philosophy.

The poet apostrophises the God of Sleep, blaming him for not closing more often the all-too-wakeful eyes of the elderly husband.

" How have I offended thee, O Sleep, placid brother of Death, that thou dost no more return to shut the eye-lids of the worthy spouse ? His old blinking orbs were formerly thy resting-place, yet nowadays I rarely behold thee alight upon them.

50

"O joy! It would seem as if the deity had hearkened to my prayer. There lolls the feeble old head, which tries vainly to keep steady. On the breast sinks the flabby chin; lo, it falls, and falls yet lower. Thus on the arm of Sleep reposeth hoary Age.

"Already from those fair shining eyes, dark, amorous and ardent, can I drink in slow draughts of the luscious poison. And in the silence I already feel that poison course through every vein, nor dare I open my lips, so full is my soul.

"But alas, what do I see? Is he awake, before ever he was sound asleep? To earth I must fix my eyes, burning with the love-light. Why dost thou mock my prayers, O Sleep, last of the gods to obey? Malign and envious, thou art the foe of lovers, and carest no more for their sorrows than for their delights." *

From this poem it becomes quite clear that the passion of the man at this date was warmly reciprocated by the lady. It is, indeed, a horrible picture that this vile poem affords us of the Chevalier, once the hero and darling of Scotland, sunk thus in a drunken slumber and waking therefrom perhaps to detect his young wife exchanging glances of no mistaken meaning with one of his own guests. We can easily conjure up such a scene—the old, old situation of the jealous elderly husband, the pretty young wife and the eager unscrupulous lover that forms the staple matter for so many a farce, which ought to move to pity and disgust rather than to uproarious mirth. The heir of a race of kings, famed in song and story, in his dismal palace of exile, fallen in age, reputation and strength, has become the prey of an Italian wife-hunter. It is a terrible travesty of the familiar fable of the lion grown old and helpless.

How long a time elapsed before the Countess yielded herself a ready confederate in this sort of low conventional intrigue we have no means of ascertaining; but it is evident that she and Alfieri were on the intimate if secret

* *Poesie Amorose* (*Anacreontica*), pp. 249-254.

51

footing of avowed lovers some time before the final catastrophe of December, 1780. Originally, so we firmly believe, Alfieri had only found a friendly hostess and a sympathetic listener in Palazzo Stuart. But the lady's interest in his literary aspirations quickly added fuel to his fire, so that it could not have been long before this "Tower of Virtue," as Alfieri himself styles her, yielded before an attack that was at once brutal, calculated and subtle in its methods. A mutual admiration of Montaigne (one of whose essays the Countess was wont to peruse regularly each morning, as she herself once told Bonstetten in a letter) * formed perhaps the first bond of intellectual sympathy between the pair. The intention to write a tragedy on the subject of the unhappy Mary Stuart, Queen of Scots, the lineal ancestress of her husband, gave further opportunities for the poet to press his suit under cover of an union of twin intellects. This play was doubtless often read aloud in parts to the Count and Countess of Albany; and possibly when the descendant of the Scottish Queen had fallen asleep as the result of weariness or of the wine-cup, there arose one of those rare but long-desired opportunities for the display of that language of the eyes, which is so graphically and coarsely described in the lyric lately quoted. The writing of the drama of *Maria Stuarda*, in short, seems an inevitable episode closely bound up with the amorous onslaught of Alfieri and the all-too-easy capitulation of the Countess. Her lack of deep religious convictions, whereof her later letters afford abundant proof, told strongly in the lover's favour; the cruel humiliating conduct of an old and repellent husband was constantly present in her mind to assist his unscrupulous arguments; whilst the intellectual sympathy between the pair was growing more imperiously insistent every day. For the actual plot of the tragedy of *Mary Stuart* was, so Alfieri himself tells us in the dedication of that drama, conceived in obedience to the wishes of his "Donna Amata" during

* *Lettres et Écrits divers*, p. 7.

52

these early days of their romantic intrigue in the Florentine palace.

"As every work of mine is yours, you must not be left for a moment in doubt that I wish to anticipate the slightest desire of yours. I have often heard that unhappy woman, Mary Stuart, pitied by you; it has given me pleasure to exculpate her in this tragedy (which I dedicate expressly to you), as much as possible from the murder of her husband generally laid to her charge. I confess I would not have entered on such a task of my own spontaneous will, partly because I take greater delight in antique themes, as richer in virtues or grander in crimes, and partly because I foresaw that I could not deal with the subject without inclining to adulation, or in some manner offending the memory of a race to which, during a long period of unhappiness, you remained attached by sacred ties. However, you shall hear me speak with my usual freedom, which, next to yourself, I deem the dearest thing in the world; and whilst I develop the truth, I will show you that for your own sake, and not because I was near you, I consecrated to you the better portion of my life, the whole of the genius that was in me, and more obsequious affection than was ever found in any other heart." *

This dedication obviously belongs to a later date than the major portion of the play itself, which was composed during the course of this surreptitious love-making in Florence; whilst the fierce tirade against Charles Stuart (already quoted as a fore-word to this chapter) was added by the poet in after years, probable during the time of his separation from the Countess in 1783.

Yet another proof of the lively interchange, presumably unknown to the husband, of literary ideas between the pair of lovers, is to be found in a curious little paper preserved in the Musée Fabre at Montpellier, wherein so many relics of the poet and the Countess of Albany have found a final resting-place. This paper, one of

* *The Tragedies of Vittorio Alfieri,* translated by E. A. Bowring.

their very few communications that have survived the hand of the deliberate destroyer, consists of a small sketch by the Countess of the heads of the four great Italian bards—Dante, Petrarch, Ariosto and Tasso—whose works Alfieri was ever perusing and striving to rival in his tragedies. Above the poets of Italy is suspended a wreath of laurels with the single Latin word *Digniori* ("To one yet more worthy of the laurels than they "), which was doubtless the method of the Countess's personal encouragement to one whose talents were as yet unknown to his countrymen. We have already noticed how Alfieri speaks of his new-found mistress as an incentive and support to his literary ambition ; and in this bit of paper we are shown proof positive of the lady's keen interest that led to this outburst of praise and flattery. On the treasured paper itself is a note in the poet's handwriting : "This I received as a gift from my lady in the year 1778 at Florence ; " whilst at the back of the sketch is indited the sonnet which contains the lines in allusion to the four bards, his special masters and models :

> *Chi son costoro ?*
> *Quattro gran vati ed i maggiori son questi.**

Seeing then, from the evidence of Alfieri's own muse already given, that a complete collusion, both of the heart and head, existed between the poet and the Countess of Albany so early as the year 1778—that is to say, barely a twelvemonth after he had made his first bow in the chambers of the Stuart palace—it is surprising to find the expected revolt or escape of the lady postponed so late, for two long years of indecision were fated to elapse with the household of the Chevalier plunged in so uncomfortable and precarious a state. No doubt the eager lover constantly urged flight to be followed by a freer union with himself and his ideals ; and such a suggestion

* Mazzatinti, *Le Carte Alfieriane di Montpellier*. (*Giornale Storico delle Letteratura Italiana*, vol. iii., p. 262.)

COUNT VITTORIO ALFIERI
From the portrait by F. X. Fabre

must have brought the usual temptations to the bewildered and undecided lady. But on the other hand, miserable as was certainly her daily life in her husband's thraldom, yet that very life had its compensations. Although her lord's tipsy habits and occasional barbarity rendered her truly wretched, yet by the inexorable unwritten law of Italian social life, she owned the inestimable boon of daily receiving and hearing her adorer, whose presence in his house, either from ignorance of his aims or from fear of Florentine ridicule, the Chevalier seems never to have resented openly. Alfieri was to the last a constant guest at the prince's table, and thus found occasional chances for the exchange of vows, plans and confidences with his charmer. Again, the Chevalier's appalling state of ill-health was a perpetual source of hope to the Countess. Any day might bring an apoplectic stroke or some fatal malady; and then the lovely and much-pitied woman would in one brief moment find herself left sole mistress of her future fate and the owner of no mean fortune. In one of her letters to Gori a few years later she alludes to her husband as " the man of iron, who lives on and on, in order that we may all die " ; and no doubt the secret hope of a sudden ending both to her spouse and to her own state of oppression and uncertainty dominated not a little her perplexed mind, which was being constantly fed, though never satisfied, with the daily sight and conversation of her lover. And perhaps—who knows ?—she was even afraid at this period of risking her rank and her wealth, of setting the whole social world at defiance in order to please a man whom some of her friends may have pointed out as a gay deceiver ; for, as we have shown, Alfieri's reputation was far from spotless, and his present protestations of undying devotion might some day be falsified. Again, though far from being a good Catholic, the Countess was not lax in the attendance to her religious duties, so that perhaps some scintilla of the moral teaching that had been impressed on her young mind in the cloisters of Mons may have caused her uneasiness at the suggestion of deserting a husband to whom she had been bound by the most solemn ties of the Church. These are at least some reasons that go to explain that long-drawn out fever of delay and indecision between the time of Alfieri's disclosure of his love to willing ears and the Countess's final step of quitting her husband's roof for ever. So far as the Chevalier is concerned, we are left wholly in the dark. It seems incredible that the suspicious irritable old man should not have had an inkling of the game that was being played around him; yet if he had really caught Alfieri in the act of making love to the wife whom he now hated as well as guarded, he would surely have found some means or other to rid his house of so dangerous and objectionable a visitor. But the poet tells us explicitly in the *Vita* that he himself was unsuspected; and if this was truly the case, then the wife-stealer must have been an adept at simulating a false friendship with the host he was engaged in injuring. We are therefore compelled to believe that for three years Alfieri was enjoying the hospitality of a home that he was setting himself to wreck in a most selfish, deceitful and altogether detestable method, a fact which must carry a sense of contempt and indignation against this man who had set himself up to teach his countrymen the means of moral and political redemption, and yet was the actual and unabashed author of so cold-blooded an act of treachery. One other person must have played a leading part in this disreputable affair. This was Madame de Maltzam, the confidant of the Countess, and it is perhaps due to her astute counsels that the final flight of her mistress was so long delayed. But in what manner, or to what extent she guided the affair, it is only possible to guess, for her name is never once mentioned by contemporary informants in connection with it.

It becomes useless, therefore, to try to apportion the true amount of guilt in the case of the Countess of Albany, concerning whose behaviour there is at this time no evidence, favourable or unfavourable, forthcoming. That

she was shockingly ill-used by her husband was decidedly
the universal opinion in Florence, and Sir Horace Mann
in commenting later on her escape gives her credit for
having been driven to this step, not out of a desire to
elope with Alfieri but in order to avoid physical injury at
the hands of the tipsy and half-mad Chevalier. " During
her nine years' Martyrdom," he writes, " she has applied
to cultivating her mind by studying Mathematiks and
reading History and Poetry, at a time when one may well
suppose that she had a great struggle with her constitution to resist the temptation of her Master, the renowned
Count Alfieri, without the least blemish to her character."*
This act of approval, however, the British envoy was
moved afterwards to modify on hearing something of the
Chevalier's side of the story ; but Mann's judgment at
this crisis is of some value in proving to us the general
consensus of belief in the Chevalier's personal violence
and in the lady's unsullied honour, however strong had
been her temptation.

The final event, which we believe Alfieri himself desired
rather to hasten than to avoid, took place towards the
close of 1780.   To the last the pair of lovers had managed
to enjoy some small share of each other's society, whilst
the seal of approval had been set on the attachment not
only by the indulgent Gori but also by the gentle Abbé
di Caluso, who had spent the whole of the year 1779 in
the poet's company in Florence.   But Alfieri, baulked
of his chances by the circumstance that Charles was
invariably present at each meeting, and also growing
exasperated at the sight of the domestic tyranny to which
his lady was being continually subjected, was daily
becoming more and more impatient.   What led to the
last scene of violence is commonly said to have been the
convivial debauch on St. Andrew's Day, November 30,
when the Chevalier, maddened by the fumes of wine and
strong waters to a point beyond his habitual condition of

* *Mann and Manners*, vol. ii. pp. 376-377.   Sir H. Mann also adds his
opinion that the lady deserves a handsome English pension on this account !

drunkenness, suddenly attacked his wife in the privacy of her bed-chamber, accusing her of infidelity; a charge which she denied with considerable warmth, so as to anger her tipsy spouse yet further. A disgraceful assault of the intoxicated man upon the young and lovely woman followed; the Countess was not a little injured and was certainly alarmed for her life, and Sir Horace Mann even hints at conduct too nauseous to relate. The piercing cries of the terrified lady soon brought the servants to her rescue, and Louise was dragged from the clutches of her infuriated husband.

It would seem that, bad as Charles' behaviour had long been, this particular escapade on St. Andrew's night was far in excess of any former acts of cruelty; and it was now that the Countess, in genuine alarm for her safety, at last applied to Alfieri, who was only too willing, to find some means of escape from a house that was not merely intolerable but actually dangerous. Leaving abruptly the course of deep study wherewith he was solacing himself for the thought of the indignities endured by his beloved lady, the poet now spent his time in applying to the officials of the Tuscan court, who, it seems, were more than ready to lend themselves to some scheme of rescue. The Pretender was considered a political nuisance in Tuscany, a country which was deeply indebted to Britain and anxious to keep in British good graces; indeed, the very presence of the Stuart Prince and his court in Florence was most unwelcome to the Grand-Duke. Both for reasons of common pity as well as of public policy, Alfieri's petition therefore was favourably received in exalted quarters, so that the only question to be considered now was, how best to effect the act of rescue, which owing to the Chevalier's constant and jealous supervision of his wife presented some difficulty.

The story of the Countess of Albany's escape is well known and has been described many times already in works dealing with the later Stuarts, so that it will be recounted here as briefly as possible. A few days after the affair of St. Andrew's night, the plot had been hatched and all precautions taken for its successful fulfilment. A certain Madame Orlandini, an Irish lady, and her *cavalière servente*, Mr. Gehegan, were admitted to the secret, which must also have been shared by Madame de Maltzam, albeit that mysterious lady's name never once appears openly in connection with the incident. At dinner on a certain day, Madame Orlandini, who had previously obtained in private the consent of the Grand-Duchess of Tuscany, suggested that after the meal the whole party in the course of their usual afternoon drive should call at the neighbouring convent of the White Nuns in the Via del Mandorlo in order to inspect some pieces of embroidery. In so innocent a proposal even the abnormally suspicious Prince failed to detect any latent plot; and accordingly a little later the carriage containing the company drove to the entrance of the convent, where the Countess duly alighted, accompanied by Madame Orlandini and escorted by Gehegan. The portress of the convent admitted the two ladies; the doors closed upon them, and this was the last sight on earth the Chevalier ever obtained of the pretty and talented wife, whom he had alienated by his cruelty but who might have grown into a devoted and useful support in his old age, had he but treated her with the tact and kindness that such a marriage of disproportionate ages especially demands.

After a long interval of waiting, the impatient Chevalier, hobbling with feeble swaying steps up to the doorway, knocked with angry strokes at the door itself, which Gehegan had declared would not open to his request. A panel of the close-barred portal was slid aside for a moment, whilst a voice from within briefly informed the amazed and indignant husband that the wife he sought had left him to seek the protection of the Grand-Duchess, which had been graciously afforded her. The panel was then shot back with force, and the Chevalier was left on the doorstep to curse uselessly to his heart's content or to bear his unexpected loss with dignity, as he might choose. In a frame of mind that can be more easily imagined than described, the lonely man returned to his deserted palace, where he took a mean revenge a few hours later in refusing to supply his runaway spouse with any of her necessary linen or apparel, which a special messenger had come to demand; and it was only some days later, at the express order of his almoner, the Pope, that the discomfited Prince acceded to the distasteful request. Here then in the dismal old palace we leave Charles-Edward Stuart on the verge of his sixtieth birthday, deprived of his wife, wounded in his honour and his personal pride, a prey to the demon of " the nasty bottle," despised by his very servants and feeling acutely his ignoble position as the merest of political ciphers in the eyes of the Pope and the sovereign of Tuscany. As for his wife, she never forgave him. Almost to the last hour of her life, her hatred was almost indecently keen and bitter against her husband,* whose defects and outrages seemed in the process of time to take on a larger and more lurid aspect. Yet the idea of regaining her by force of the law rather than by entreaty was for some time prominent in the bereft Prince's wandering brain, so that at first he left no effort untried to accomplish his object. But neither the Pope nor the Grand-Duke would pay the smallest attention to his demands, and indeed the only person anxious to effect a reconciliation between the pair seems to have been the worldly old Princess of Stolberg, who made one feeble attempt to persuade her daughter to return to her husband. Failing to gain sympathy from the Pope or the Grand-Duke Leopold, the Prince now fell back on the pious and learned Monsignore Antonio Martini (the eminent translator of the Bible into the Italian tongue), who was greatly embarrassed by the enraged husband's persistent appeals. A letter from the unwilling prelate to the

* Except in her highly insincere letters to the Cardinal of York.

Cardinal of York on this subject is therefore of some importance, seeing that Alfieri and the Countess considered Martini's action as having been largely responsible for their separation two years later in Rome. That the Archbishop was most anxious to avoid any participation in the matrimonial affairs of the Count and Countess of Albany is quite obvious both from the language and the tone of the following letter, which is dated November 2, 1781, within a year of the actual occurrence.

" YOUR ROYAL HIGHNESS AND EMINENCE,—Had I not full knowledge of the extreme piety and goodness of Your Eminence, I should not presume to trouble you with this letter, dealing with a painfully delicate matter, which owing to my official position places me in a grave dilemma.

" The Signor Comte d'Albany has implored me several times to come to see him at his palace, and has even himself struggled to reach my own house more than once in order to consult with me, so that at last I felt bound, out of mere civility, to pay him my respects in person. The motive of his anxiety to meet me was explained by himself the very moment I entered his cabinet, and this motive was his fixed desire to start an action here for the restoration, as he terms it, of his lady consort. I did and said all I could to calm his fury, but to no purpose. Finally I begged him to wait awhile, so as to give me time to reflect well on so difficult and delicate a case. Within the last few days, however, he has been pressing me for an answer so impatiently, that I therefore appeal to Your Eminence to deign to suggest to me what I ought to do under the circumstances, wherein a husband of such rank claims the right to recall a wife who has left him (so he alleges) without just cause. The kindness I received of Your Eminence some months ago in Rome, and your own virtues and experience, must make you excuse this step on my part, to which necessity alone compels me. I do assure you I shall do neither more nor

61

less in the matter than what you yourself suggest to me. . . ." *

Meanwhile the romantic story, doubtless much distorted and exaggerated, of the lady's flight and of her husband's impotent wrath became the sole topic of conversation in the scandal-loving society of Florence. Her case was at least considered as exceptional, so that sympathy with the ill-treated wife and an universal belief in her innocence were everywhere expressed, whilst the abandoned spouse was, of course, the subject of combined scorn and amusement.—"The mould for any more casts of Royal Stuarts has been broken," writes the delighted and much relieved Sir Horace Mann to his English crony, " or what is equivalent to it, is now shut up in a convent of Nuns under the double lock and key of the Pope and the Cardinal of York, out of the reach of any Dabbler who might foister in any spurious copy " †—a remark that clearly exhibits the real cause of the British envoy's late anxiety and present sense of relief at the turn affairs had taken. By degrees the details of the incident spread over Europe, and finally reached British shores, where, however, the humiliation of the Stuart Prince aroused little compassion or, indeed, any interest whatsoever ; it was scarcely alluded to in the journals and in the art of caricature the news only produced a feeble and scurrilous print of the Chevalier and his runaway wife in company with a mischievous Cupid holding a burnt-out torch.

Whilst the outside world of Florence was thus engaged in discussing her private affairs, the Countess of Albany herself remained quietly in the shelter of her chosen convent, utterly exhausted with her late feverish adventures and awaiting an answer to an imploring letter she had promptly despatched to her brother-in-law, Henry Stuart, Cardinal-Duke of York. Her position in her own eyes was scarcely an enviable one. She had, indeed, taken a leap in the dark. If she were at last released from an

* Reumont, *Gli Ultimi Stuardi*, pp. 70, 71.
† *Mann and Manners*, vol. ii., p. 376.

odious servitude to a tipsy master, on the other hand she was likely henceforth to be totally deprived of the society of the one person on earth, whose presence had made her willing to endure all the tyranny she had suffered for the past three years. It is reasonable therefore, to presume, that but for her genuine fears for her life at the hands of her husband, she would have rested content to bow to her domestic afflictions, provided only she were assured of the daily visits of her lover, and would have awaited with all the patience available the release that she hoped in the course of nature was not so far distant. By this time bound heart and soul to Alfieri, and caring for nought else on earth, the quiet convent must have seemed to the unhappy and distracted woman merely an exchange of one prison for another. Her future position, which lay entirely in the hands of her worthy but prudish brother-in-law, troubled her greatly. Would she ever, she wondered, be able to evade the irksome restraint of the cloister, so as to meet with her lover; or had the Cardinal the firm intention of shutting her up from the outside world so long as " the man of iron " lingered on ? Such were doubtless her thoughts at the time she received the expected answer from Henry Stuart, whose kind but vague letter invited his sister-in-law to return to Rome under his powerful protection.

" FRASCATI, *December* 15, 1780.

" MY VERY DEAR SISTER,—I cannot express to you the sorrow I have felt on reading your letter of the 9th of this month. Long ago I foresaw what has at last happened, and your escape being made with the approval of the Tuscan Court has fully justified your conduct. You may rely, my very dear Sister, on my own kindly sentiments towards you, for up to the present moment I have always sympathised with your position ; though, on the other hand, I beg you to recall the fact that I had no share whatsoever in bringing about your indissoluble union with my Brother, beyond giving my formal consent

to a marriage whereof I had received no previous intima-
tion. As to its consequences, no one more than yourself
can understand the impossibility of my assisting you in
the smallest degree during your subsequent troubles and
trials. Under the circumstances, nothing can be wiser or
more convenient than for you to come to Rome and live
in a convent, so I have not lost a moment in going into
Rome expressly to serve you by arranging this matter with
our very Holy Father, whose kindness towards yourself
and me I am unable to relate adequately. I have thought
of all things essential to your case, and I am glad to say
the Holy Father has approved of all my suggestions. You
will reside in the convent where the Queen, my mother,
remained some time, and for which the King, my father,
had a special veneration. It is the least restricted convent in Rome. French is spoken there, and some of its
inmates are persons of rank. . . .

"It is enough to say that you may rely on being in good
hands, and that I shall never fail openly to admit my protection of you as a duty owing to you in your present
situation, since I am perfectly convinced you will be ready
to accept the counsel and advice I may occasionally give,
with no other object in view than that of your own good
before God and man. The Nuncio [in Florence] has
been well instructed, so that your departure may be conducted safely and agreeably, and you must therefore
follow his instructions. I fancy you will be accompanied
by Madame de Maltzam,* and by two maids at most.

"Finally, my very dear Sister, remain calm and allow
yourself to be guided by those who are attached to you,
and above all do not tell a soul that you never intend to
return to your husband. Do not fear I should ever urge
such a step, unless a miracle were to take place. But in all
probability God has permitted the past in order to induce
you to lead a holy life, so that all the world may thereby
admit the purity of your aims and the reasonableness of

* Called here Madame de Marzan : one of the very rare allusions to this
lady in contemporary letters.

your conduct ; so also we may hope by the same means He intended to convert my Brother. . . .

"Your very affectionate Brother,
"HENRY CARDINAL." *

A careful study of this verbose and rambling but truly sympathetic letter is especially important, if the reader wishes to understand the exact terms on which the upright Cardinal invited his sister-in-law to Rome, and to estimate how far those terms were compatible with the existence she hoped or intended to lead under his protection. From the tone of the letter it is easy to see that the Cardinal-Duke, with his utter ignorance of human weakness, was wholly unsuspecting of any possible complication, save that of incompatibility of temper, in this late domestic upheaval in his brother's house. Yet at this moment he was apparently no less obtuse than the rest of the wise world, for the name of Alfieri was being mentioned on all sides merely in the light of a chivalrous and disinterested friend, who out of sheer compassion had helped to connive at the lady's flight. That he was really guiltless so far, he himself states in a rather vague passage of the *Vita* where, after protesting his own blameless conduct in his attitude towards the Countess, he proceeds to say : " It is sufficient to state that I rescued my Lady from the tyranny of an exacting and ever-tipsy consort, without however compromising her honour in the least degree, and without causing any scandal to the world at large. In any case all who have known or have seen the peculiar circumstances of her very harsh imprisonment, which was killing her by inches, will realise that this was no easy matter to conduct and bring to a happy conclusion." †

Let us then at this precise point affirm our perfect belief in the innocence of the Countess of Albany, without caring to ascertain whether such innocence were partly

* St. Réné Taillandier, *La Comtesse d'Albany—Revue des Deux Mondes* 1861.

† *Vita*, vol. ii. p. 83.

the result of the perpetual espionage of the husband, who rarely allowed his young wife out of his sight, even for a moment ; for, as Alfieri relates, " he was always present with her, or at best in the adjoining room." She had therefore a perfect right to ask her brother-in-law for the protection which he readily granted on her request, as we have seen. She had then the approval of the Cardinal, the Pope and the Grand-Ducal court of Tuscany for her revolt ; whilst her position was regarded for once by Italian society with universal sympathy rather than with condemnation, so convinced was everybody of the horrors she had been forced for years to endure in her husband's house. Save for the concealed secret passion for her deliverer that was consuming her, the Countess might well have been envied as a fortunate woman to have escaped on such easy terms from her late slavery, and to have this prospect of an honourable retirement before her in Rome. Thither the Pope, Pius VI., himself invited her in a letter full of kindly interest,* and ere the month of December had drawn to a close, a travelling coach with an escort of well-armed servants set out from Florence bearing the Countess towards Rome. A report of the time tells us that Alfieri himself in disguise and with pistol in hand accompanied her carriage ; but no such incident is mentioned in the *Vita*, so presumably the picturesque statement has no foundation in fact. Thus, despite the fierce but unavailing appeals of the lonely husband, the Countess of Albany was enabled under official approval to quit the scene of her late trials and to make the journey to her new abode in safety.

* Reumont, *Appendix*, pp. 313, 314.

66

CHAPTER V

THE SECOND VISIT TO ROME

" Life, what a hard thing it is ! For myself it has been one
long bout of suffering for the last eleven years, all except the two
years I spent with the Friend in Rome, and even then I was
living in the midst of alarms."—*Letter of the Countess of Albany
to Francesco Gori, written in the autumn of* 1783.

Arrived safe in Rome at the Ursuline convent in the
Via Vittoria, where the suite of rooms once occupied
by the ascetic Queen Clementina Stuart had been hastily
prepared for her reception, the Countess of Albany was
welcomed in the most affectionate manner by the
Cardinal-Duke of York, who found his sister-in-law,
to his deep distress, in a fearful state of nervous collapse
after her late trials and experiences in Florence. Louise
was indeed glad of the change with its sense of relief
that no more could her " nautious tyrant," as Mann
styles the Chevalier, assault or torment her ; and for
the moment she was perhaps ready to remain quietly
in this peaceful retreat, where she was regarded with
special interest and attention by the inmates

Meanwhile Alfieri, too anxious and too perturbed to
linger in Florence after the flight of her whose absence
made the beautiful city appear odious and gloomy to
his lover's eye, hastened southward on the flimsy pretext
of a necessary visit to Naples, though it seems needless
to state that he halted at Rome on his way thither, so
early as the second month in the New Year, 1781. From
having loathed and abused, in one of his early sonnets,[*]
Rome and the Papal dominions, the susceptible poet

[*] *O vuota, insalubre regione.*

67

now confesses that he found the Eternal City the most tempting spot in the whole world. He duly called upon the Papal officials, who regarded him as the legitimate and honourable *cavaliere servente* of the distressed lady now immured in a nunnery; whilst with the permission of the Cardinal-Duke he was allowed to hold a short interview with her under the usual conditions in the guest-room of the Ursuline convent.

" I came," so he relates this experience in the pages of the *Vita*, " I saw her (but, O God ! my heart seems to break now at the mere recollection of it), I saw her behind a grating, less tortured than in Florence, but for a certain reason no less unhappy. For we were separated, and who could tell how long that separation might endure ? And yet I solaced myself amid my tears that here she could at least gradually recover her health, could breathe a freer air, enjoy quiet sleep, and no more be trembling for fear of that dire ever-present shadow of her tipsy husband." *

Alfieri remained only a few days in Rome, but during his short sojourn he was busily employed in interviewing various officials with the determined but artfully veiled intention of obtaining additional freedom for the well-guarded Countess. The eager lover's efforts in quest of this object knew no bounds. Every argument, every species of flattery, and we may add, every sort of untruth were adduced by the Count to make the Roman authorities relent in their severe regulations with regard to the runaway wife of the Chevalier. Alfieri, the republican aristocrat, who had hitherto railed at priests and kings, and at priestcraft and king-craft, now showed himself an adept courtier, and was evidently guilty of an amount of artifice and dissimulation of which he felt bitterly ashamed in his heart of hearts.

" Love softened my austere nature and drove me to devise the most cunning schemes, to which otherwise

* *Vita*, vol. ii. p. 86.

I should never have stooped for the whole world. . . .
I abased myself to pay visits (of ceremony), even to make
my court to the Cardinal, her brother-in-law, on whose
decision depended all hope of her liberty, and whom
we both constantly kept flattering. I shall speak no
more at length concerning these two brothers (Charles-
Edward and Henry Stuart), since all the world at that
date knew them well ; and although Time will ere long
have buried them in oblivion, it is not my business to
draw them forth from obscurity. I can say no good
word for them, and at the same time do not wish to say
anything ill. However, my conduct in Rome at this
crisis affords the most perfect testimony to my boundless
devotion for my Friend, in that I should have thus
lowered my proud nature before such people."[*]

This hypocritical apology for his illicit endeavours
to deceive the Cardinal of York and the clerical authorities, as well as the insolent but vague abuse levelled at
the kindly if obtuse prince of the Church he was bent on
hoodwinking, must cause us to become rather sceptical as
to the constantly advanced claims of Vittorio Alfieri to be
regarded as a noble character. As his own biographer,
he is not likely to exhibit his conduct in a worse light
than its actuality, yet it would be hard to find a
more unfair account of a particularly low trick played
upon a man of real virtue and simple goodness such as
the Cardinal of York. How far the Countess of Albany
was guilty of abetting her lover already at this early
stage, in setting out deliberately to deceive her excellent
brother-in-law with his innate horror of a love-intrigue,
it is difficult to say. Alfieri certainly describes this
pair of secret lovers as busily engaged in the mean game
of chicanery and flattery, so that in that case she cannot
be acquitted of a share in the scheme, though in a less
degree than the Count who certainly acted as her
instigator.

Most reluctantly leaving the Countess, " as delicacy

* *Ibidem*, p. 87.

69

compelled him," and abandoning his already partially successful occupation of toadying and winning over the Papal officials, the poet proceeded to Naples, whilst the Countess remained in her convent, still agitated over her new cause of anxiety, and in consequence but slowly recovering her broken-down health. The following letter, dated April 23, 1781, is one of the first letters in the correspondence that opens from this time onward between the Countess and the unsuspecting Cardinal, who was undoubtedly attributing the lady's continual state of nervous depression solely to her recent ill-usage at the hands of the drunken Charles-Edward, and was very far removed indeed from having the faintest inkling that the sympathetic Count Alfieri, who had taken so much disinterested trouble in the matter, could be aught else than a loyal and honourable friend of his own sister-in-law.

" *To my very dear Brother the* CARDINAL DUKE OF YORK
at FRASCATI
"*April* 23, 1781.

" . . . If you could see me now these days, my dear Brother, you would think me bad tempered, but I am only out of spirits and have such headaches that I can hardly speak. So I hope you will rest thoroughly assured that I am very happy; indeed it would be impossible for me to feel otherwise with such a brother as yourself. So never believe that I am cross, I beg you. Farewell, my dear Brother, keep me in your good graces, and be always persuaded of my tender affection.
" Your affectionate Sister,
" LOUISE." *

During the interval of Alfieri's absence at Naples, where the restless poet was impatiently awaiting a suitable moment to return to Rome, the petition of the Countess to be allowed to leave her present place of honourable

* British Museum. Add MSS. 34, 634, / 25.

but irksome confinement was being discussed by the Cardinal of York and his friends. Fortunately for the lady, the reigning Pope, Pius VI. (Gian-Angelo Braschi, of Cesena), was easy-going, not to say indulgent to human weakness; and consequently an interview between the good-natured luxurious pontiff and the pretty winning wife of the Stuart Prince with her graceful manners, her opportune tears, and her air of injured innocence, created a most favourable impression. This private colloquy, which according to Sir Horace Mann took place in the sacristy of a church, was followed by the Pontiff's plea to the anxious Cardinal not to press too hard the incarceration of so lively and innocent a creature within the walls of a gloomy nunnery which she pined to quit; whilst Henry Stuart, only too willing to please his sister-in-law to whom he was sincerely attached, showed himself quite ready to follow the opinion of his august temporal and spiritual sovereign. Public propriety would be satisfied, it was suggested, if only the solitary lady were allowed to inhabit her brother-in-law's palace; and as fate would have it, no arrangement could have suited both the lady and her lover more perfectly. For the Cardinal, practically living at his episcopal city of Frascati, across the Roman Campagna, rarely spent a night in his huge official palace of the Cancelleria, one of the finest of the early Renaissance secular buildings of Rome, which had been erected for Girolamo Riario, the favourite of Sixtus IV., in the sumptuous days of the Della Rovere and the Borgia. The Countess of Albany, now installed in a fine apartment on the second floor of this splendid mansion, was therefore destined to live practically in absolute independence, and yet to enjoy the very valuable and indeed indispensable qualification, of dwelling under the roof of her husband's brother, who was not only the wealthiest and most distinguished but also, perhaps, the most respected of all the members of the Sacred College. In vain did the helpless drunkard, the deserted

71

husband in Florence, storm and protest against the liberty now allowed his wife, and against the presence of Alfieri, who had returned to Rome in the middle of May; his mouthpiece, Prince Corsini, only got a severe lecture for his pains from the Pope, who now diverted half the Chevalier's Papal allowance of 12,000 crowns to the use of the Countess; whilst as to Alfieri, Pius declared that the great poet honoured his capital by coming to dwell therein. Furious letters to his brother Henry, always wrapped up in his daily life of pious duty and regal entertainment at Frascati, made no impression on that determined and obstinate prince, now that he had made up his mind to place the fullest confidence in his sister-in-law's discretion and modesty; whilst we have already mentioned the Chevalier's failure to win the good offices of the Archbishop of Florence. Louise, Countess of Albany, therefore came to take up her abode indefinitely in the palace of the Cancelleria under the happiest of auspices, with the full approval of Pope, Cardinal, and of Roman society in general.

In certain of its aspects, the Rome of Pius VI. was an ideal spot to inhabit.* The present holder of the See of St. Peter was strongly imbued with the notion of making the Eternal City once more the centre of the liberal arts, whilst he was a sincere admirer of his Medicean predecessor of the Renaissance, Leo X., who with the same end in view had even succeeded in carrying out for a few years some of his magnificent schemes. As far as was possible, a repetition of the far-off Leonine Age was being attempted; vast schemes of building in the city and of the draining of the Pontine Marshes were being undertaken; fresh aqueducts were being constructed; and a new sacristy was being added to the colossal basilica of St. Peter's by this imitator of the splendour-loving Medici. Rome was crowded with artists, actors, singers, sculptors and every sort of professional personage that could instruct or amuse. The

* Silvagni, *Corte di Roma*, chapters xiv.-xix.

world of fashion from all parts of Europe poured in a
ceaseless stream into the Papal capital, and all were
cordially welcomed thither, whatever their nationality,
their creed, or even their character. At this period,
just before the deluge of the unexpected French Revolution, the life and gaiety of Rome were remarkable.
Balls, *fêtes*, assemblies, operas, ceremonies followed in
an endless circle; and if the substructure of all this
pyramid of social splendour and activity were rotten
and the Papal exchequer rapidly approaching a state of
bankruptcy; what did such drawbacks matter to the
frivolous members of society, who danced, gambled,
feasted, and generally enjoyed the pleasant existence
that the place at this time afforded to its citizens and
its guests? To have sighed and fretted in a convent,
amidst so much pleasure and social stir, would indeed
have been too cruel a privation for the Countess of
Albany, all eager as she was to taste of the many delights
that love and liberty could furnish. It was therefore
as much due to the indulgent nature of the Pope, as
to the complaisant notions of the trustful Cardinal,
that Louise owed her freedom and her happiness. Henry's
consent to the arrangement once given, then it became
nobody's business henceforward in that pleasure-seeking
and corrupt throng to point out later that the lady was
perhaps making an undue and improper use of that state
of independence, which she had been at such pains to
acquire. But for the time being her position was secure
and well defined. As the sister of the royal Cardinal
Stuart; as the acknowledged and wronged wife of a
titular king; as a German princess in her own right,
the Countess of Albany at once took rank in Roman
society as one of its most exalted leaders, yielding the
palm alone in this respect to the haughty Princess Rezzonico, niece of Pope Clement XIII. So charming and
witty a princess was naturally accepted by all with the
greatest delight as a welcome addition to their assemblies,
and the wealthiest prelates and nobles vied in entertain-

73

ing so interesting and agreeable a lady, who never risked
her popularity by insisting on the royal honours which
her quarrelsome spouse had always demanded so per-
sistently a few years before in this very city. The Cardinal
of York, to his credit be it said, took little part in this
extravagant existence, contenting himself with visiting
the city from Frascati only to attend to certain church
ceremonies or to despatch the business in connection
with his many offices. This aloofness from social pleasure
was, however, far from being shared by his fellow members
of the Sacred College, of whom Cardinal de Bernis, the
French Ambassador, was especially celebrated for his
gorgeous banquets and his sumptuous mode of living.
This prince of the Church, whose elegant but trivial
poetry had won him the nickname of " Babet la Bouque-
tière " from the venomous tongue of Voltaire, possessed
a fine palace in the Corso, and his splendid entertainments were imitated by his aspiring but less wealthy
colleagues. At such scenes of fashion and amusement
the Countess was a constant visitor and, indeed, her face
was rarely absent from the more noticeable of the receptions in the great Roman palaces. Amidst such gay
surroundings, however, was seldom to be remarked the
handsome Piedmontese Count with his stern features
and flowing ruddy hair, who contented himself with
frequenting the comparatively few literary *salons* of the
city, notably that of Madame Pizzelli.*

Almost immediately on his return in May from Naples,
the Countess had taken further steps to ensure the goodwill of her easily duped brother-in-law, who, as she
herself speedily perceived, was as eager to condemn
any moral irregularity as he was slow to detect its presence.
To produce a good impression in his mind with regard
to Alfieri was her main object, and with this intent she
had promptly purchased a rare copy of Vergil (always

* Silvagni, vol. i. p. 229. Chapter xviii. of this fascinating work deals
with Alfieri in Rome. *See also* B. Magni, *V. Alfieri in Roma.* (*Il Buona-
rotti*, May, 1864.)

the favourite pagan author with Italian ecclesiastics), which she despatched by Alfieri's hand as a gift for the Cardinal's library in the seminary of Frascati, which he was now engaged in furnishing with its necessary complement of books.

"*May* 15, 1781.

"Since I had noticed, my dear Brother, that your fine library lacked a good copy of *Vergil*, and since I knew of a most beautiful example, I send you the very book; and I take the liberty of sending it to you by the hand of Count Alfieri, who has dined to-day at my house, and has told me he was going to-morrow to pay you his respects. I hope, my dear Brother, you will do me the honour of accepting my gift as a mark of my tender and sincere attachment towards yourself. Would that I could give you proofs of it every hour of the day! But rest fully persuaded that I am as devoted to you as if I were your own sister, and accept the assurance of a boundless affection.

"Louise." *

The poet prepared in characteristic fashion to settle in Rome with the fixed purpose of enjoying thoroughly what were now the three ruling passions of his life —namely, his Lady, his books, and his horses. Before leaving Florence he had even taken the step of abjuring his rights as a Sardinian citizen, since every subject born in Piedmont was liable to various acts of summary interference on the part of its Government, which his proud independent soul fiercely resented. To obtain his freedom therefore, and to become quit of the galling restrictions of the Piedmontese law, which compelled the subjects of the King of Sardinia to publish all their writings at Turin under heavy penalties for infringement, and which also required all landed proprietors to apply for passports when leaving the realm on every occasion,

* British Museum. Add MSS. 34, 634, / 29.

75

Alfieri had decided to divest himself of the greater portion of his hereditary estates of Cortemilia. By a legal donation therefore to his sister Giulia, wife of the Conte di Cumiana, the poet performed an act which was undertaken rather from reasons of personal convenience than from brotherly generosity.* By reserving to his own use the annual sum of 50,000 *livres*, he was now rid of all obnoxious obligations to the Piedmontese law, and also exempt from any further trouble in connection with the landed property whence he drew his income ; the annual sum reserved being fully sufficient to provide him with all the luxuries he might desire. Free as air then, the Count Alfieri, " comte piedmontèse et dipiedmontisé," was now able to hire the beautiful Villa Strozzi on the Esquiline at the very moderate rent of ten *scudi* a month. It was a lovely spot in those far-off days ; a picturesque villa surrounded by vineyards, olive groves and gardens, which enclosed many an ancient rose-red ruin half-shrouded in tangled masses of verdure. In this charming retreat within the walls of the city, yet far enough removed from the human noise and stir that he so cordially detested, Alfieri set to lead an ideal existence at no great distance from his " Donna Amata " installed in the great Palazzo della Cancelleria. Many hours a day he worked with the true literary zest on his unfinished tragedies, supporting himself on the most wholesome and frugal food, for he had long abjured the use of wine and all rich dishes. After a light meal at midday, he was wont to ride furiously over the rolling stretches of the grassy desolate Campagna, bounded by its ring of historic mountains and dotted with many a ruined Roman tomb and arch, that aroused his poetic nature to composition. Sometimes these rides in the clear crisp air were not solitary, for the beloved lady herself was occasionally wont to accompany her lover on the back of the favourite " Fido," for Louise was a capable

* The story of this " Donazione " is described at length in a special chapter of the *Vita*, vol. ii. pp. 60-74.

and intrepid horse-woman. The study and the exercise for the day being both completed to the poet's satisfaction, he usually spent the evening with the Countess, all of which daily routine he describes with loving emphasis in the *Vita*.

"During these two years (May 1781, to May 1783) in Rome I led a truly happy existence. The Villa Strozzi, near the Baths of Diocletian, afforded me a delightful retreat. The long mornings I spent wholly in study, never moving from the house, except for an hour or two spent in riding over those boundless solitudes of the deserted neighbourhood of Rome, that invited me to reflect, to mourn, and to compose verses. In the evening I descended into the city, whence I returned never later than eleven o'clock to my hermitage, restored by the welcome sight of Her for whom alone I lived and laboured. A life more free, more cheerful, more simple in the suburbs of a great city one could never find, nor one more congenial to my nature, character and occupations." *

Alfieri also speaks of his life at this period as being *onesta*,† and certainly he seems to have been very cautious and discreet in his hours of visiting the Countess and of the length of time he spent beneath her roof. Doubtless the prudent Madame de Maltzam supervised the movements and meetings of this pair of lovers, who were still half hoping to hear almost daily news of the sudden death of the lady's husband, concerning whose increasing ill-health reports were being constantly brought from Florence. In any case, it is evident the amount of attention paid by the poet to his sister-in-law aroused no anxiety in the mind of the good Cardinal; and if Henry Stuart seemed satisfied with this state of things, who in Rome was qualified to criticise this intellectual friendship? Provided only the rich and powerful Cardinal of York was content to protest and champion

* *Vita*, vol. ii. p. 110.

† *Cf.* the Sonnet *Alta è la fiamma, che il mio cuor consuma* (*Poesie Amorose* p. 153).

77

his sister-in-law (as he did even against his own brother), then it was nobody's business to interfere in the arrangement, or even to hint at the smallest impropriety in the romantic attachment between a great lady living apart from her husband and her chosen *cavaliere servente*. And yet it must have been patent to any thinking person, that the same cavalier continuing to wait on the lady after her flight elsewhere could not be regarded in the same category of social indulgencies, which admitted of such an anomaly, as the *cavaliere servente* himself. Be that as it may, no one in Rome, priestly or lay, seems to have raised an eyebrow at the pair, concerning whose close friendship nobody was so wanting in tact or courtesy as to inquire whether it proceeded from the head or the heart, or from a commingling of both senses, as it did in reality.*

To strengthen his position with the Roman authorities, the poet also laid aside with ease for the time being his austere republican ethics, making every effort to win the good graces of the Pontiff, whom he had so roundly abused a few years before. Apparently Pius bore Alfieri no ill-will, for he was received with the utmost cordiality at the Quirinal, where the Pope, to the intense but, of course, concealed disgust of his kneeling suppliant, patted the republican cheek in the most familiar and friendly manner, much as the Medicean Pontiff Leo X. had once embraced the disappointed Ariosto when openly seeking coin and not kisses at the Roman court.† Not only, however, had the ashamed but persistent lover to endure this act of humiliation, but his pride in his Muse was also destined to encounter a severe but quite unintentional rebuff from the well-meaning Pius. In order to make himself more secure of the Papal favour

* For the non-platonic side of this romance, *see* the Sonnet *Sovvienti la fra la temenza e speme,* which is excluded from all Alfieri's printed works, but is to be found in Fabris' *Studii Alfieriani (Appendix,* p. 231). *See also* Bertana, p. 189, on this point.

† *La mano e poi le gote ambe mi prese,*
E'l santo bacio in l'una e l'altra diede.

for his own private ends, the poet finally decided to present to the Pope the dedication of his *Saul*, generally considered the best of his tragedies. To his intense surprise and unspeakable mortification—for he deemed his offer one of exceptional attraction—the Pope politely declined the proffered distinction, excusing himself on the ground that so close a connection between the tiara of the papacy and the buskin of the despised stage was most unsuitable and, indeed, absolutely impossible. It is, however, only fair to add that Alfieri admits his reproof on this occasion with candour and humility in the *Vita*, and acknowledges that his snub was thoroughly well deserved, since his offer of the dedication had been tendered in a spirit of base deceit and with an ulterior object in view.* Nevertheless, by means of flattery and dissimulation he was enabled to obtain and hold the approval both of the Pope and the Cardinal during his two years' residence in Rome, so that, but for an unforeseen accident, he might have retained this advantage until such time as the expected demise of the lady's husband had removed the sword of Damocles, ever hanging above their heads during this second phase of their love-idyll.

Alfieri and the Countess seem to have been fairly circumspect in their conduct to the world at large, and as not a few of their meetings were arranged in secret, it is highly probable that their rides together over the rolling sward of the Campagna, wherein both delighted, were unknown to any save to Madame de Maltzam and to the Count's confidential valet, Elia, now in the employment of the Countess of Albany.

In the long hours of study or of riding the poet, it seems, was wont to console his temporary solitude with the absent lady's miniature that he invariably carried, stopping at spare moments to apostrophise the smiling face, as one may infer from the following sonnet composed about this time :

* *Vita*, vol. ii. p. 104.

79

Thou art, thou art Herself ! so deftly painted,
Each cherished feature seems with life to glow.
The rose-bud mouth, the bosom lily-tinted,
The dark and lustrous eyes so well I know.
Concealed within my breast this Image sainted
Accompanies my steps where'er I go,
I touch and fondle it as one demented,
I press is to my lips to whisper low.
Ah, then it seems to smile at mine emotion
And even speak ; " Call not those kisses lost
In vain caprice ; for such is the devotion !
Whereof your absent Friend makes constant boast,
That in the future with a double portion
She'll recompense all that your love has cost."*

It is easy to imagine the delightful existence the pair
were leading at this period : Alfieri working diligently
and successfully at his self-set task in a pleasant retreat
on the Esquiline ; the Countess enjoying her fill of the
social gaiety of the Roman capital, and both ever wrapped,
present or absent, waking or sleeping, in their secret
love, which a possible exposure and the dreaded sense
of a forcible separation made all the dearer and sweeter.
Alfieri now was in the full bloom of his manhood and
in the first fervour of that career of his literary ambition,
which formed one of the strongest bonds between the
lady and himself. His handsome face, his reputation
for profound learning, an attractive eccentricity, and
his evident devotion for the lovely wife of the Pretender,
all combined to invest his vigorous personality with a
halo of romance in the eyes of those fashionable persons,
whose assemblies he rarely deigned to honour with his
presence, preferring early hours and simple fare to the
splendid balls and banquets held in the Roman palaces.
Of the compelling charm of the Countess at this date
we have ample testimony. Her beauty, which was
increased rather than diminished by a pallor of the
complexion that had found its origin in her late life of ill-
usuage and anxiety in Florence, was radiant and renowned ;
indeed, the intervening years since her last visit to

* *Tu sei, tu sei pur dessa ! amate forme* (*Poesie Amorose*, p. 125).

Rome had given her more mature grace, had enlarged
and improved her mind, so that she was now considered
in truth a *donna intelletuale*, and no mere aspirant to that
term ; whilst her caustic wit, for which she had been
noted from her childhood, had doubled in point and
pungency. She was known to be the idol and the
Egeria of the erratic but brilliant poet, who tried (but
all too feebly and with transparent effort) to show to
the world that nothing save a mutual love for letters
bound him to the side of so exquisite and exalted a
personage. Thus the wit, learning and loveliness of the
Countess ; the handsome person, the sad reputation
and the noble ideals of Vittorio Alfieri ; the convenient
blindness of the pious Cardinal of York ; continued
for nearly two years topics of whispered conversation
in the *salons* of Rome, where all society was vastly amused
and very far from being shocked at the rumoured intrigue
between the pair, both of whom, it so chanced, were in
the good graces of the Pope and the Roman court.

In such a transitory condition of affairs, it seems quite
evident that sooner or later the two lovers must some
day be expelled from this paradise, wherein they
were straying under false pretences. Yet such was the
indifference of the Roman officials, and such the obstinate
belief of the Cardinal in his sister-in-law's integrity,
that the intimacy proceeded unchecked month after
month ; whilst no appeal from his brother in Florence
could move the Cardinal to see matters in the same light
as the outraged and protesting husband, who perhaps
had persons in Rome to spy upon the pair and to report
their delinquencies. On the contrary, Alfieri was growing more popular in Rome, thanks partly to the efforts
of the Countess and partly to his own anxiety to place
on the stage one of the tragedies he had recently completed, the *Antigone*, founded on the touching Greek
drama of Sophocles. For this purpose the handsome
Duchess of Zagarolo and the Duke and Duchess of Ceri,
members of the great Papal families of Odescalchi and

Rospigliosi, were induced to act with the poet himself, who undertook the part of Creon, for the play only required four persons on the stage in all. After some hesitation, it was decided to present the drama in the newly constructed theatre of the Spanish Embassy in the Piazza di Spagna, and thither on an evening in November 1782, the whole of Roman society was invited to witness the Count's tragedy. On the occasion of the event a modish and inquisitive throng, lay and clerical, Roman and foreign, assembled in the official palace of the Spanish Embassy. The Sacred College was well represented, its most conspicuous absentee being his Royal Highness and Eminence of York, who rarely attended entertainments in the city, fortunately on this occasion for the author of the play and for his distinguished friend, whose expected presence was evidently looked forward to by certain of the invited guests with more gusto than the severe dialogue of the tragedy itself. Conspicuous among the glittering crowd with the gorgeous dresses of the gentlemen and the powdered hair and diamonds of the ladies appeared the scarlet robes of the gallant old Piedmontese, Cardinal Gerdil, immensely proud of the genius of his fellow countryman, and especially honoured by the host, the Duca Grimaldi. Cardinal de Bernis was, of course, noticeable with his devoted Princess Santacroce as usual beside him, whilst the names of the great ladies and nobles of Rome who were present would fill several pages. To the seat of honour over all was conducted the Princess Rezzonico, niece of Pope Clement XIII., and known usually as the "Senatrice," of which title this influential woman was especially proud. Yet although the beauty and splendour of the regal Princess Rezzonico dominated the whole room with its courtly prelates, its resplendent gentlemen and its bejewelled ladies of fashion, the real queen of the evening was the lady whom ten years before the Swiss, Carl-Victor Bonstetten, had dubbed "Regina dei Cuori." As Louise, Countess of Albany, entered the

crowded theatre with her delicate pale skin illumined
by the soft light of hundreds of wax candles, in her
magnificent court dress and with the historic jewels
of the Stuarts and the Sobieskis sparkling in her bodice,
in her soft fair hair and on her breast, the whole company
was seized with overwhelming admiration or envy, as
the case might be. All guessed or knew the secret tie
that bound her to the author of the tragedy they were
about to witness, and it became a second and a yet more
interesting occupation to turn from the sorrows of
Antigone on the stage to study her radiant and intelligent
face each time her lover appeared upon the boards to
act for her and for her alone. Thus the pleasure-loving
world of Papal Rome gained a double entertainment
that memorable evening, and the Countess of Albany
a double triumph from the effect of her own beauty
and from the impression that her lover's genius created
on all around her.

After the curtain had been rung down for the last
time, the distinguished quartette of amateurs been
applauded, and the last strains of Cimarosa's tuneful
melodies had died away, a buzz of conversation arose
from the gaily-coloured mass of fine ladies and their
squires, as the host led the way to a great saloon where
supper was served to his many guests. A hundred
servants in liveries of canary with red stockings, the
royal colours of Spain, attended to the wants of these
elegant creatures, offering on silver salvers cakes, jellies,
sweetmeats and above all delicious ices flavoured from
an old recipe and served in little cups of spun sugar,
a pretty novelty which aroused much mirthful admiration. On all sides the author was being congratulated
by the first persons of Rome, whilst the lady was assuredly
conscious that the complimentary speeches made by all
present to Alfieri were largely directed to herself, who
was universally regarded as the poet's source of inspiration. Of all the triumphs in the course of a long and
chequered career, the reception in the Spanish Embassy

with the performance of *Antigone* perhaps afforded her the greatest satisfaction. She had been recognised thereat as indeed the Queen of Hearts, and all Rome had hastened to offer real or pretended homage to her beauty, her rank, her talents and, above all, to her skill in attracting to her feet so illustrious a lover. The acting of *Antigone* at the Spanish Embassy indeed marked the zenith of the success and happiness of the Countess, and as not unfrequently happens in such a case, its sunny brilliance only portended the coming of the dark storms of sorrow.*

The destruction of this fool's paradise came about (as was perhaps inevitable under such circumstances) with appalling suddenness. Towards the end of March 1783, the news reached Rome that the lonely Chevalier was at last lying at the point of death in his dismal Florentine palace; and this information, which must have raised for the moment the high hopes of the lovers, induced the Cardinal of York, though with great reluctance, to proceed to Florence. But the vitality of Charles Stuart was truly marvellous, for when the Cardinal arrived on the scene, the prince was already out of immediate danger and fully conscious. In his brother's sick-room then (if we can trust Alfieri's own account) the Cardinal was for the first time brought to realise his own equivocal position in allowing the existence of a scandal which was patent to all in Rome, save to the unsuspecting guardian of the lady herself. At first it seems Henry refused to believe in his brother's version of the story, but the arguments used by the priests of his own household and those whom Archbishop Martini (whom the Countess calls a busybody in one of her letters to the Cardinal) had sent to minister [to the supposed dying penitent, were fully able to persuade him of the truth of Charles' allegations. Burning with a not unnatural anger at the trick which had been played upon him, he returned to Rome with the firm intention

* Silvagni, *Corte di Roma*, cap. xviii.

of putting a step without delay to the intimacy between the Countess and Alfieri which he had hitherto sanctioned. Such a step was quite conceivable, but the poor Cardinal, who could rarely hold his tongue under any mental excitement, must needs talk of the matter before all sorts of persons, and even go so far as to hasten to the Pope with his tale of grievances. To the lady herself he wrote a curt note, forbidding her to receive Alfieri again in his palace of the Cancelleria ; whereat the Countess, smothering for the time being her wrath and dismay, at once set to propitiate and deny, whilst promising to carry out her brother-in-law's command. In the meantime she appealed apparently to the Pope, who would perhaps have listened to her plausible arguments but for fear of offending the Cardinal of York, for the latter now had lashed himself to a white heat of passion against the poet for having taken such advantage of his easy disposition and unsuspecting nature.* Already at the Cardinal's eager request a mandate had been issued, bidding Alfieri quit Papal territory ; and though it is possible he might have been allowed to remain temporarily at the Villa Strozzi, if he promised faithfully nevermore to attempt to visit the Countess, he saw the obvious necessity of his departure, before a further order of the Roman Government might compel him forcibly to leave the States of the Church. To this decision the Countess herself in a letter full of despair unutterable also urged her lover, and thus on the morning of May 4, 1783, were " Psipsio and Psipsia " torn apart, the latter to remain in a city filled with gossip and curiosity concerning herself, and the former to carry his egotistic tears of grief and humiliation to the sympathetic Gori, the friend of his heart, at Siena. In the *Vita*, Alfieri refuses to admit his actual expulsion from Rome, but with the enmity of so powerful a personage as the Cardinal of York, the issue of an order of compulsory removal must have been merely a matter

* *Last of the Royal Stuarts*, pp. 155–159.

85

of time. "Expelled or not expelled," comments the unkind Signore Bertana, "it is merely a question of expression. He left Rome in fine because he was not allowed to stay there any longer!"* Alfieri's own account is perhaps worth quoting here to see how he glosses over this most unpleasant incident in his life.

"It was the fourth day of May in the year 1783—which will ever be, and has been till now, my bitterest remembrance—that I then removed from Her who was more than half of myself. And of the four or five separations from Her undergone by me, this was the most terrible for me, since every hope of seeing her again was so uncertain and remote. . . . And thus did I leave my only Lady, my books, my villa, my peace and Myself in Rome, travelling thence like a man damned and distraught."†

Here then we shall leave Alfieri for the present wending his way in intense misery of separation and shame towards the faithful Gori at Siena, whilst we continue to trace the fortunes of the luckless woman he had abandoned so unwillingly. Whatever her feelings towards her brother-in-law must have been—and the fact that she had been deceiving him and wronging the honour of his House for the past two years could not have made her less bitter or unreasonable—the prudent Louise was determined to keep silence and not to quarrel with him. The possibility of an enforced return to the nunnery in Via Vittoria, or even of a patched-up reconciliation with her hated husband, spread a terror in her mind, so that she was determined, even if she had been deprived of her lover, at least not to lose her liberty also. In the letter therefore that she wrote to the Cardinal-Duke, she assumes her innocence; maintains the dismissal of Alfieri is a mere vexatious caprice of the Cardinal's, which she has hastened to put into practice, however distasteful; and only blames her brother-in-law for making public a matter which might have been

* Bertana, p. 197. † *Vita*, vol. ii. p. 109.

settled without any scandal whatsoever. This letter, which we quote here, is a very good example of the whole series of evasive, intentionally misleading letters she wrote to the Cardinal between 1781 and 1784. She flatters her correspondent continually; she is for ever appealing to his kind heart; she exhausts herself in protestations of duty and affection; yet she never once attempts to excuse or explain her conduct with regard to Alfieri; whilst it is fairly evident from her later allusions to the Cardinal that all the time she both hated and despised him.

" Sunday Evening.

" According to the advice you gave me, my Brother, for which I thanked you at the time, because I believed the matter was quite private, I have induced Monsieur le Comte d'Alfieri to leave Rome. He went this morning. I should have sought to hasten his departure, but after serious meditation and after consulting with the most sensible of my friends I concluded that an abrupt and apparently enforced exit would have given colour to those disagreeable but ill-founded rumours on my conduct, that are only too prevalent. Well, in any case, your wish is fulfilled and your advice followed. The only grievance I feel is that the matter has aroused gossip which injures my reputation and my sense of honour. See what unpleasantness you would have spared me, if (as we had originally agreed) *you had confided your views of the matter to myself alone*, and had not most unnecessarily informed the Pope; in short, if you had not allowed yourself in your first excitement to follow a course of action (and in this I appeal to your kind heart), which you must now perceive was most distressing to myself, not only because I am your sister-in-law, but because I am a woman. Do not, however, dread that from this time onward I am going to load you with reproaches; for I shall avoid doing so. I shall only recall the marks of affection I have received from

87

you in the past, whereof I shall always retain the warmest recollection. In spite of all that is just past, I feel a devotion no less sincere, of which I entreat you, my Brother, to accept the assurance.

" Your very humble and obedient Servant and Sister,
                                    " LOUISE." *

Towards the lady herself, now he had expelled the intruder, who was guilty of imperilling the good name of the Royal Stuarts, the Cardinal bore no ill-will, and perhaps even felt vexed with himself for having squelched this equivocal friendship in so ruthless and blundering a fashion. He now did all that was possible to revive the Countess' drooping spirits, and to make her forget the loss of her treasured *cavaliere servente*. Already he had been generous in the extreme to his sister-in-law, but he now offers to bestow on her, by way of consolation apparently, certain of the Stuart diamonds enclosed in a chest at Frascati, adding, however, that he fears some legal restrictions may possibly prevent his obtaining them for her. To this Louise, whose grief and desolation were in reality far beyond being appeased by any gift of jewels, returns a graceful if an insincere reply to the guardian who had deprived her of her lover.

" . . . I have thought a second time about the diamonds, and if you have the smallest scruple about opening the strong box, I beg you to do no such thing. I note your anxiety to please me, and that suffices. I only ask for your affection, and for nothing else in the world. As your brother's wife I am the proper person to have the diamonds, but there seem to be certain objections which you have no power to overrule. In any case everybody will hear you wanted to give them to me, for I shall tell this to all my friends. It is a proof of your affection and confidence in me, so be assured I am grateful to you." †

* British Museum. Add MSS. 34, 634, / 51.
† British Museum. Add MSS. 39, 634, / 55.

So many contradictory versions exist of the pother that ended in the abrupt departure or expulsion of Alfieri from Rome, that perhaps the following account from the pen of a celebrated Englishwoman, living in Rome at that very time and a lifelong friend of the Countess of Albany, may be inserted here, since her statement is in all probability exactly that with which the Countess satisfied her many questioners and sympathisers at the moment. The writer is no less a person than Miss Cornelia Knight (the devoted attendant of the Princess Charlotte of Wales, concerning whom she wrote a memoir of no small historical value).

" There was much ill-natured gossip this year on the subject of the Countess of Albany and Count Alfieri. The moment the Countess heard that the Pretender was lying at the point of death, she forwarded the news to Cardinal York at Frascati, who instantly hastened to Florence to see his brother. On his return to Rome, he spoke only a few cold words to the Countess, but informed the Pope it was his brother's wish that his wife should either dismiss Count Alfieri or go into a convent. The Countess thereupon wrote a letter to the Pope, in which she cleared her own character, and declared that if Count Alfieri's visiting her gave his Holiness any displeasure, she was quite sure she could prevail on that gentleman to leave Rome. The Pope replied that he approved of her conduct, and had no doubt of its correctness, but as the Cardinal disapproved of the Count's visits to her house, it might be as well to request his absence, taking care, however, to do it in such a manner as not to offend him." *

In opposition to Miss Knight's, or rather the Countess' own version of the affair, we may quote that of Sir Horace Mann, which is even wider of the mark, for the British envoy, who had formerly been convinced of the lady's ill-treatment in Florence, now veers round and seems to take the husband's part, much as had been done by

* *Autobiography of Miss Cornelia Knight*, vol. i. pp. 77, 78.

the Cardinal of York, whom he rudely calls the silliest mortal that ever existed. In his letter to Horace Walpole, dated April 26, a week before the hurried exit of the *cavaliere servente*, Mann states :

" I formerly gave you an account of the *fracas* in the Pretender's family, by the elopement of his wife, whom everybody then pitied and applauded. The tables are now turned. The cat, at last, is out of the bag. The Cardinal of York's visit to his Brother gave the latter an opportunity to undeceive him, by proving to him that the complaints laid to his charge of ill-using her were invented to cover a plot formed by Count Alfieri who (by working up Tragedies, of which he has wrote many, is most expert, though he always kept behind the curtain) had imposed upon the Great Duke, the Pope, and the Cardinal, and all those who took her part. All he said on that subject, at a time that he thought himself and was supposed by everybody to be in the most imminent danger, made a great impression on his Brother, who on his return to Rome exposed the whole to the Pope, and obtained an order from him to Count Alfieri to leave the Pope's State in fifteen days. Not content with that satisfaction, the imprudent Cardinal (for a more silly mortal never existed) published the whole of the Countess' intrigues with Alfieri.

" This has exasperated all the Roman nobility against the Cardinal, insomuch that instead of considering the Delinquencies of the Parties, their wrath is turned against the Publisher of the Scandal, and they compassionate the situation of the disconsolate Lady, who, I really believe, will marry the Count a week after she becomes a widow." *

One plain fact emerges from these two widely divergent and equally inaccurate accounts, namely, that it was the chief complaint of the Countess of Albany, guilty or innocent, that the dismissal of Alfieri, which might have been carried out soberly and discreetly, was made by

* *Mann and Manners*, vol. ii. p. 400.

the imprudent Cardinal an event sufficient to arouse scandal and gossip, so that his sister-in-law's character became immediately a theme of comment and discussion in every Roman *salon*. The majority pitied and upheld her; a few blamed or jeered; but praise or blame or compassion seemed all alike obnoxious to the Countess of Albany, who had been utterly humiliated by the result of her brother-in-law's hasty action. A sudden visit to Rome from the Princess-Mother of Stolberg-Gedern, obviously undertaken with the intention of coaxing or coercing her rebellious daughter into a reconciliation with her husband, only served the more to exasperate the mind and harden the heart of Louise, who openly despised her frivolous and worldly mother.[*] Sore stricken both in her heart and in her pride, the lady was glad indeed to exchange a city filled with tattle concerning her late misfortunes for a peaceful villa in the cool Alban hills near Genzano, whither on the advice of the Cardinal she now retired for the summer months.

[*] Vitelleschi, p. 463.

CHAPTER VI

SEPARATION

" By life or death will our sharp trial be ended ?
Yet since upon a single thread, I know,
Frail as may be, our future is suspended,
Guarding thy life in mine I forward go."
V. Alfieri to the Countess of Albany

On reaching Siena the dejected poet at once sought the house of Francesco Gori, whose modest dwelling is still pointed out to the stranger as one of the sights of the city, and is now distinguished by a tablet to commemorate its connection with so many of Alfieri's trials and triumphs. Here, in spite of Gori's soothing presence, Alfieri gave vent for some weeks to the most profound and unmanly grief. He refused to see any member of his once appreciated *crochiette saporito*, save his host ; and no doubt the tale of his late misadventures and indignities in Rome soon became the talk of the quiet old city. At length, somewhat recovered from his unseemly paroxysm of mingled grief and shame, he set forth with saddle horses to make a pilgrimage to the places associated with the four great Italian poets, whom he especially revered and whose equal he certainly fancied himself. Thus he visited the tomb of Dante at Ravenna, the house of Ariosto at Ferrara,* the home of the learned Bembo at Padua, and other scenes recalling events in the lives of the literary giants of Italy. Amid so many recollections of the glorious past, the poet gradually regained his studious

* Lady Holland in her *Journal* relates that she saw Alfieri's signature appended at the foot of Ariosto's famous MS.: " *Vittorio Alfieri vede e vennerò*, 10 *Giugno*, 1783."

habits, whilst the news of the recent and reluctant acknowledgment of the United States of America by monarchical
England once more aroused the old republican afflatus
(which had been lulled to sleep in Papal Rome) to result
in his ode to " America Libera." Returning to Siena,
Alfieri resumed his interrupted work of revising and
polishing six more of his tragedies, which he was anxious
to publish in the autumn at latest. Easier in mind and
once more engrossed with his literary ideals, he was now
able to look more calmly upon life itself, and even to
buoy up his sunken spirits with the hope of a possible reunion with his lady, which is certainly expressed in the
following sonnet :—

> Who dares deprive me of that face so charming,
> Wherein both chastity and beauty meet,
> Inviting love, yet evil thoughts disarming,
> By its own smile, so artless and so sweet ?
> O what barbarian hand with force alarming
> Hath broke the fountain of my life's retreat ?
> Hath dimmed those eyes that once my passion calming
> Filled heart and brain with every thought discreet ?
> Hate, envy and hypocrisy ay ready
> To don the mantle of mock piety
> Have caused my tears ; and yet I do not dread ye,
> Accursèd band, because the day is nigh,
> When seated all-triumphant by my Lady,
> I shall with poet's scorn your spite defy.*

This sonnet at least speaks plainly of hope and restoration, as well as the poet's intention of avenging himself
and the lady for the " hypocrisy " of the guilty Cardinal
and his advisers, although an unprejudiced critic might
be led to consider this failing had been shown in so small
degree by the complaining lovers in their late efforts to
hood-wink that pious prince of the Church. But we
are left very much in the dark as to the exact behaviour
of Alfieri at this critical period of his life and fate, for
though he was writing constantly, perhaps daily, to the
heart-stricken woman at Genzano the whole of this

* *Chi mi allontana dal leggiadro Viso* (*Poesie Amorose*, p. 145).

summer, not a line of that correspondence has survived to tell us the true and exact tale of their plans, their sorrows, their hopes, their fears. That Alfieri in the first uncontrollable outburst of his fury and disappointment had even meditated suicide (seriously or merely in a poetical sense it is impossible to say) is proved by a sonnet, composed apparently to assure his lady that for her own sake and for no other reason was he willing to preserve a life which had grown hateful to him since their enforced separation.

> O Lady mine, alone thou knowest the reason
> Why overwhelmed with shame I yet consent
> To eke existence out, for my decision
> To perish means thine own dear life is spent.
> Wherefore I count such tempting thoughts for treason,
> Which counsel steel with merciful intent ;
> Whilst in my ears I hear thy voice of passion
> A solitary life-in-death resent.
> Ah me, how helplessly my limbs are banded
> In iron shackles of resistless woe !
> By life or death will our sharp trial be ended ?
> Yet since upon a single thread, I know,
> Frail as may be, our future is suspended,
> Guarding thy life in mine, I forward go.*

Here Alfieri urges his " Donna Amata " to take courage, to trust to her lover's unselfish determination not to destroy himself, and to wait till the snapping of that frail thread, the life of the invalid husband in Florence, which could not now be long postponed. Efforts to meet secretly with her whom he adored as the better half of himself, he seems never to have contemplated for one moment ; whether from fear of compromising further the lady's character or from a poet's peculiar sense of his own luxury of grief, we are wholly unable to decide. Thus separated by many leagues, the pair of unhappy lovers passed through that memorable and odious summer, consoling themselves with futile hopes and vague plans for meeting at some future date.

* *Tu il sai, donna mia vera, e il sai tu sola* (*Poesie Amorose*, p. 177).

Towards the middle of October, however, Alfieri took a step which appears strange in an ardent lover, who had been so lately prating of suicide and vengeance. This was his fixed intention of travelling to England in order to buy horses, an expedition which would naturally remove him further than ever from Rome and his "Donna Amata." It is useless to analyse the reasons for this sudden resolution, except to suggest that Alfieri, being such a mass of egotism and inconsequence, was profoundly indifferent to the feelings of the unhappy woman, who undoubtedly was deeply hurt thereby, though she was loyal enough never to question her lover's action or to protest against his leaving Italy. All letters, however, dealing with this matter between the lovers have perished, during *l'anno disgraziato per tutti i due*, as the Countess herelf records in a manuscript copy of Alfieri's sonnets, so that we can only guess at the nature of the poet's arguments and the lady's pleadings.

We have stated with truth that none of the love letters passing between the Countess of Albany and Alfieri are to-day in existence, but by a strange chance five of the lady's letters still remain intact to give us a valuable clue to her feelings. These were, however, addressed not to Alfieri himself, but, strange to say, to his bosom friend Gori, with whom the Countess had at this time but a very slight personal acquaintance. They were discovered more than a quarter of a century ago by the talented writer, who conceals her real name under the title of "Vernon Lee," in the Communal Library of Siena, where she found these faded but most valuable pieces of paper amongst the late Signor Giuseppe Porri's collection of un-edited letters of the Countess to her Sienese friends. Only a small portion of this most important and interesting literary "find" was, however, translated and given to the world in "Vernon Lee's" *Countess of Albany*, so that a complete translation of these five fugitive epistles, that have escaped by some rare chance both the pious hand of the destroyer and the erasing finger of Time,

95

cannot be regarded as superfluous in any detailed biography of the Countess of Albany. The letters are undated, with the exception of one, which merely bears the words " *Genzano, Martedi le* 19 " ; but from internal evidence it is fairly easy to arrange their due order, and also to conclude that they were written and despatched some time during the late summer or early autumn of that aforesaid year of calamity for "Psipsio and Psipsia," namely, 1783.

The five letters in question are composed in a tolerable Italian that is perhaps superior to the Countess' usual medium of French ; and, indeed, it may be noted here that it was only at Alfieri's instigation that she had undertaken to study and acquire the language of the country of her residence. As usual, stops are conspicuous by their absence, so that occasionally the sense is somewhat obscured by the absence of them. Only in one place in Italian literature are these five letters apparently reproduced in their entirety,* and only portions of them have been translated into English ; but it would seem that a rapid perusal of this torrential outpouring of a wild devotion is essential to all who care to understand and realise something of the true living character of the Countess of Albany, who appears herein so utterly different a creature from what the remainder of her voluminous edited correspondence leads us to suppose. "Vernon Lee" rather arbitrarily calls the contents of these human documents " an excited, unconsecutive, unceasing, discursive, reiterating gabble of hysteria ; eager, vague, impotent thoughts suddenly vanishing and as suddenly coming to a dead stop ; everything rattled off as if between two sobs or convulsions." † Whether or no the reader will wholly endorse this description, no one can fail to be convinced of the genuine, absorbing, overwhelming, irrational, and absolutely unselfish devotion of the Countess for her lover ;

---

* R. Tomei-Finamore, *La Comtessa d'Albany e il suo Carteggio Senese.* (Rivista Abruzzese, 1892.)

† Vernon Lee, p. 132.

and it seems a pity that the many blind admirers of Alfieri and the many mean detractors of his "Donna Amata" cannot be brought to realise the vast depths of devotion which the poet had at his command.

I

"GENZANO, *Tuesday the 19th.*

"DEAR SIGNORE FRANCESCO,—I do not understand why I have received no news of the Friend by the ordinary post. I am very anxious about it. I hope I shall get news to-morrow. If only you realised how miserable and depressed I am! It seems to me that my load of wretchedness increases daily. I do not know how I am to exist without the Friend. I meditate self-destruction. I do nothing but weep, nor can I ever think upon him save with utter torment. Music alone deadens my grief somewhat, and I spend my whole day playing on the harp, and that because I know the Friend would be pleased if I learned to play well. If you could only guess at the horrible thoughts that cross my mind! Sometimes I believe in, and sometimes I fear for, the Friend's recollection of me. He may desert me, and yet I ought to desire such an ending for his own sake. But I am not strong enough to make so great a sacrifice, when he is essential to my happiness and to my very existence, so that without feeling secure of him I no longer wish to remain in this world of sorrows. What do I here save eat, drink, and sleep? Useless creature that I am! I have neither peace nor joy in store, unless I recover the Friend. I live in a state of constant agitation, in a place that I abominate, and amongst acquaintances with whom I have not an idea in common. If this state of things is not brought to a speedy end, I shall have to take some violent action. O dear Signore Francesco, how your own heart must sink at seeing the Friend so distressed! Would that he were able to remain with you! But I expect he will want to travel and to wander far away.

G

97

However, if travel distract his mind, then I ought to approve of it. His welfare counts before mine, and I am ready to sacrifice everything in order that he may be happy, so deep is my love for him. O God, what a fate is mine ! Who knows how it will all end ? My life so far has been full of sorrow, but I have had one compensation for it in finding in him a friend who loves me. Give me news of the Friend's health ; my own is pretty good. Farewell, dear Signore Francesco."

II

"Dear Signore Francesco,—I am truly grateful for your sympathy. You cannot even in imagination conceive of our misery. My own grief is no whit less than our Friend's. There are moments when I feel my heart torn asunder, as I reflect on what he must be enduring. My sole consolation, and it is no small one, is that you are with him. Never leave him alone. He is worse, and I know how keenly he appreciates your company. You are the only person who does not irritate him, and to whom he always gladly returns. O dear Signore Francesco, in what a sea of sorrows are we sunk ! And you yourself also ; for our troubles are your own. I live no more, and were it not for the Friend, for whom I reserve myself, I should refuse to eke out this hateful existence.* What am I doing in this world ? I am but a useless inhabitant of it. Yet why should I suffer, since it profits nobody ? But the Friend—I cannot decide to abandon him, and he is necessary for his own fame ; and so long as he lives, even if I have to crawl, I shall go on suffering and living. Who knows what will be the end of this Man ? This Man in Florence who has been ill so long a time ? He seems to me to be formed of iron to destroy us. You will tell me, to reassure me, that he cannot last long ; but I see matters clearly. I don't suppose this last illness has given him a

* Compare Alfieri's similar sentiments expressed in the sonnet already quoted as to his reason for not committing suicide.

fresh lease of life, but I do think he can hold out very easily for a year or two longer. Of course he may at any moment succumb to the gout in his chest. What a brutal thing it is to expect one's happiness through another's death! O God, how it degrades the soul! Yet none the less I cannot refrain from this desire. Life, what a hard thing it is! For myself it has been one long bout of suffering for the last eleven years, all except the two years I spent with the Friend, and even then I was living in the midst of fears. And you, perhaps, are not happy; for with a heart like yours that would be an impossibility. Whoever is born with a sympathetic nature can never enjoy peace. I commend the Friend, and particularly the Friend's health, to your keeping. My own health is tolerable. I take great care, and pass much of my time in bed, which seems to soothe my disturbed nerves. Farewell, dear Signore Francesco. Keep your friendship for me. I deserve it, because I realise its true worth."

III

"DEAR FRIEND,—I am so grateful for the interest you display in my unhappy plight, which is indeed a terrible one. Time only serves to aggravate it, nor shall I ever find any relief for my sorrow, save in the presence of our Friend. Neither peace nor rest can I expect. I would surrender the remainder of my life to spend one whole day with him, and then expire contented. My devotion to him is unalterable, as is his towards myself. Who knows when I shall see the ending of my trials? Who knows if I shall ever see it? That Man does not seem likely to pass away. His legs are become useless, yet he survives despite his malady. You advise me not to practise on the harp. But I apply myself to it, because the Friend would be pleased at the idea of my playing well, and the mechanical task I set my fingers to perform prevents me from brooding over my sorrows. Not that the mere act of playing soothes me, but that the music does me some trifling

99

good. I read and translate the tragedies of the Friend,
so far as my head permits me. Is not his second volume
a masterpiece? I am deeply impressed with the
Agamemnon. There is an overwhelming majesty in that
drama. Agamemnon is indeed the king of kings. The
Orestes too is fine, but not equal to the *Agamemnon* in my
opinion. The *Rosmunda* will delight you. I do not
know what fault the critics will find in this trilogy of
plays, though no doubt envy will make them scatter abroad
some sharp abuse. But the Friend will revel in the fame he
deserves as a king of men with the soul of an ancient Greek
or Roman, for he can make his characters speak according
to nature, and not after the style of the French dramatists.
But you know more about these matters than I; and yet
who more than myself knows how to venerate the genius
of our Friend? I grieve to think of his leaving you, but
travel is necessary to him, so I hope he will wander far
afield and thereby recover his health. I flatter myself
you will continue to give me news of him. I am deeply
attached to you. Your letters have caused me to realise
your sympathetic heart. Such a thing is rare, and rarer
still is a heart such as yours. My health is good, but I
suffer somewhat from the weakness both of nerves and
digestion. But that is nothing compared with the
anguish of my heart. I have my moments of despair,
when I could throw myself out of the window, did I not
remember that I must preserve my life for our Friend,
since it belongs to him. I have a fixed horror of my life,
which is so firmly rooted in my mind, that I ask myself
now and again : ' Why am I alive ? What am I doing
here ? ' But then the Friend's image returns to my
mind, and I go on enduring in patience. Oh, forgive me
for unburdening my thoughts to you ! You alone understand my case, and you alone, after the Friend, realise
the anguish of a loving heart. Yes, you ought to come and
visit me this winter. It would afford me real comfort.
Farewell, dear Signore Francesco. Keep your friendship
for myself, your friend."

IV

" DEAR SIGNORE FRANCESCO, FRIEND OF US BOTH,—I do my utmost to keep a brave heart. I study all I can. Music alone distracts, or rather deadens my thoughts, and I play daily for many hours on the harp. I am glad to do so, for I know how earnestly the Friend wishes me to become proficient, and therefore I apply myself to it as much as possible. I only exist for his sake. Without him life would be odious and unendurable. I do nothing in this world. I am useless here below. Why should my suffering be of no avail ? But there is the Friend, so here I must remain. I believe implicitly in his love for me. And yet in my transports of grief, I also grow frightened lest he may find somebody who would cause him less suffering than I, somebody with whom he could live happy and contented. I ought to desire this end, but I lack strength. Yet I trust in him to such a degree, that immediately I grow pacified on remembering that he has told me such a thing cannot and will not happen. I love him more than myself. It is a close union of soul and mind that we ourselves alone can understand. In him I find every thing I can require, and he is all in all to me. Nevertheless, I have to endure his absence, although I feel certain that if I took one decisive step, I should be the happiest woman alive. Nevermore would I think on the past, for I should live in him and for him all the rest of my days.

" I care for nothing in this world, neither for luxury nor for position. All is vanity in my eyes. A peaceful existence with him would suffice for all my needs. And yet I have to languish far, far away from him. What a horrible life ! I am glad to think you realise how deeply the Friend loves me ; and I assure you that, after him, you are the person dearest to me, believe me, dear Signore Francesco. If the Friend goes to England this winter, I hope you will come to see me. Your presence will prove a true source of consolation to me. My health is fair. I am troubled with my nerves, but that is nothing worth mentioning. I commend the Friend to your care. Make him attend to his health. I have derived much satisfaction from the copy of the *Agamemnon*, which is well printed on good paper. I have read it with great pleasure, the first pleasure I have felt since last May. I can only allude to its style, which seems to me far more easy and less laboured. Farewell, dear Signore Francesco. Retain your friendship for me, as I keep mine intact for you."

V

" DEAR FRIEND,—So you will bear our Friend company so far as Genoa! How fortunate you are! How I envy you your opportunity of seeing him, whilst poor I am deprived of his presence! But you too will lose him, and then, indeed, your heart will ache. For myself, it is like the shadow of death to learn of his departure from this land, and especially his departure from the side of so devoted a friend as yourself. But on the other hand, I believe this journey is essential to his well-being, so that I must sacrifice my own feelings for his good, as indeed, I would sacrifice my very life, if it could be of any use to him, or in any degree contribute to his happiness. But then I know I must guard my life for his sake, so as some day to render him happy. Thus I am doing all that is possible. I take exercise on horse-back. I go early to bed; I am very careful of myself. But my heart is sore stricken, and I am scarcely alive, but rather drag along my wretched existence, which I cannot endure much longer. One way or another it must come to an end. As for myself, I am ready for anything. Life is but a burden, to which I am in no wise attached. Indeed, without him I abhor it. I am utterly useless. What can I do? I hope all this will be changed, and that I shall yet rejoice in living for our Friend, and that we three may yet some day be reunited together in a land of liberty. Wish me well, I pray you, for I am wholly yours; and do not forget to charge the Friend to take care of his health, I entreat you."

Whatever degree of blame the Countess of Albany may have incurred by her recent deceitful conduct towards her unsuspecting and generous brother-in-law, no one can deny the severity of the punishment she was now undergoing. Torn with feelings of fear, of jealousy and of hopeless devotion for her absent lover, utterly cast down with womanly shame from the late humiliation she had undergone in Rome, and kept by the Cardinal's injunction in a state of semi-confinement, the lady must indeed have spent a distressful summer in that hill-set villa near Genzano, " close-latticed to the brooding heat and silent in its dusty vines," where the indignant Cardinal-Duke had placed her. Here this royal Mariana of the South was compelled to weep and fret, pining so that her beauty was visibly fading beneath the burden of her sorrow. In a state of endless uncertainty, that was but a shade less terrible than despair itself, the " Donna Amata " of Alfieri passed those months of torment in durance amid the lovely scenery of the Alban hills. We can imagine her sitting the live-long day of enervating heat in the close-shuttered room, employing the wingless hours in playing on the harp or vainly striving to keep her wandering thoughts fixed on some favourite volume of abstruse learning, or perhaps reading through and annotating the tragedies of " the Friend " with bitter-sweet emotions.* All day long the silent house echoes with the dry shrill chirrup of the cicale in the trees without, and the great spaces of the dim rooms seem haunted by the presence of the beloved one, who is never for a moment absent from the inmost thoughts of the forlorn lady. With a mind torn in agonies of speculation and

* *See* Diomede Bonamici, *Tragedia d'Oreste di Psipsio, paragonata con quella di Voltaire, di Psipsia.* (Livoruo, 1903.) This labour of love of the Countess " will appear puerile to the reader, since both spelling and syntax are cynically disregarded."

suspense as to her lover's constancy (and Alfieri's reputation for this virtue was none of the best, as many a candid friend no doubt had often informed her), and yet
with the fixed determination never to distrust or suspect
him, the Countess dragged out the weary summer days in
alternate phases of hope and misery. The thought of
Alfieri's departure, as she tells Gori in one of her letters just
quoted, was like the shadow of death for her, to whom the
poet's presence meant life itself. To console her, she had,
indeed, his letters and his sonnets (the latter of which
she copied out carefully in a volume that is now preserved
in a Florentine library); she had the constant company
of "the tender and faithful" Madame de Maltzam; and
when the erratic and selfish poet ceased to write and inform her of his own sorrows and movements, she had the
comfort of receiving letters concerning him from the
worthy Gori. Yet despite such truly valuable supports
as the kind sympathy of Madame de Maltzam and the
sensible advice of Gori, the continued suspense of the
unhappy woman must have been terrible in the extreme,
and when we seek to condemn her duplicity and her
illicit devotion to a self-centred hedonist such as Alfieri,
we must remember that if the sin were great, the punishment proved almost too severe for the offence.

> She rising from her bosom drew
>   Old letters breathing of her worth,
> For " Love (they said) must needs be true
>   To what is loveliest upon earth."
> An image seemed to pass the door,
>   To look at her with slight and say
>   " But now thy beauty flows away,
> So be alone for evermore." . . .
>
> But sometimes in the falling day
>   An image seemed to pass the door,
> To look into her eyes and say,
>   " But thou shalt be alone no more."
> And flaming downward over all
>   From heat to heat the day decreased,
>   And slowly rounded to the east
> The one black shadow from the wall.

" The day to night," she made her moan,
" The day to night, the night to morn,
And day and night I am left alone
To live forgotten and die forlorn."

So marvellously does this description apply to the actual
case of the harassed and love-stricken Countess of Albany
in the solitude of her Italian villa during the long long
summer months of 1783, that it would almost seem as
though a greater and more human poet than the rough
and selfish Vittorio Alfieri, had been moved in after years
to record in imperishable verse the well-deserved sufferings of the unhappy " Donna Amata."

Compared with the anxiety and agitation endured for
so many months by his lady, the burden of Alfieri may
be reckoned light.   True, he had first appeared in May at
Gori's hospitable house in Siena weeping and raving, but
Time had rapidly set to healing the wounds he had lately
received in Rome.   Long talks at Siena with the friend
of his heart ; a visit to the sympathetic Abbé di Caluso at
the family castle of Masino near Vercelli ; complacent
meditations at the literary shrines of Northern Italy ;
the resumption of his dramatic work in order to prepare
his tragedies for publication in the coming autumn ; and
the composition of amatory poetry expressive of his late
emotion, were able to some extent to deaden the effects
of the late shock to his self-esteem and to soften a little the
agony of separation from his lady.   His unabated passion
for horses also stood him in good stead at this juncture,
and the prospect of another visit to his beloved England
with the object of purchasing further additions to his
stud now served to distract his mind, which had taken on
a violent longing to quit his native land.

About the middle of October therefore, he set out
from Genoa, whither he had been accompanied so far by
Gori, and travelling by way of Antibes and Avignon proceeded to Paris.   In the French capital, which he always
professed to detest cordially, the poet was a witness of the
historic ascent of the Mongolfier Balloon, which greatly

interested him, and is described by him as " a grand and marvellous spectacle, both from the view of poetry or of history, and an invention worthy of being called sublime, provided there were but some chance of its being adapted to fill some need of humanity." * Leaving Paris after this unique experience, he crossed the Channel to reach London late in the year, where he passed his time, so he tells us, in unprofitable idleness and in selecting fourteen horses, the exact number of the plays he had written. After four months thus spent in London, he prepared to return to Italy with his string of horses, and in his *Vita* gives a graphic account of the various difficulties he himself and the farrier engaged to assist him had to overcome on their journey southward.

Leaving for the moment Alfieri struggling, like Hannibal, to conduct his horses across the snowy passes of the Mont Cenis, let us return to the lonely and disconsolate Countess. It seems from later letters of hers, that Gori was able to redeem his promise of spending part of the winter in Rome, which must have afforded the lady some degree of pleasure, or rather some diminuation of her abiding grief. This period is also somewhat remarkable for a correspondence which had sprung up between the Countess of Albany and the Countess Monica Alfieri, the mother of the Friend ; a pious, simple and unsuspecting old lady who was still living with her third husband in the family house at Asti. Although the two ladies never once met in the whole course of their existence, the mother of Alfieri had from the first taken a lively interest in the charming princess her idolised son was supposed to have rescued from the clutches of a cruel husband. Messages to and from the mother and the mistress of the poet were frequently conveyed during the recent two years' sojourn in Rome, and we now find the Countess of Albany placed in the peculiar position of supplying the anxious parent with information as to her son's whereabouts. In the ensuing letter, the news

* *Vita*, vol. ii. p. 127.

of the death of one of the Countess Monica's grand-
children has evidently inspired the condoling sentences of
the Countess of Albany, whilst the rather cryptic allusion
to the possible extinction of the Alfieri family is sometimes
considered as a hint by the runaway wife of Charles Stuart
that some day in the future she herself may become the old
lady's daughter-in-law and perpetuate the ancient line of
Casa Alfieri, though the remark was certainly not accepted
in this sense by the unsophisticated mother of the poet.

"*Le* 29. . . . [The date is almost certainly November 29, 1783].

" I have learned with much sorrow, Madame la Comtesse, from Monsieur, your son, of the loss you have sustained. I assure you, Madame, that I have felt your grief
as keenly as if it had been my own. It is a terrible thing
to lose a beloved child ; but still, Madame, there remains
to you a son who loves you dearly. And though circumstances prevent him from dwelling with you, be assured
that he loves you no less in his absence. At present he is
in Paris, and he will certainly go to see you on his return
in the spring. If he has not already paid you a visit, it is
on account of the lateness of the season which has made
him wish to hasten his journey. But I know that before
his departure he has had his tragedy of *Merope* printed,
wherein, Madame, he gives you a public proof of his devotion and respect. Rest assured that his heart is full of
these sentiments towards you.

" I fully understand how sad it is for you to live so far
from him, and how sad also has been the loss of your grand-
child ; it is, indeed, a hard trial which God summons you to
bear. But I hope, Madame, that, if circumstances change,
you will not see the extinction of a family to which you
are attached, and that you will yet find your chief source
of consolation in Monsieur le Comte Alfieri. . . . I shall
sometimes give you news of the Count Alfieri. He is very
well, but his health required this little tour [to England]
after his severe exertions in finishing his tragedies. . . ." *

* Bernardi and Milanesi, *Lettere Inedite di V. Alfieri*, p. 62.

In another letter, dated April 3, (1784), the Countess who all her life was fond of painting portraits of her many friends, alludes to a likeness of Alfieri which she had lately sent to the simple old lady, who had requited this gift with a present of some dried fruit.

" I am very grateful to you, Madame, for the preserves you have sent me, and I am delighted to hear you were pleased with the portrait. It was the likeness to him that made me take the liberty of sending it you. Monsieur, your son, was due to leave London the first day of this month. He intends to travel with the horses he has bought in England. You know they are his ruling passion, and being in England he could not refrain from buying them. . . .

"As to my husband, he is better. But I assure you, Madame, I cannot be so deeply interested in him, as you imagine, since during the nine years I lived with him, he rendered me the most miserable creature alive. If I do not actually hate him, it is due to simple Christian precepts which tell us we must forgive. He drags on a wretched existence deserted by all, without relatives, without friends, and in the power of his servants. But it is his own fault, for he never could live with anybody. Forgive me, Madame, for entering with you into these details, but your professed friendship for me has induced me to speak plainly to you. Pray rest assured of my gratitude for the interest you take in my welfare, &c. &c." *

This uncompromising reply to the Countess Monica's inopportune inquiry as to the health, temporal and spiritual, of Madame d'Albany's husband is almost contemporary with a letter of the Countess to the Cardinal of York (to whom she was still inditing letters full of a gushing but wholly insincere affection), announcing the successful issue of a series of negociations for a legal separation from Charles-Edward, which had been pending throughout the early spring months, and in which the lady doubtless

* *Ibidem*, pp. 63, 64.

found the most efficacious of remedies for her late love-sickness. The prospect of obtaining even her partial liberty was, indeed, a hopeful outlook, so that the Countess wrote in the most coaxing terms to her brother-in-law, whose consent and approval thereto she was naturally most eager to secure. The fact is that during the past winter, King Gustavus III. of Sweden, travelling in Italy under the name of Count Haga, had become intimate with the derelict Chevalier at Florence, and had promised him more financial support after hearing the pitiful, though greatly exaggerated, complaints of his poverty. This, however, the King, after first consulting with the Countess of Albany and Cardinal de Bernis in Rome, only undertook to obtain on condition that the prince agreed to settle his conjugal difficulties on the reasonable basis of a legal separation *a mensâ et thoro ;* and by pushing forward this scheme the good-natured monarch conceived he was doing a real service to each of the ill-mated pair. Charles Stuart had by this time presumably given up all hope of ever recovering possession of his erring wife, or even of ever persuading the Cardinal of York to assist him to that end ; consequently, though loth to loosen the matrimonial bonds of his hated consort, for the sake of the increased income promised on certain conditions by the Swedish king, he now gave a grudging consent to his proposals. Roughly speaking, the terms of this instrument were to include the total renunciation by the wife of any income from the Royal Stuarts during her husband's lifetime, although she was at once to receive the annual pension of 60,000 *livres,* which had been settled on Charles-Edward's bride, and not on himself, at the time of the marriage in 1772.* In this manner, the lady would not truly, as Sir Horace Mann admitted, for the present

* *Le Livre Rouge* (Paris, Baudouin, 1790), the book of the official entries of the pensions granted by the French court, particularly emphasises this point, namely, that the subsidy was the personal property of the wife and not of her husband, though apparently it was paid over to the latter.—" By royal decree of September 1, 1776, there was conferred on the Countess

"receive a shilling from the Stuart family, and was only to receive a jointure of 6,000 crowns after her husband's death, a poor equivalent for what she had lost." * Charles himself at first made strong representations to the King of Sweden against his liberated wife being permitted to bear his name; and it is a curious coincidence that the pair, whether by accident or by design, henceforth spell their assumed title in different forms, the Countess as *Albany*, and her husband as *Albanie*.

So important but melancholy an event as the separation from his absent spouse gave occasion to the unhappy Stuart prince to draw up another of those semi-royal manifestoes which he loved to compose in the grandiose language of a real reigning monarch and to seal with the Royal arms of Britain; and thus run the terms of the mandate admitting his consort's power to live apart from himself—

"We, Charles, legitimate King of Great Britain, on the representations made to Us by Louise-Caroline-Maximilienne-Emmanuele, Princess of Stolberg, that for sound reasons she wished to reside at a distance separated from Our person; that circumstances as well as Our common misfortunes have rendered this event useful and necessary for Us both; and in consideration of all the arguments she has adduced to Us, We declare by these presents that We freely and voluntarily give Our consent to this separation, and that We do permit her to live from henceforth in Rome, or in any town she may consider most convenient, such being Our pleasure. Given and sealed with the seal of Our arms in Our Palace at Florence, April 3, 1784."

And at the base of this imposing document is added a final sentence in the poor King's crabbed penmanship:

the sum of 60,000 *lire*, paid in that month, which seems to have been continued indefinitely till the fall of the French monarchy. Charles-Edward's payment only dates from February 1785, and was 30,000 *lire*." (Mazzatinti, *Le Carte Alfieriane. Giornale Storico*, vol. iii. pp. 47, 48.)

* *Mann and Manners*, vol. ii. p. 409.

"We approve the writing and all contained therein. C. R." *

It was on the receipt of this welcome capitulation of her husband in his attitude of opposition that the Countess wrote off in high glee to her brother-in-law at Frascati the following letter.

"*Wednesday, April 7, [1784].*

"MY DEAR BROTHER,—I have not been able to speak to you sooner of a project for a separation that the King of Sweden has proposed for my husband and myself. I lend myself the more readily to it, as I hope thereby to prove that I am very far from seizing on the fortune of your Brother, as he declares, and it is without any regret that I now restore him not only the 1000 *écus* that you pay me, but also the 3000 which by my marriage settlement constitute my own pin-money. And I agree equally that he shall take back his diamonds from Rome. It is a sacrifice I should have made long ago, had I not considered that my honour required for the present and the future for me to keep this pension, as a positive proof that in leaving my husband I had the approval of those whose opinion was precious to me. I have, therefore, declined to surrender my claims except under an arrangement with him that shows we are living apart by mutual consent. The King of Sweden has undertaken the task, and I am completely in his hands with regard to all my interests, while he is kind enough to act both as a friend and as a relation. To my great surprise Stuart † has this very morning brought me the agreement signed, and it is now once more in the possession of the King of Sweden. As soon as I get it, I shall inform you of its contents, being certain, my very dear Brother, that you will rejoice with me that I am at last at the end of my difficulties with my

* *Hist. MSS. Commission Reports. Tenth Report, Appendix*, part vi. p. 235.

† John Stuart, the Chevalier's trusted Major-domo at Florence, to whom his royal master left a legacy.

Husband, and that he himself is finally quit of his financial embarrassments which I believe are genuine, since
Stuart says so. I feel, therefore, some pride in helping
him, and in surrendering my additional money in order
to procure him the necessary income. May Heaven
grant him some measure of repose and content in his old
age! And may you, my very dear Brother, be persuaded that my expressions of gratitude and affection
towards yourself are as unalterable as is the sincere
attachment wherewith

"I am, Your affectionate Sister,

"LOUISE.

"Allow me, my dear Brother, to wish you *les bonnes
fêtes de Pâques*, and a thousand good things!" *

This optimistic letter, however, failed to prove acceptable to the Cardinal-Duke, who, besides being shocked
at the idea of any legal separation, also resented the
financial arrangements which were being made without
his previous consent between the pair, imagining, rightly
or wrongly, that the income which the Countess offered
to restore to her husband was his own property and
neither that of the lady to bestow nor of Charles to
accept. A testy and ungracious reply was therefore
despatched to the anxious Countess of Albany, who
must have felt greatly exasperated at this unforeseen
check to the smooth procedure of these negotiations,
which meant ultimate freedom for herself.

"MY VERY DEAR SISTER,—I am so busy these days,
that I have scarcely the time to reply to your letter, and
therefore I confine myself to assuring you that nobody
in the world ought to desire a settlement between yourself and your husband more than I; but I can never
approve of a separation, whose sole aim is interest.

"I cannot, and ought not, to interfere in any arrangements you two may devise together, but I bid you remember that everything you have received from Cantini

* British Museum, Add MSS. 34, 634, f. 63.

(my steward) since you have resided in my palace of the Cancellaria has come from *myself*; and that the said Cantini has my orders to pay it to you so long as you live with me. It is a piece of insolence therefore on my brother's part, this disposing of money which is mine, as though it were his own, and without my knowledge, so that I feel compelled to acquaint him with my own opinion of his conduct in the matter. And I beg you once for all, my very dear Sister, not to annoy me further on this point, for really it quite upsets my health, to have my brother expecting me to carry out every scheme that comes into his head, by force of abuse and without any acknowledgment of his obligation.

" I wish you a very happy Easter, my very dear Sister." *

Though not actually daring to retort in a spirit of annoyance to this very unsatisfactory answer to her letter, the Countess strove to argue and reason with her obstinate brother-in-law, setting forth the advantages her decrepit husband would reap from the already half-completed settlement between the pair. How far these kindly and considerate sentiments with regard to her husband's future welfare were prompted by her own intense longing for independence or by a genuine wish to see his financial position improved, we leave to the reader to decide after what has already been written on this point.

" MY DEAR BROTHER,—I hasten to send you an exact copy of the mutual arrangement concerning our separation, which is based solely on the conviction we both hold as to the impossibility of living together, owing to our incompatibility of temper, and with the example before us of other persons no less distinguished than my Husband and myself, who have been placed in similar circumstances. You see now that your unhappy Brother is only obeying reason and not interest (as you suggest) ;

* British Museum. Add MSS. 34, 634, *f.* 65. This letter is marked and dated, " *Letter of Reply of H.R.H. to Madame, his Sister-in-law, written Friday, April* 9, 1784."

and that he is not dealing with what is yours, since it is of my own motion and with full knowledge of his needs that I surrender back to him what he promised me for my pin-money and you told me should be paid me here in Rome.

"I repeat, it is a sacrifice that I am making, and one which I believe I ought to have made earlier save for certain objections. Be assured, my Brother, the King is in need, and I should feel ashamed not to aid him. Stuart will be able to tell you that during his last illness he had not the wherewithal to pay for the Masses said on his behalf, and when Stuart wrote to you, there was but six sequins in the house. I assure you, my Brother, that without the pension from the Apostolic Chamber in addition to the fifty thousand *livres* from France he cannot possibly exist. I used to imagine he was hoarding, but I have examined the bankers' accounts, and I have seen that he was speaking the truth, so that I felt myself bound to assist him. You know, my dear Brother, that I thought the same thing, when you suggested to me to keep the diamonds over which I have certain claims (all except the large stones you possess equally with your brother). But I never could have done a thing which would have made everybody exclaim, and being bound in conscience and in honour I cannot refuse him his request any more than can you yourself. How is it possible, my dear Brother, that with your gentle heart and with your ingrained sense of justice and integrity, you cannot realise it is better for us to be separated on proper terms ? Have you no satisfaction in my generosity towards your Brother (seeing that it is a proof of my own forgiveness of his evil conduct towards myself), or in my efforts to render him happy, by surrendering this money ? It is an excess of attention on my part to have informed you at all, for you would never have found it out ; and is it not better for him to live comfortably during the brief remainder of his life, and for you to be left in peace, and myself also ?

What need then to irritate him by writing to tell him that he is disposing of *your* money, since it is I who am dealing with my own property and am bestowing it of my own free will ?

" Farewell, my dear Brother, I beg you to be convinced of my tender attachment, which I shall always preserve.
                              " LOUISE YOUR SISTER.

" I beg of you to return the copy I am sending you. Tuesday Morning." *

The captious opposition of the Cardinal was eventually frustrated by the tactful intervention of King Gustavus, whose letter to the grateful Countess of Albany shows that the legal separation was already well on the way to completion early in the summer of 1784.

                              "PARIS, *June* 13, 1784.

" MADAME LA COMTESSE,—I have just received on my arrival in Paris the letter you have kindly addressed me from Rome, and I was greatly pleased with your gift of the rare and interesting medals struck at the time of your wedding. I shall deem myself happy, if I have been of any service in softening your lot. I consider you can rest quite easy, Madame, as to your brother-in-law's attitude in this affair. Matters are now well advanced, and they cannot be put back. I shall not cease my own efforts to uphold the terms of separation I have already drawn up, but I believe all is well, and financial arrangements are alone likely to cause any trouble. I also expect that the Cardinal-Duke's visit to Florence will only result in increasing the bitterness of feeling between the two brothers. I trust the waters [of Baden] will benefit your health, and I look forward to our next meeting, when I hope to prove to you the

* British Museum. Add MSS. 34, 634, f. 67.

warm friendship wherewith I have the honour to be, Madame la Comtesse, your good friend,

"GUSTAVUS." *

This cordial letter from the Swedish king may be said to mark the final stage in these negotiations, which were now sufficiently advanced to allow of the Countess of Albany being considered free from all marital control before the summer of 1784, almost exactly the inauspicious anniversary of Alfieri's expulsion from Rome.

* Reumont, *Appendix*, pp. 206, 207.

CHAPTER VII

REUNION

*" Giunto il di 16 Agosto presso la Mia Donna, due mese in circa
mi vi sfuggirono quasi un baleno."*
Vita di V. Alfieri, vol. ii. p. 148

THUS formally released from the galling tie that bound
her to the husband that she loathed, the Countess now
requested permission to leave Papal territory for a season,
in order to spend a portion of the summer at the baths
of Baden, in Switzerland, since her health had been
gravely impaired by her late anxiety and agitation. The
Pope gave the necessary consent without demur, so that
the Countess was travelling northward by way of Bologna
towards her destination in June, in which month Alfieri
was slowly traversing the Lombard plains with his string
of recently purchased English horses, fourteen in all, on
the road to Siena. Overjoyed at the unexpected news
of his lady's legal release from her tyrant, he was sore
tempted, so he tells us, to abandon his cavalcade and to
pursue the Countess towards her goal, but prudence
happily prevented his carrying out so rash a project,
which would at once have made people put the worst
construction on their well-known friendship. Alfieri
therefore continued his course towards Siena, where he
was warmly welcomed by the delighted Gori, by Teresa
Mocenni, by Mario Bianchi, by the Arch-priest Luti, and
by the other members of the *crochiette saporito.* But
to remain long at Siena, whilst his lady, just escaped from
her late prison of the Eternal City, was equally longing
for a meeting, seemed unendurable to the impatient

poet. Already, no doubt, subtle plans were being laid both at Siena and at Baden for a meeting that might be kept a most profound secret, and in those distant days, when the world was not blessed with journalistic spies, railways or telegraph wires, the success of such an arrangement was well within the range of the practical. It was evidently the astute Madame de Maltzam who came to the rescue of the perplexed and still separated pair of lovers, with her ingenious suggestion that the Countess should retire to her family castle of Martinsburg near Colmar on the Rhine, whither Alfieri could in due course of time proceed to visit her without anybody being the wiser. The necessary preliminaries and precautions were taken; the Countess moved from Baden to Colmar; and a little later Alfieri, leaving his whole stud behind at Siena in charge of the long-suffering Gori, set off with haste all alone, reaching Colmar on August 16, after twelve days of rapid travelling. " Here," so he records, " I found at last Her whom I had ever been calling and seeking; Her of whom I had been bereft for the last sixteen months "; * and again, in a marginal note to one of his poems, he alludes to this joyful reunion of " Psipsio and Psipsia " after an enforced interval of tears and anxiety: " On the seventeenth day of August, 1784, at eight in the morning, at the inn of the Two Keys, in Colmar, I met Her and fell speechless from plenitude of my joy."†

Two months were spent in this hidden retreat of Martinsburg, which for the next few years enters largely into the life of this celebrated pair of lovers, and will therefore be described later. Here Alfieri, recovering his spirits and his poetical fervour in the close presence of his " Donna Amata," once more set to the task of writing or revising his tragedies, so that under these present happy auspices were begun the dramas of *Agis*, *Sophonisba*, and *Myrrha*, the last-named being considered by some critics one of the finest of his works. This

* *Vita*, vol. ii. p. 147.   † Vernon Lee, p. 134.

stolen period of perfect bliss was, however, doomed to sudden interruption from an unexpected quarter. Scarcely had Alfieri and the Countess settled down to their peaceful life of unclouded happiness, than the news came from Siena first of the illness and then the death of their beloved friend, Francesco Gori, who expired on September 3, at the age of forty-six. This sad event, which was duly announced to the poet by Mario Bianchi, came as a crushing blow to the lovers in the midst of their mutual ecstasy. Alfieri, always emotional and unbalanced, was of course absolutely overwhelmed with sorrow, and in his Autobiography he speaks of the support afforded him in his grief by the consoling presence of his Lady. Writing to Bianchi, who henceforth steps to a great extent into the void caused by Gori's death, he thus describes his sensations :

" O God, I know not what to say or to do ! I ever seem to see him and hear him, and I talk with him, and each smallest word or thought or act of his returns to my mind, and gives me continual throbs of pain in my heart. I have lost something I can never find again— a true, good, upright, unselfish and devoted friend. This treacherous world does not produce such things, and I do not look for them. . . .
" The Person who is dearest to me (after whom came easily our ' Checco ') knew and understood him, and she too is inconsolable at such a loss." *

This meeting, near Colmar, which had been brought about apparently through the good offices of Madame de Maltzam, was, as we have already said, of a clandestine nature, being utterly unknown to everybody with the exception of Gori (now dead) and of one other friend, the Chevalier Mario Bianchi, who had probably been made acquainted with this circumstance by the devoted " Checco " on his death-bed. A postscript to the letter we have just quoted is therefore highly illuminating

* *Lettere Inedite di V. Alfieri*, p. 118.

119

in connection with this attitude of strict secrecy, which was, of course, intended to preserve the lady's name from further scandal. " It is needless," writes the poet, " to remind either you or Teresa [Mocenni] not to give the smallest hint as to my whereabouts. However, if the fact of my writing to you is ever mentioned, you can always say my letters came from a villa near Venice."[*]

And again, in the next letter, Alfieri reiterates his warning, telling Mario to salute the Arch-priest Luti warmly, but on no account to give him the address. Later, in the following summer, he reminds his correspondent of his full direction at Colmar, bidding him send all letters " à Madame la Baronne de Maltzam, chanoinesse de Mijet, à Colmar, en Alsace."

Together then the pair of mourners for Francesco Gori mingled their tears, and henceforward found but a chastened pleasure in the six remaining weeks of their residence in pleasant Martinsburg, which for the sake of enhanced prudence was brought to a close about the middle of October.

From Colmar the pair proceeded southward by different routes ; Alfieri travelling towards Siena, which he found a desert without the presence of his beloved Gori and soon exchanged for Pisa ; whilst the Countess made her way towards Bologna through Piedmont. On her way thither she apparently made an effort to pay a visit to Alfieri's mother, the old Countess Monica, at Asti ; but according to her own account (and there is no reason to doubt her statement) the country roads were so heavy and impeded after the late autumnal rains, that she could obtain no coach in Turin for the purpose and had therefore reluctantly to abandon her project. Nevertheless, it does not appear that the Countess made any further attempt to visit the old lady. At the end of November the Countess of Albany was staying at Genoa, whence she wrote one of her many letters of pseudo-affection to the Cardinal of York, whom she presumed to be

* *Lettere Inedite*, p. 118.

wholly ignorant of her late carefully contrived escapade at Colmar, and was still most anxious to humour. The letter, which is important only as showing the farce of sisterly affection being still vigorously enacted, contains the usual terms of flattery as well as some sharp remarks about "the King" in Florence, who had recently received in his house Charlotte Stuart, the natural daughter that he had repulsed so unfeelingly ten years before in Rome.

"GENOA, *December* 1, 1784.

"MY DEAR BROTHER,—I have received your letter from Turin. I am well aware of the proofs of affection you gave me, and I shall always try to merit them. I know your heart well, and your kind thoughts, of which you have afforded me proofs on many occasions. As to your Brother, nothing surprises me in his behaviour. I know him so well, that I consider him capable of going to any length of absurdity. I was cognisant of all his late nonsense in Florence, and surrounded by Irish friends he will go on thus, and even make these people baronets. I assure you, my dear Brother, that it will only be with his last breath that he will cease to commit follies. I am about to leave for Bologna, the fourth day of this month. I expect to remain some time with my old friend, the Princess Lambertini. I hope, my dear Brother, that your health is good. I have met the Marchese Grimaldi here, who is grown fatter and more youthful. Monsignore Codronchi at Turin did me many services. He is a good creature. Farewell, my dear Brother. Receive assurance of the affection I bear to you for life, but which I cannot express as well as I could wish.

"Your affectionate Sister,
"LOUISE."*

In deciding to spend the winter at Bologna the Countess was able to keep within the allotted limits of the terms

* British Museum. Add MSS. 34, 634, *f.* 68.

of her legal separation, which permitted her to reside
only in Papal territory, so that she was thus able to avoid
Rome with its unpleasant recollections of the past and
its many tattling tongues; also, in all probability she
was most anxious to elude the vigilance of the Cardinal
of York, or rather of his surrounding host of spying
friends and sycophants. In addition to these advantages,
she was comparatively near to Alfieri at Pisa, so that
twice a week letters passed regularly between the pair,
"again torn asunder, and yet near neighbours," as the
latter expresses it; adding that this situation was at
once a source of consolation and of martyrdom to him.
The Countess meanwhile remained the whole of the
following five months in the house of her friend, some
eleven years older than herself, Donna Mariana Lambertini,* *née* Nobili of Lucca, who had been married
ten years before to Prince Giovanni Lambertini, a great-
nephew of Pope Benedict XIV. The Cardinal-Duke,
still blissfully ignorant of the late meeting near Colmar,
was probably satisfied with his sister-in-law's residence
in so correct a household, for he seems to have corre-
sponded occasionally with her throughout this winter
on friendly terms. The following letter commenting
on the bestowal of the Order of St. Andrew on his
daughter Charlotte, seems to be the last in point of date
that has been preserved of all her letters to the Cardinal :

"BOLOGNA, *December* 24, 1784.

" . . . I am quite comfortable in this place. I am
staying with the Princess Lambertini, of whom I am
very fond and whom I am helping to divert in her present
situation, for she has just been brought to bed. Her
husband is full of attentions towards myself, and antici-
pates my wishes, as does also the Cardinal-Legate, whom

* Not to be confused with Donna Giulia Lambertini-Bovio, in whose
house died Charlotte Stuart, Duchess of Albany, in 1789, and some of whose
letters to Cardinal York are included in *The Last of the Royal Stuarts*,
pp. 187, 188.

LOUISE, COUNTESS OF ALBANY
From the pastel by Pompeo Batoni

I see daily. The Casa Angelelli has done every service possible for me. I suffered a good deal from the cold on my journey hither, and I greatly dread the passage over the mountains on account of the snow, which is very deep. The King continues to do a thousand absurdities in Florence, although he can scarcely move from one room to another by reason of his swollen legs. His illness does not, however, prevent him from bestowing the Order of St. Andrew at the end of a banquet on his Daughter and on a certain Lord who attends him. It is all very ridiculous. Farewell, my dear Brother. Keep well, I beg you, and retain your kindness and affection for me, and rest assured of my lasting attachment to yourself.

" Your affectionate Sister,
" Louise." *

Throughout the whole of the opening months of 1785 a most active and regular correspondence was proceeding between the Countess at Bologna and Alfieri at Pisa. Not a single line of a single letter has, however, survived, and we are therefore left wholly in the dark as to the ideas and suggestions thus exchanged. Fortunately, on the other hand, we possess a clear account of Alfieri's life at Pisa drawn from his many letters addressed jointly to Mario Bianchi and his mistress Teresa Mocenni, who equally shared the poet's confidence. To Mario and Teresa he often complains of the monotony of his daily existence and of the hardship of separation from his lady; he admits his own morose and moody temperament; and mentions his determination in future never to discuss literature with a soul of his acquaintance : " I have decided nevermore to talk of books or letters on any consideration; and to anybody that engages me upon the Muses, I shall reply by discussing horse-flesh."

As the season advances and the days grow longer and

* British Museum. Add MSS. 34, 634, f. 70.

warmer, Alfieri supplies his friends at Siena with detailed accounts of his daily occupations, which serve well to illustrate the eccentric, self-centred nature of the famous Italian dramatist, who at this period lived solely in himself and for himself, caring little for the feelings of those around him, but rather enjoying his reputation for aloofness among the people of Pisa, and loving to be noticed and pointed out by all as the great Count Vittorio Alfieri of Cortemilia, Italy's patriotic tragedian.

"I take exercise here on the fine broad roads, whereon I spend all the time I am not actually at table or in bed. What a charming existence! And thus engaged you will find me, despite all my late sorrows and anxious moments. But now I breathe again, and in the mornings I have once more started to read in bed. I study *Pliny's Letters* and peruse Ariosto a little. I go out riding with a copy of Petrarch in my pocket, and thus am I restoring my mental equilibrium by slow degrees. . . .

"I ride fifteen or twenty miles daily, after which I return to my lodging, for I am a man, or rather (to speak truth) a creature of habits which I cannot break without doing myself great violence. I should like to be with you two at Siena, but I cannot leave my horses behind me here; indeed, they constitute my one and special care, and now that I ride so much more, I am fonder of them than ever. My friend the Cavalier —— and myself ride out each morning, and drive in the afternoon. Sometimes we visit the theatre and occasionally go to see an invalid friend at the baths of San Giuliano, whilst during the course of the day I manage to sleep a good deal, read a little, and revise my dramas. . . . I often think on 'Checco' during my morning ride, saying to myself, 'This place, this city, this river would delight him'; and then I weep, and read out of the volume of Petrarch which I always keep in my pocket. Then I think on my Lady, and again I fall to weeping; and thus do I live my life and long for death, deploring I

have no reason for committing suicide. Thus in the midst
of this dismal but not desperate state of affairs do I feel
my soul dead and my heart buried, and I no longer
recognise my true self. Such I am at present; perhaps
I shall change later, in the event of which I shall inform
you. I should be only too pleased to distract my thoughts
with your company, but I have not sufficient energy to
start upon the road to Siena." *

The allusions contained herein to an unhappy frame
of mind and to anxieties of a private nature, such as he
can only hint at to his friend Mario Bianchi, are connected
with a curious and sinister incident, which is not
mentioned in the *Vita*. Alfieri's Autobiography, in
fact, whatever may be said of its veracity as a whole,
is certainly not guiltless of that convenient elimination
of disagreeable facts which the lawyers have designated
suppressio veri. The truth is, that these months at Pisa
were passed in a state of great suspense by the poet,
and also presumably by the Countess, although we can
only judge of her feelings and position from the existing
letters of Alfieri to Bianchi. A new and unexpected
source of danger and exposure had all at once appeared,
and to explain it we must return for a moment to the
earlier years of the poet's life.

From the age of sixteen Vittorio Alfieri had always
been attended by a valet named Elia, a faithful and
obliging servant through all his wanderings and early
adventures, whose name is frequently mentioned by
his master in the first half of the Autobiography. For
many years Elia had endured with good-natured resignation the sharp tongue and even the personal violence
of his erratic master, who on one occasion had almost
killed the unfortunate valet, by a terrific blow on the
temple with a silver candlestick, for accidentally pulling
his hair whilst dressing it before the mirror. The man
nearly succumbed from the shock and loss of blood, but

* *Lettere Inedite, Op. Cit.*

his devotion to his hasty master was such that he declined
to leave his service, and merely revenged himself by
keeping ever in his pocket the blood-stained bandage
that covered his broken head, and this he was wont to
dangle before Alfieri's eyes whenever the Count again
showed signs of giving way to his ungovernable temper.
Alfieri, as well he might, placed full confidence in the
discretion and attachment of such a domestic treasure,
and consequently when he came to dwell at the Villa
Strozzi, in Rome, he invited Elia to join the household
of the Countess of Albany, with the evident object of
his acting as a confidential messenger between himself
and his lady.   In this manner therefore Elia must have
become closely acquainted with every move and interview of the pair; he was doubtless present during the
stolen meeting at Colmar; and his knowledge of the
risk run by the Countess in thus deceiving the Papal
authorities and in breaking the spirit of the terms of her
late legal compact with her husband must have made
it all-important to keep this witness both contented and
silent.

Nevertheless, for causes which it is impossible to
discover at this distance of time, the Countess actually
dismissed this man from her service in the spring of
1785, and sent him back to his original master, although
at the same time allowing him a small annual pension
of 400 *livres*.   The following letter, addressed by Alfieri
to his sister, the Comtessa Giulia di Cumiana, at Turin,
throws a good deal of light on the late conduct of the
once highly valued Elia, and it also shows us the firm
and drastic manner in which Alfieri could meet with
and overcome an exceedingly dangerous and disagreeable
antagonist; for there can be little doubt that Elia had
attempted to blackmail the Countess, who must have
offered her servant this bribe of an annuity for life in
order to induce him to leave Bologna and to re-enter
the service of his former master, as being more competent
to deal successfully with so troublesome a fellow.   It

is an ugly incident, and one that is very little known, but it finds its echo many years afterwards in some sweeping remarks of the Countess to Teresa Mocenni about Italian men-servants in general : " It is your Christian charity," so she writes to Madame Mocenni, " that prevents you from distrusting men-servants. As to myself, I am less Christian, for I hold it for a maxim that every servant is a thief, and I act on that principle. This class of human beings is utterly vile, and is ever at perpetual war with us. They are always seeking to injure us, and we must be ever on our guard against them."

It was undoubtedly the Countess' unpleasant experiences about Elia which prompted these sentiments, as will be gathered from the contents of the letter from Alfieri to his sister, which has already been mentioned.

" Elia finally leaves to-day for Turin, and will arrive there directly. I must now tell you, and with the deepest regret, that I have been deceived in this man for over twenty years, and for these last four years, during which time I have placed him in the service of the Countess of Albany, I have clear evidence to convince me that he is not only a thief, but also that he has every vice whereof a man is capable. He is inquisitive, untruthful, impertinent, blustering and babbling. Being such, the Signora Countess was compelled to dismiss him this summer before setting out on her travels. He was sent to me, and I should have made no objection to retaining him, had he chosen to stay quietly in my house. But in spite of repeated warnings, he has never ceased from pestering the Signora with letter after letter, each one more impertinent in tone, in order to induce her to receive him back into her service. Beside this, he has caused mischief in my small household by abusing me ; and, worst of all, seeing the Signora is determined not to take him back, he has had the impudence to speak ill of her both in the *cafés* and in my own house, saying things that are partly true, and (needless to say) partly false, invented, and absolutely astounding.

"This behaviour, which renders him equally noisy, indiscreet, ungrateful and rascally, has decided me to send him back to Turin, so that he may nevermore set foot outside it. Out of kindness, however, and so as to put him still more in the wrong, and also on account of his long and faithful service on my former travels, I have decided to leave intact his pension of 1000 *lire*, which I assigned to him at the time of my donation to yourself, and which he then deserved though he deserves no longer. So also the Signora, for the four years he has remained in her service, is willing to allow him an annuity of 400 *lire*. But neither of these pensions will he obtain save under the following conditions, which Elia has signed and which I keep beside me. These are as follows : he is never to leave Piedmont, or indeed Turin itself; and never to write either to the Signora, or to myself, or to any member of our households. Besides, he is to understand clearly he is never to speak either well or ill, to any person or in any way, of the Signora, who rewards him beyond his merits and now deeply regrets having made him such a gift. As to his mentioning myself, he can say what he pleases; but I shall not permit any remarks about the Signora, and I beg you to warn me at once of the slightest whisper. I have also written in the same strain to the Abbé [di Caluso] and to Damiano, who will know how to deal promptly with the difficulty."*

The wretched and cowed Elia dared not apparently defy the wrath or vengeance of his former master, for we find him still drawing his pensions, presumably on the conditions laid down, in the year 1793, when Alfieri, on account of his financial losses from the French Revolution, suddenly cut down his old servant's allowance from 1400 *lire* to 400. "You will do me a service," so he

* Bertana, pp. 211–213.

again writes to his sister in October 1793, " by making
Elia understand he is never to write to me ; nor to pester
others ; because my mind is absolutely made up ; and
that if he annoys me, I shall never again pay him more
than the 400 *lire*. If things change for the better in
course of time, and if it be possible, I shall resume giving
him the extra 1000 *lire*. . . ." *

Elia's dismissal is also noted elsewhere, for Charlotte
Stuart, recently created Duchess of Albany, describes
the circumstance to her father's brother, the Cardinal,
whom she was then engaged in doing all in her power
to conciliate. This ambitious young woman, after years
of neglect, was being now petted and adored by her
father, who had even gone so far as to declare her legitimate, much to the annoyance of Henry Stuart. Being
most anxious to reconcile the two brothers, for this
purpose she was actively trying to persuade the reluctant
Henry of the guilt of the Countess of Albany. On
June 4 she therefore addressed to the Cardinal, whom
she had not yet met, the following letter, evidently
inspired by an intense malignity in the writer, who,
as the mouthpiece of her father, as well as from her own
private feeling of jealousy, ever abused the Countess,
and was bent on creating a rupture between her and the
Cardinal-Duke. The date is June 4, 1785, a few days
prior to Alfieri's letter to his sister.

" Monsignore,—According to various pieces of information received, I consider it my duty to inform
Your Royal Highness that Alfieri is, they say, seriously
annoyed with Madame on account of his jealousy. He
scolded her for preferring a certain Elyot. Meanwhile
that servant of his [Elia] has been dismissed by her,
presumably for other reasons of the same nature. Finally,
it is rumoured that a German, by name Count Proly [?],
has followed her to Paris. Alfieri makes no secret of
his anger and says everything possible that is nasty.

* *Ibidem*, p. 214.

What causes us alarm is that this man [Alfieri] has taken a house here in Florence for four months, and that the King is in constant danger of meeting him, much to his annoyance and alarm. Moreover, this objectionable movement of his seems like a deliberate insult to my august father. Forgive me, Monsignore, if I pass the limits of your permission to acquaint you so far as is possible with what is going on." *

As the letter contains one serious mis-statement, namely, that Alfieri had taken a house in Florence for the summer months, it is not unreasonable to suppose that the other innuendoes contained therein are either false or distorted pieces of gossip. The fact was, that Alfieri came to Florence for two or three days to attend a *fête champêtre* in the Boboli Gardens, and then returned at once to Pisa. As to the statements concerning the two mysterious men who are said to have aroused Alfieri's suspicions or jealousy, we know nothing of such persons, and there is no mention of their names in Alfieri's Autobiography or in his private letters to Mario Bianchi. As the whole of the long correspondence between the Countess and Alfieri during this period has been destroyed, there is no evidence to show either way whether or no the Countess had been guilty of any flirtation serious enough to rouse the slumbering spirit of jealousy in her lover; but we consider the charge itself highly improbable, seeing the extreme devotion of the pair and their constant plans for a reunion in the coming autumn. On the other hand, a determined attempt had been made to storm the heart of the poet at Pisa during the winter months by a certain Venetian lady staying in Pisa, who had fallen head over ears in love with the handsome poet, after watching him daily ride or drive in the environs of the town. Possibly the unscrupulous Charlotte, only too eager to seize upon any scandal connected with the pair, no matter how ill-authenticated or

* Reumont, *Gli Ultimi Stuardi, Le Comtessa d'Albany e V. Alfieri.*

improbable, had heard some vague story of a flirtation or a quarrel, which she had immediately out of malice assigned to the detested wife of her father. That is our own opinion; but, as we have said, there is no definite basis to decide upon the extent of the truth or the untruth of Charlotte Stuart's charges, since all letters on the subject have perished. Alfieri in one or two of his letters at this time to Bianchi certainly alludes to his deep anxiety about his Lady; but this attitude, we think, is wholly due to his alarm at the possible results of Elia's tales, more or less correct, of the late meeting at Colmar, which the valet, turned rogue, had been scattering abroad at Pisa, and probably also at Bologna. An exposure of this sort would naturally mean at least the breaking of all existing ties between the Cardinal of York and the Countess (a catastrophe the latter was particularly anxious to avoid); and it might even cause complaints to the French court, so as to imperil her annuity of 60,000 *livres*, to say nothing of a further loss of her reputation. This prospect was surely sufficient of itself to account for the inquietude of Alfieri concerning his lady, and we firmly believe this to have been its sole cause. Whether the Countess had got wind of her lover's platonic and mild intrigue with the charmer at Pisa,* we do not know; but we feel confident that from the point of jealousy, the Countess alone of the pair had the smallest ground for complaint, whilst we have the poet's own statement for her magnanimity towards his various peccadilloes.

Already the Countess had with the Pope's permission long ago exchanged Italy for France, on the plea apparently of a desire to be near her sister the Duchess of Berwick. In April she had left Bologna, and was already in Paris; nor had she any intention of returning to Italy until such time as the querulous old invalid in Florence should have given up the ghost. She there-

* For a brief account of this episode *see* E. Copping, *Alfieri and Goldoni*, p. 117.

fore spent the summer in Paris, and then, by preconceived arrangement, again slipped off to Madame de Maltzam's pleasant castle of Martinsburg, where she was joined by Alfieri in the early part of September. The poet again warns Mario Bianchi before his departure thither to be very careful not to divulge his true address, but to mention England as his destination. He also begs his Sienese friend to keep him well informed as to the movements of Charles Stuart, telling Mario and Teresa that the chances of his returning to Italy depend solely on the changes that would naturally ensue upon the death of that perennial stumbling-block to the happiness of himself and the Countess, "which we have already agreed to think no more about and have put on the list of things impossible."

This time Alfieri fully intended to remain at Martinsburg for the whole winter, and accordingly he travelled thither with his new secretary, a studious youth named Gaetano Polidori,* whose name is fairly well known in English literature as the grandfather of the poet-painter, Dante Gabriel Rossetti.

Here for the second time a blissful and all-too-brief space of two months sped by in each other's company, and it is very difficult, from the obvious delight wherewith the pair found themselves reunited after a year's interval, to imagine there can ever have been the smallest foundation for the malign insinuations of the embittered Charlotte Stuart, who was undoubtedly devoured with a double portion of rancour, jealousy and uncharitableness so far as her father's erring wife was concerned. Towards the end of November the pair had again to separate, the Countess returning to Paris, and Alfieri remaining on at Martinsburg, "our home," after first escorting his lady so far as Strasburg, where "with the deepest grief he was forced to leave her for the third time," so he relates in his *Vita*. His chief consolation

---

* For an account of this Polidori, *see* A. D'Ancona, *Un Segretario dell' Alfieri* (*Varietà Stoiche e letterarie*, Serie I. Milano, 1883).

now, so he informs Bianchi, is that he can by staying
on at Colmar receive letters from her at short and regular
intervals, and this is the main reason of his own decision
not to return to Italy. The same letter also contains
a detailed description of their temporary home of Martinsburg and of his own daily life in the absence of his lady.

"COLMAR, *November* 29, 1785.

" . . . I cannot come to see you this winter. The
reasons are that, in the first place, I want to be near my
Lady [in Paris], and here at Colmar I can reach her within
four or five days, and can send and receive news twice
a week. With such a devoted heart as hers, my resolution is fully justifiable, though I must also add my own
laziness. I dwell in the place where I have been with
her, where I have high hopes of seeing her again, and
where I have my books, my manuscripts, my secretary,
and all the implements of my art. The house is well
situated, very cheerful, convenient and in good repair.
My horses are together in a clean and ample stable. I
hear no gossip of any kind, and I see nobody. I am
three miles distant from the town, which is near enough
for convenience, yet far enough for me to escape
its many nuisances, cobble-stones, noises and tiresome people. All these attractions have induced me to
remain.

" I shall describe you my situation, and how pleasant
the country seems. . . . The house is placed on an
eminence of no great height, but sufficient to afford
a complete view over the whole plain so far as Old
Brisach on the Rhine, just as one sees your own villa of
Montechiaro from Siena, about fifteen Italian miles
away. At the flanks are two gentle slopes covered with
vines, whilst behind them the hills rise gradually to
terminate in forest. The house, which here they call
a castle, is isolated and at a furlong's space from a hamlet,
that lies hidden to one side of it, so that its squalour
is not offensive to the eye, and one need not pass through

133

it to reach the castle, unless so disposed. The stables form a separate building, fifty yards below the castle, right underneath us but not causing any annoyance. The interior of the house is not large, but it is adequate. It is scrupulously clean, very light, and, thanks to its stoves, very warm. At this moment I am writing from a turret, which juts out from an angle of the castle. It has three windows and a small stove, and is bright as a lantern, and so delightfully warm that I am now writing at an open window. The life I lead is this.

" I awake before six, light my lamp and read and write in bed till ten. Having dressed, I call my secretary, and revise the *Sallust* and the *Tragedies*, which are almost ready for copying. Thus till mid-day I remain in my bedroom. Then after a light meal, I go to the stables, and ride or drive during my leisure hours till four. On returning home, I dress my remaining hairs, which for greater convenience I have now tied into a queue. I dine and proceed to my cabinet, where I think of my friends, write to my Lady, and read some book for amusement. At eight or a little earlier I visit the stables to see the horses fed, talk to my favourite nag Achille, look into expenses, argue with my man about oats and hay, and at nine go to bed.

" In this uniform life I pass my days, and I miss neither the gossip nor the amusements of the town. Only one thing I yearn for, and that is my Lady, and yourself, and the Teresina, and the Abbé [di Caluso], and that grand unique friend, for whom desire is useless, since nevermore shall I see him again. . . ." *

This description of the *château* of Martinsburg, locally known as Wettolsheim, affords us an interesting and minute setting to the existence led by the Countess and Alfieri during these few years. The castle itself was still standing, though greatly modernised, in 1882, as Baron von Reumont relates in his valuable account of

* *Lettere Inedite*, pp. 174–177.

Alfieri in Alsace; * whilst the lovely rich scenery of
the valley of the Rhine remains almost unchanged from
the far-away time when Martinsburg was inhabited by
"the foreign princess and the Italian nobleman who
was not her husband," as the pair are traditionally said
to have been described by the peasants on the estate.
We get a few glimpses here and there of these sojourns
near Colmar, notably in the reminiscences of Gaetano
Polidori, who hated his employer Alfieri, and saw next
to nothing of the Countess of Albany, though dwelling
beneath the same roof with her. Polidori's account †
includes one vulgar and highly improbable anecdote
concerning the lady, together with some sharp and rather
spiteful remarks upon the foppishness of that would-be
antique Roman republican, Vittorio Alfieri himself,
with his scented ruddy locks, his flowing cloak of blue
lined with scarlet, and his intense but carefully concealed
craving for admiration from the very people he most
affected to despise. Polidori's reminiscences have all
the appearance of issuing from a jaundiced mind; but
we have, on the other hand, some more pleasing and
also more authentic accounts from various visitors to
the castle of Martinsburg, including the poet Ippolito
Pindemonte and the eminent German antiquary, Baron
Joseph von Lassberg, a nephew of Baroness de Maltzam.
The learned Lassberg stayed at Colmar during the autumn
of 1786, and as the result of his close observations there,
he has left us a most attractive picture of the Countess of
Albany, as she appeared to him at the age of thirty-four.

"The Countess was then shining in all her beauty.
In stature a trifle above the middle height, her figure
was firm but not too robust, whilst in all her movements
she expressed grace and dignity. Her thick hair, of a
light chestnut hue, almost touched the ground. Her

* *Alfieri in Alsazia.* (*Archivio Storico Italiano*, 1882. Serie v. vol. x.
pp. 210–222.)
† D'Ancona, *Un Segretario dell' Alfieri.* *Op. Cit.*

sky-blue eyes exhaled love and sweetness. A well-formed mouth showed rows of even teeth, white as ivory. Her complexion was most delicate, but the roses of her cheeks had partially faded, from the sufferings she had undergone owing to the behaviour of her husband. Her feet and hands were shapely, whilst her conduct and manners pointed to high breeding and a kindly nature. Her voice was somewhat louder and shriller than is usual in her sphere of life. She danced, sang, drew, played the harp and the spinet, and rode better than one commonly sees in persons of her rank. Her tastes were mostly serious, and though she owned the gift of conversation in a marked degree, nobody could accuse her of loquacity. She was agreeable to all, and withal kind and generous to the poor. One needed to understand her thoroughly to appreciate her, but such appreciation was permanent." *

During the year 1786, the break, which had so long been threatened between the Cardinal of York and his sister-in-law, came actually to pass. In spite of her behaviour in Rome in 1783, the Cardinal had continued to correspond on terms of friendship with the Countess, nor could his brother's angry appeals, now joined with those of Charlotte Stuart, induce him to believe in the existence of " lo scandalo con Conte Alfieri," as it was termed. In vain did Charlotte, as the secretary of her indignant father, argue and insinuate in her letters; the Cardinal remained firm in his belief in the lady's

* Reumont, *Gli Ultimi Stuardi*. There has been much dispute as to the exact colour of Madame d'Albany's eyes, which Alfieri invariably describes as *negri* or black; Bonstetten as of a *bleu foncé* or dark blue, and this writer as of a *bleu céleste* or sky-blue. The real fact seems to be that her eyes were of a changing chameleon hue, appearing now light and now dark to the beholder, a peculiarity which constituted in itself no small charm. Most of her portraits, however, exhibit the eyes of a decided blue, in spite of Alfieri's judgment upon them. Compare on this subject the interesting contribution by " Hermentrude," to *Notes and Queries* (3rd Series, vol. viii. p. 164), who discusses the matter at some length with quotations from the sonnets of Alfieri.

present innocence, however imprudent or misleading he might have deemed her past conduct. But in the autumn of 1785 he graciously accorded a personal interview to the Chevalier's daughter at Perugia, where the damning evidence then adduced by this astute young lady finally opened wide the Cardinal's eyes to the continued existence of the intrigue. No doubt, the statements which the rebellious Elia had let fall had reached the Chevalier and his daughter, so that they had probably had little difficulty in discovering the secret meetings at Madame de Maltzam's country-house. Once convinced, though sorely against his will, for he seems really to have been fond of his sprightly and (apparently) affectionate sister-in-law, Henry Stuart now seconded the desperate efforts of his brother in order to stop the lady's pension from the French court, which rendered her sufficiently independent to defy her husband's accusations of misbehaviour.

The Cardinal therefore now began to demand not denials of guilt (with which he had hitherto shown himself fairly satisfied), but explanations of her movements since the summer of 1784; and to these searching questions the Countess had, as may well be supposed, no reply to return, beyond professing her undying affection and her complete innocence. With this general and vague answer to his direct query the Cardinal was no longer ready to rest content, and ere the year 1786 was brought to a close, the long-averted rupture was brought about. Lengthy documents were now drawn up by the Cardinal-Duke, setting forth the lady's late iniquities, and refusing to hold further communication with her till she had cleared her name, or had at least refused evermore to be visited by Alfieri. In vain did the Countess plead and promise ; the Cardinal proved obdurate, though he constantly stated his readiness to overlook the past, provided she would put herself in the hands of Cardinal de Bernis or some mutual friend, who would undertake to cut off all future communication between herself and her lover. This suggestion the Countess continued to evade, so that her brother-in-law now openly distrusted all her promises and protestations for the future. " It cannot be denied " (so runs the preamble of a long *Memorial* of the Cardinal's on the conduct of his sister-in-law) " that the Count Alfieri has been the origin, the cause, the instigation, and the agent of the utterly deplorable and irreparable differences between the Royal Brother and his Consort, and also in consequence between the Lady-Consort and the Cardinal-Duke." *

Secure in the possession of her French pension (perhaps through the good offices of Queen Marie-Antoinette, whom she had known as a child), the Countess was able to withstand the double attack of the Stuart brothers to bring her to her knees by depriving her of the means of existence ; but there can be little doubt that she felt very acutely the final discovery of her late intimacy with Alfieri by the Cardinal. She had evidently hoped to keep his valuable approval and friendship to the last, and possibly but for the determined action of Charlotte Stuart she might never wholly have lost them. Having, however, lost irretrievably that on which she evidently set the highest consideration, the Countess henceforth rarely alludes to her brother-in-law, who in his turn nevermore addressed any private letter to her. How artificial and deceitful her whole conduct must have been to him throughout these six years, is made manifest by the unkind and satirical comments upon him and his foibles which she made later at a time when his misfortunes and his great age should have ensured him the warmest sympathy. Nothing in short can be more callous or unsisterly than the remarks she allows herself to indite to her friend Teresa Mocenni in the spring of 1800, when the Cardinal of York, old, infirm and bowed down with his enforced wanderings, was resting for a few days at Siena on his return to Rome from the late Conclave of Venice.

* British Museum. Add MSS. 30, 478, *ff*. 207–210.

"MY DEAR TERESA," she writes on May 17, "I write to warn our good Arch-priest that the Cardinal of York is going to settle at Siena . . . until such time as he can return to Frascati. It will be very pleasant for the poor Archbishop [Zondadari], who will be ruined if he has to keep this incubus for any length of time in his palace. He won't sleep a night in Florence, on account of myself whom he wishes to avoid. He is very whimsical and very dull, and he bores every one he meets. When he was on the open sea [between Messina and Venice] he wanted to have the ship stopped at his pleasure, as if such a thing were possible! He belongs to a race of amphibious creatures, who are intended to be *seen from a distance*, but whom an evil chance has brought close to our eyes. All that class would appear similar, if one had to live with any one of them, as in the case of that stage-figure, my brother-in-law."

And again, in a letter of a week later, the writer remarks : "You will see the Cardinal of York at Siena, and no doubt he will be as silly there as he is everywhere else. Mercifully for the Archbishop, he is going to stay at the monastery, so that this visit will not ruin him. I expect you will enjoy his company for some time."

In a third letter, of May 31, the Countess asks the Abbé Luti to give a polite message from herself to Monsignore Cesarini, but to give it without the knowledge of his master the Cardinal, "*who hates me like Lucifer*"!

In the autumn of 1804 the Countess spent some time in Rome, in order to consult with the sculptor Canova about the monument she was proposing to erect to Alfieri; but though her brother-in-law, from whom she had years before received such generous treatment, was fallen into his dotage and sunk in a state of senile childishness, the Countess never once went to Frascati to visit him, although his feelings for herself cannot have been wholly devoid of affection, if only for the sake of times long past, when she had so willingly and seemingly so gratefully availed herself of his protection and the glamour of his name. For the old man, the picturesque gentle Pretender, the Cardinal-King Henry IX., turned to forgive the woman who had once accepted his bounty, and then deceived and even maligned him, by bequeathing her in his will as a memento a valuable picture and a gold watch with her cipher. And these the Countess accepts with a profession of affection and sympathy which we hope rather than believe to be genuine, declaring she was quite satisfied with the thought of her brother-in-law's dying recollection of herself, " had he left her only a pin for remembrance." * It is pleasant to think of this graceful forgiving act of the pious and much abused Cardinal ; but the whole story of the behaviour of Louise, Countess of Albany, towards her brother-in-law forms undoubtedly one of the most disagreeable and discreditable episodes in a career which is certainly not devoid of a good many blemishes.

* *Hist. MSS. Commission Tenth Report. Appendix.* Part vi. p. 249.

CHAPTER VIII

DEATH OF CHARLES-EDWARD STUART

*" Oui, l'adultère a beau s'entourer de mille excuses et se parer
de tous les prestiges de la poésie ; l'heure de la punition finit
toujours par sonner. Sous une forme ou sous une autre, le juge
invisible sait attendre les coupables. Certes, on ne peut blâmer
la Comtesse d'Albany de s'être soustraite aux mauvais traitemens
de Charles-Edouard ; dès le jour où il viola tous ses devoirs,
Charles-Edouard n'avait plus de droits sur elle. Une fois libre
cependant, une fois arrachée à ce joug odieux, comment absoudre
la femme qui ne sut pas se respecter ? "*

ST. RÉNÉ TAILLANDIER, *La Comtesse d'Albany*

THE open breach between the Countess and the Cardinal
of York, as well as authenticated reports of the renewed
relations between the Countess and Alfieri, soon caused
the veil of concealment to be removed. Setting at
defiance both her brother-in-law's fulminations and the
opinion of the censorious world, the Countess now induced
the poet to return with her to Paris in the winter months
of 1786 ; whilst with regard to this change in his plans
Alfieri writes to Bianchi from Colmar on October 5.

" . . . Since the latter part of August my Lady has
been here, and till lately I have been in uncertainty as
to my plans. But she has at last persuaded me to go
with her to Paris for the winter, and return to Colmar
in May, now that the business matters between her
husband and herself have been settled. Paris is to me
always the most insufferable spot . . . but the presence
of the Beloved beautifies everything, and I proceed
thither solely for her sake. So you will not behold me
for a year's space,

" Siena put new life into me, because I was busy there all day long, and possessed three or four friends who put up with my vagaries, and amongst whom I could pass pleasant evenings so as to gather fresh strength for the coming day. Paris, even with my Lady, will bore me to death, for I cannot suffer fools. I shall, however, take the line of quizzing them, and of making notes for future comedies. I shall be forty years old * next January, and on my birthday I shall divest myself of the buskin, my tears and the mask of tragedy, since I mean to consecrate the next six years and no more to satirising everything in this world that deserves mockery ; whilst the remainder of my life from forty-six onward I intend to spend in keeping silence, and in printing, polishing and revising my works." †

On December 5, therefore, Alfieri left Colmar somewhat unwillingly in compliance with the wishes of the Countess, so that by the middle of the month he was installed in the city which he had abused at various times as " that Babylon ; that *cloaca maxima* of putrefaction," &c.‡

To Mario Bianchi he accordingly writes on December 26, telling of his arrival.

" . . . I left Alsace with my Lady on December 5th and we reached Paris on the 15th, after a somewhat tedious journey owing to the bitterness of the weather, although so far we have had no snow, only roads deep in mire. Despite this, you can imagine that travelling thus all alone with the Better Half of Myself I did not suffer much from the discomfort of the vile roads. Here we do not inhabit the same house for propriety's sake ; and I am lodging a short distance away. We have, however, grown so used to being together at the villa, that I feel consequently some annoyance ; and besides, this city has always been hateful to me. This is my fifth visit to Paris in the last eighteen years, and were

* In reality thirty-eight.
† *Lettere Inedite.*   ‡ *Op. Cit.*

it not for my Lady, I should refuse to endure it for a day." *

They spent the whole winter and spring in Paris, the poet detesting the city despite the presence of the Countess, and missing keenly his horses, his books and the repose of Colmar. Early in the summer of 1787 they returned to Martinsburg, where before many weeks had passed, Alfieri was prostrated by the serious illness (the direct result of over-work) which had long been hanging over his head. Throughout this stubborn and prolonged attack, he was nursed by his Lady as well as by the faithful Abbé di Caluso, who had recently come to Colmar to spend some months with his friend, and it was chiefly due to their combined exertions that the invalid was rescued from the clutches of death. By the middle of September, Alfieri was pronounced out of danger, so that he was able to inform his correspondent at Siena of his convalescence.

"COLMAR, *September* 15, 1787.

" See, I can only just breathe, or hold up my head after a mortal illness, wherewith I have been threatened for the last two years, and which I warned you of in my last letter from Geneva. At last it seems as if Nature had run her course, for since the eleventh of August till to-day I have not set foot to the ground, whilst it was but three days ago that they were able to ward off a terrible attack of dysentery. But now I feel myself radically cured, after having been given over for dead for twenty days. . . .

" I was in good hands, for where could I expect to find more devoted nursing than between my *Donna Amata* and the *Amico Letterato* [Caluso] ? " *

During the long days of convalescence, the beloved Lady and the learned Abbé found some difficulty in

* *Ibidem.*

143

distracting the busy mind of their restless patient, and various little artifices were resorted to in order to attain that end. One of their efforts has been noted once or twice as illustrating the naturally shallow mind of the Countess; but surely any attempt to coax an invalid into forgetting his pains and grievances ought not to be condemned, merely because it may happen to be of a trivial character? It would seem that among the many persons who were now openly visiting the distinguished tenants of Martinsburg, some relations of Madame de Maltzam used occasionally to attend at the house. One of these ladies living at Colmar chanced to possess a pretty little girl of six, who was a special favourite with the Countess, and one day the latter, regarding attentively the extreme beauty of this child, thought to concoct a pleasant surprise for Alfieri, who was still kept to the sofa, although warmly dressed. Accordingly, the little Lina was attired as a Cupid and hidden at the bottom of the invalid's sofa, behind a curtain, which was suddenly drawn aside to exhibit a living picture of the God of Love. In after years the child herself, then Madame Lina Beck-Bernard, used to relate this simple little episode at Martinsburg, which, as we have already stated, has sometimes been adduced in evidence of the innate vulgarity and silliness of the poor Countess of Albany, who was thereby merely guilty of a small effort to amuse her sick friend, and was apparently in league with the serious-minded Abbé di Caluso in this matter.

"The Countess of Albany noticed me at the house of my cousin Madame de Maltzam (who was then lending her house to the Countess and to Vittorio Alfieri); I was then six years old with curly hair and rosy cheeks. The Princess declared I was like Cupid, and asked leave of my mother to bring me to Wettolsheim (Martinsburg). She had a vest of pale rose-coloured silk made for me and a tunic of sky-blue muslin, to the back of which were fastened some gauze wings sewn with peacock's feathers.

To complete my character of Love, I carried a bow and a gilt quiver, and in this guise I was set at the end of a large yellow damask sofa with a canopy of yellow damask overhead. On the sofa itself was stretched Count Alfieri, enveloped in furs, although it was the height of summer." *

According to one account, the poet, in spite of his weak state of health, became very excited at this sudden apparition of Cupid, and set to spouting verses in so theatrical a manner that the human deity took alarm and started to howl; whereupon the child was hastily removed, and her terror was only appeased by being driven back to Colmar in Alfieri's phaeton.†

The summer of 1787 is also remarkable for a determined effort on the part of the old Countess Monica Alfieri to induce her son to leave the Countess of Albany in order to marry a young wife, an heiress and a member of a distinguished Piedmontese family.‡ The true relations between the pair at Colmar were now so well known, that at last even the innocent old lady living at Asti had grown to realise the nature of the dominating influence wielded by the royal Princess, whom her son had (so chivalrously and so unselfishly, as she once considered) rescued from the power of a drunken husband. The poor mother had made her proposal by means of Alfieri's guest, the Abbé di Caluso, as an old friend of the family, and she does not even seem to have contemplated the possibility of her letter being commented upon by all three—her son, the Abbé and the Countess. One can imagine the reception that this suggestion must have caused in that charmed circle of intellectual souls, and how this artless appeal must have raised a triumphant smile of amusement on the face of the " Donna Amata,"

* Reumont, *Alfieri in Alsazia*.
† R. de Bourdellès, *Études Italiennes*, p. 151. (Quoted from an article by M. André Hallays, in the *Journal des Débats*, April 27, 1906.)
‡ *Vita*, vol. ii. pp. 174, 175. Vernon Lee, pp. 142-145.

who was still waiting for news of the death of her husband, now installed in Rome, and with his daughter Charlotte reigning in the old palace of the Santi Apostoli. Still, behind her mocking laughter and open smiles, there must have lurked some real sense of bitterness at the thought of the good old Countess Alfieri's recent enlightenment as to her romance, so that no doubt she lamented, though in the strictest secrecy, the withdrawal of the Countess Monica's approval, as she had already, also in secret, bewailed her rupture with the Cardinal of York.

Alfieri, who had not even sufficient curiosity to inquire the name of the domestic paragon suggested by his mother, briefly replied that such an idea could not be entertained, seeing that his present age, his pursuit of literature and his own unconcealed theories on the state of matrimony absolutely precluded such a notion from his emancipated mind. This decided refusal to her plea, though couched in vague but affectionate terms, must have come as a sore blow to the anxious mother, who felt only too plainly how useless it was to try to separate her son from the royal siren that had enthralled him. From time to time the poor lady made feeble efforts to induce the wanderer to return to Asti, or else expressed timid doubts as to his soul's health. Indeed, letters passed with tolerable frequency between mother and son, but all those of the former are imbued with a hopeless sadness, for the Countess Monica had realised at last the waning of her influence, never a very strong one, over her brilliant son. Alfieri, on his part, always shows himself gentle and conciliatory; he seeks to parry her plain questions with soothing answers; he speaks of his constant affection for her; and does what he can to allay her alarms or suspicions concerning the ungodly life she conceives him to be leading with the Countess of Albany at Colmar and in Paris. Seeing how essentially self-centred and impatient of all restraint he was, Alfieri seems to have behaved with more consideration

146

towards his mother than might have been expected from the general tenor of his career.

" I want to tell you for your consolation," so he writes from Paris a year or two later, " that I am less bound to the world than you suppose. I live a very retired life in this city, going to bed every evening at ten, rising at five or six, and studying all day till two; whilst I am truly convinced that one can serve God and please Him in every condition of life." * And again—

" You ask me if I have a good spiritual director. Really, I do not wish to run the risk of hypocrisy by saying I hold long and frequent discourses with him, but sometimes I recognise and argue with a certain Corsican Capuchin, who is a man of most saintly and exemplary life." †

The following letter, which is the last the Countess Monica was fated to address to her absent but dearly loved son, especially stirred Alfieri, for it seems to have aroused in him a genuine desire to revisit the parent he had so long neglected. But his filial resolution was made too late. His tears flowed freely, so he tells us; but there was an influence behind that held him back from immediately carrying out his intention, and six weeks after this last pathetic appeal by the old Countess Monica, the hand that wrote it was stiff in death, so that the priceless opportunity of obeying an aged mother's last request was lost to him for evermore.

" Asti, *March* 13, 1792.

" . . . Console my old age, I beg you, by giving me your news and by removing from me the anxiety I have experienced on your account, since by reason of my advanced age I can no longer support myself with the hope of seeing you again. And I believe, if you *did* come home, you would soon perceive that my face is no longer that of the portrait you possess of me, but is in reality that of a corpse, as no doubt the Person (who

* Mazzatinti, p. 219.   † *Ibidem*, p. 220.

147

you say means to accompany you) will tell you. I do not believe it possible she can feel the smallest jot of affection for myself, since I have never even been granted the opportunity of meeting her. I should like to think that the affection for me she professes was the result of a tie, that would allow your temporal happiness to give place to the salvation of your soul. That would indeed be a real consolation to me, and the sole one I can desire ; since, my dear Son, I love you with a love that is equally maternal and Christian, making me wish for you those good things which can alone satisfy the human heart in this life, in order that later we may be united by the mercy of God with Him for ever. I ' embrace you tenderly, as your most affectionate Mother." *

Six weeks later, on April 23, in her seventieth year, died the mother of Vittorio Alfieri, lamenting to the last the continued absence of her son, caught, as she not unnaturally conceives, in the toils of the Countess of Albany, whose attitude she here criticises with a bitterness that is none the less powerful for the writer's restraint of language.

After having paid a visit, together with his Lady and the Abbé di Caluso, in the autumn of 1787 to the celebrated printing-press recently set up by Beaumarchais at Kehl, near Strasburg, Alfieri and the Countess returned to Paris for the winter months. In the following February there arrived the long expected and long delayed news of the death of Charles-Edward Stuart, strangely enough in the gloomy palace that had witnessed his birth, on January 30, 1788. He expired peacefully in the arms of his daughter Charlotte, who had certainly tended the poor half-imbecile hero with loving care and devotion for the past three years, and who deserves in consequence the gratitude of all those persons who take a genuine interest in the career of the Young Chevalier alike through stormy and through sunny days. The tidings

* *Lettere Inedite*, p. 564.

of his end made a great impression, if we are to credit Alfieri's statement, on the wife who was thereby changed into the widow of a legitimist sovereign. The circumstance is set forth with much edifying reflection in the pages of the *Vita*, and the passage certainly calls for some passing comment.

"The February [of 1788] had scarcely begun when my Lady received news of the death of her husband, which took place in Rome, whither he had retired after leaving Florence two years before. And although his demise had been for some time foreseen on account of the frequent attacks he had suffered for months past, and although she now found herself a widow and wholly free, and had also in no wise lost a friend in her late spouse, yet to my astonishment I perceived that she was in spite of all not a little stricken with a grief that was decidedly sincere and perfectly natural, for hypocrisy never entered into that most frank and incomparable heart of hers. And indeed, despite the disparity of age, her husband might have found in her an admirable companion and a true friend, if not a loving wife, had he but refrained from harassing her continually with his peevish, cruel, and drunken ways. This piece of evidence I owe to truth itself." *

This account is, of course, highly reasonable and proper, but somehow the words have not the ring of truth notwithstanding Alfieri's last sentence. It is hard to believe the Countess could really have been thus smitten either with sorrow or with remorse, when the event awaited so long and so urgently had at length come to pass. Monsieur St. Réné Taillandier goes so far as to declare that *cette brillante pécheresse* must have felt envious of the privileges won by Charlotte Stuart in being permitted to minister to the dying Chevalier,†

* *Vita*, vol. ii. p. 185.
† *Revue des deux Mondes*, vol. xxxi. pp. 291, 292.

but there is not a scrap of evidence, except these highly suspicious remarks by Alfieri, to suggest that the lady owned any feelings save those of hatred for past ill-usage towards her husband. If she *did* shed tears; well, then, the statement made above as to her heart being incapable of hypocrisy, must have been a gratuitous untruth, for the Countess could not in reason be expected to mourn for one she detested and whose death at last left her free and comparatively wealthy. In strong conflict with the passage in the *Vita* lately quoted is the remark let fall by Alfieri in the course of a letter to Mario Bianchi a fortnight or so later.

"PARIS, *February* 23, 1788.

" In your letter you give me good news in telling me you hope to escape the trammels of matrimony. I congratulate you, and bid you hold firm to your resolve. We have just learnt here, about ten days ago, of the death of the Person in Rome, but so far we can hardly credit the news, so convinced were we of his immortality. Despite all this, nothing will now change the tenor of our existence, and I fear from henceforth I shall never-more be able to stay anywhere in Italy for long."*

Thus it will be seen that the cold callous allusion in a private letter to Bianchi and the edifying homily in the Autobiography (composed for the benefit of the public) are at variance in the account given of the reception of the news of the Chevalier's death; and such a circumstance of itself makes us somewhat disinclined to place the full confidence we could wish in some other important passages about himself and the Countess, which Alfieri has inserted in the *Vita*.

This particular letter to Mario Bianchi affords us also a clear glimpse into Alfieri's mental views on the subject of marriage, especially when taken in conjunction with his reply to his mother's recent suggestion for his own

* *Lettere Inedite*, p. 203.

betrothal. It was at one time commonly reported (mainly, one would suppose, with the object of sacrificing to the proprieties) that Alfieri and the Countess had been married, though with the greatest secrecy, so soon as the death of the Chevalier permitted the performance of such a rite. Not only, however, is there not a tittle of evidence in support of this alleged marriage, but there is every reason to suppose that for several causes the pair held aloof from encountering a tie against which Alfieri had always inveighed and which the Countess, following her lover's views in all things, likewise regarded either with disdain or indifference. There is not a hint in any of the Countess' later letters to her confidant Teresa Mocenni of such a step, whilst the sentence just given from Alfieri's private opinion, vouchsafed in confidence to Mario Bianchi, shows us his real sentiments very plainly. Moreover, what would the pair have gained by changing their existing state of liberty into one of social convention ? As Signore Bertana rather bluntly puts the question from a worldly and practical point of view : " to obtain the countship of Cortemilia in exchange for that of Albany would be but a poor bargain for the lady ; whilst Alfieri did not want a simple countess for his wife when he had a queen for his mistress. And besides what could be in worse taste than to substitute the poetry of love contained in this unique union for the vulgar bond of matrimony ? " * Indeed, despite one or two apocryphal anecdotes to the contrary, it is pretty certain that Alfieri and the Countess never even dreamed of passing through the ceremony of marriage, but continued to lead the same life after as before the death of the lady's husband. One thing, and one thing only, might perhaps have operated to induce this pair of lovers to embrace matrimony, namely, the existence of children, who would have been legitimised in law by a subsequent union. As this sole argument on behalf of formal matrimony was lacking, the pair were

* Bertana, p. 219.

therefore content to live on as formerly, though in a freer and more open manner. In fact, the old idea that Alfieri became the husband of his " Donna Amata " has almost vanished in modern opinion, though if any further proof were needed for our statement, we may perhaps mention the curious little memorandum, in Alfieri's own hand-writing, amongst the manuscripts at Montpellier, which protests against himself and the Countess of Albany being classed together as a married couple and therefore liable to the incidence of the *tassa famigliare* which was imposed on the citizens of Florence in the year 1801 ; and in which he declares that " the Countess of Albany and the Count Vittorio Alfieri, having arrived together in Florence and inhabiting together Casa Gianfigliazzi, ought not either together, and still less singly, to be accounted liable for the so-called family tax." *

This simple denial of the marriage-tie in the course of casual business ought to be conclusive evidence on this point, although it would be easy to give many more proofs of the improbability of such a ceremony having ever taken place either in Paris, or later in Italy. It has sometimes been said that the Countess desired the sacred bond, but that Alfieri refused to humour her wishes in the matter. It may have been so, but it does not seem likely, for the Countess had nothing to gain and much to lose by an open marriage. As widow of a royal personage—and nobody could with reason deny that appellation at least to her late husband—Louise of Stolberg was both a privileged and an interesting celebrity ; as the wife of an Italian count who wrote poetry, her position in that social world wherein she loved to shine would have been seriously diminished. As to her character being rehabilitated by such a step, the exact opposite might possibly have been the result, seeing that she always stoutly maintained that the tie

* Mazzatinti, *Le Carte Alfieriane di Montpellier.* (*Giornale Storico della Letteratura Italiana*, vol. iii. p. 381.)

binding her to Alfieri was one of the intellect and not one of the heart ; and although nobody seriously credited this theory, yet it was perhaps better to carry such a fiction to its logical conclusion as a widow, as she had hitherto done as a wife living apart from a tyrannical husband. Such an existence, moreover, gave the Countess a sense of property in her talented lover (of whom it is needless to say she was inordinately proud), which marriage would at once endanger. In conclusion, then we may state it as a positive fact, that the Countess and the poet were never married, and that any declaration to the contrary is devoid of truth and even of probability, and has evidently been invented by well-meaning persons merely in order to throw a veil of respectability over this curious and indeed unique intimacy. The precise situation of the pair has been admirably summed up by " Vernon Lee," in the following passage from her biography of the Countess, and we cannot do better than to call in her valuable opinion to aid and intensify our own.—" Alfieri and the Countess did not get married, simply, I think, because they did not care to get married ; because marriage would entail reorganisation of a mode of life which had somehow organised itself ; because it would give a commonplace prose solution to what appeared a romantic and exceptional story ; and finally because it might necessitate certain losses in the way of money, of comfort and of rank." *

One result of her husband's death was greatly appreciated, in that from the opening months of the year 1788 the Countess of Albany became entitled to receive the annual income of 6000 *scudi* which had been settled upon her in the event of her widowhood With her pension from the court of France in addition to this jointure (to say nothing of the large annuity which Alfieri drew from his sister, the Countess Giulia di Cumiana, in compliance with the terms of his donation made in 1778), the Countess was now enabled, as a free and

* Vernon Lee, p. 149.

tolerably wealthy woman, to rent a suitable *hôtel* in the Rue de Bourgogne, where she might indulge her taste for social entertainment to the full. Such a house with such a mistress was naturally able to attract within its doors all that was best in Parisian society, both fashionable and intellectual, and only very few persons of the great social world were inclined to look askance at the widow of a British Pretender, merely because of her romantic attachment to the greatest Italian poet of his day, so that the drawing-room in the Rue de Bourgogne soon came to rank as one of the most popular and frequented of the *salons* in Paris, then vaguely restless but apparently unsuspecting of the vast political upheaval that was in store As in the case of her brother-in-law, the Cardinal-King at Frascati, a certain amount of regal display was observed by this charming and affable *Reine d'Angleterre*, as the Countess was commonly styled by certain of her acquaintances, although the use of such a title, however agreeable to the secret pride of the lady, was never insisted on save in the case of her own servants. A cosmopolitan crowd of all that was modish, witty, learned, and even revolutionary in Paris, was wont to throng her *salon ;* so that it is easy to believe that the Countess was thoroughly happy during this brief period, wherein she could command at one and the same time the open devotion of her distinguished lover and the admiration of the cultured set of the first capital in Europe. Sir Nathaniel Wraxall, who had known the Countess a few years previously in Florence and had then been greatly struck by " her fair complexion, her delicate features and her lively as well as attractive manners," was amongst those persons of British birth who were admitted to the receptions of this acknowledged queen of Parisian society.

" I passed an evening at her residence, the Hotel de Bourgogne, situate in the Faubourg St. Germains, where she supported an elegant establishment. Her

154

person then retained great pretension to beauty, and her deportment, unassuming but dignified, set off her attractions. In one of the apartments stood a canopy with a chair of state, on which were displayed the Royal Arms of Great Britain, and every piece of plate, down to the very teaspoons, was ornamented in a similar manner.

"A numerous company, both English and French, male and female, was assembled under her roof, by all of whom she was addressed as Countess of Albany; but her own domestics, when serving her, invariably gave her the title of *Majesty*. The honours due to a Queen were in like manner paid her by the nuns of all those convents in Paris which she was accustomed to visit on certain holy days or festivals." *

In order to understand the vogue and attraction of these parties in the Rue de Bourgogne, we must imagine all the celebrities of ante-revolutionary Paris passing through her rooms, remarking in their passage with amused smiles or genuine sympathy the royal dais with its pitiful royal adornments. There were the brilliant Madame de Stael (to whom the Stuart Pretender's widow was always her *chère souveraine*); the sprightly and clever little Madame de Flahault, whose first husband was fated to lose his head beneath the guillotine at no distant date; the great dramatist Beaumarchais; the poet André Chénier; the morose painter David; and a host of other literary, scientific or artistic luminaries. The Papal nuncio, Monsignore Dugnani, was wont to attend; and many an ambassador including the Imperial envoy the Comte Mercy d'Argenteau (her own cousin); whilst amongst the members of the entirely fashionable set came such persons as Madame Joséphine de Beauharnais; and her own sisters the Duchess of Berwick and the Comtesse d'Arberg. This existence in Paris, half-modish and half-intellectual, exactly suited the

* H. B. Wheatley, *Memoirs of Sir N. W. Wraxall*, vol. i. pp. 214, 215.

temperament of the Countess of Albany at that date; and doubtless she would gladly have reigned for ever as the acknowledged and flattered queen of a *salon* in the aristocratic Rue de Bourgogne.

The sparkling repartee of Madame de Stael, the cheerful and intellectual conversation of the novelist Adèle de Flahault, the recitations of Chénier and Beaumarchais had the effect of investing her receptions with a peculiar and an envied charm, so that the first intellects of France were only too pleased to admire or to be admired amid such brilliant and delightful company as that over which the still beautiful woman presided with so much tactful grace. Witness in proof of her power the following note from Beaumarchais, who had been eventually persuaded by the Countess to read aloud the manuscript of his *Mère Coupable* in the presence of herself and her invited guests.

"Paris, *February* 5, 1791.

" Madame la Comtesse,—Since you are absolutely set on hearing my very severe play, I cannot gainsay your wish; but please observe, that when I want you all to laugh, it is to be with regular outbursts; and when you are to weep, it must be with real sobs. A middle course is hateful to me.

" So ask whom you choose to my reading on Tuesday, but keep away all your friends with callous hearts or dried-up souls, who look down with contempt on these sorrows we find so delicious. That class of person is only fit to talk about the Revolution. But have some sympathetic women and some men with real hearts; and then we can pour out tears in torrents (*pleurons à plein canal*) I promise to give you a sweetly sorrowful treat, and I am, Madame, your servant with respect,

" Beaumarchais " *

It is, however, very doubtful whether the Countess' satisfaction in her daily life in Paris was shared by her

* *Revue des deux Mondes*, vol. xxxi., p. 594.

male companion. In these great aristocratic and fashion-able assemblies of the Rue de Bourgogne, the poet found himself overlooked and overwhelmed. For the Parisians knew little and cared still less about the history or fate of the Italian drama, and not a few of them were wholly unaware of the extreme importance of the haughty Piedmontese count, who was a poet and also (which to them was perhaps in many cases his sole title to their consideration) the official lover of that charming self-styled Queen of England whose *salon* they chose to haunt. Certain, of course, of the literary celebrities of Paris were inclined to appraise the tragedian at his proper worth, amongst them being André Chénier, with whom Alfieri struck up a close friendship; but, broadly speaking, the conceited and self-conscious poet found himself and his ideals sadly neglected by that Parisian throng wherein he shone with a reflected glory rather as the friend of Madame d'Albany than as the modern representative of the old Roman republican spirit of his native Italy. Reduced chiefly to the intimate society of Ippolito Pindemonte and other Italian friends, strangers in Paris like himself, he must often have thought regretfully of those long-past happy days in Siena, where he had been the idol and the master of that charming little band of provincial scholars and congenial com-panions, the *crocchiette saporito* of his early days.

" I always envy you your *coterie*," so he writes to his friend Bianchi, " whilst I lament my own misfortune in having ever to be where I do not want to be. But we shall meet again. I am sorry it will not be possible for us to live together once more, but the only part of Myself which owns any value, namely, my scribblings, you will always be the first to peruse. And I am anxiously awaiting an opportunity to send you those Odes, and especially the Dialogue about the Friend, which I am perhaps more impatient for you to possess than you to receive." *

* *Lettere Inedite*, p. 203.

This last allusion is to a short work Alfieri was then composing in order to render honour to the memory of the late Francesco Gori, and this task known as the *Virtù Sconosciuta* was amongst the various writings he was then preparing for the press, for he passed much of his time (which might otherwise have perhaps hung heavy on his hands) at Didot's famous printing-house. Thus did the pair spend the three years in the French capital prior to their visit to England, in society and surroundings that were probably as distasteful to the man as they were congenial to the woman.

CHAPTER IX

THE VISIT TO ENGLAND

" If England owned an oppressive government, both the country
and its people would be the most backward in the world. With
a vile climate and a poor soil, what it produces is without taste ;
and it is only the excellence of its government that has made
England a habitable country. Its natives are dull, without
genius or ideas, and dominated by the greed of money-making ;
for there is nothing in all England that cannot be obtained for
a smaller or greater quantity of money."—LOUISE, Comtesse
d'Albany, *Souvenirs de Voyage en Angleterre*

WITH the death of Charles-Edward Stuart the pair
seemed to be definitely fixed in Paris, whether Alfieri liked
it or not. The poet gave up for the present all hope of
returning to Italy, or even to Colmar, whence he removed
all his horses, dividing his stud between himself and the
Countess for the sake of convenience and economy. His
days were chiefly occupied in literary work (which included the writing of the first and longer portion of his
celebrated Autobiography, to which we have so often
alluded) ; and in supervising the edition of his dramas
which Didot was engaged to publish. Little apparently
did either of the pair realise the strength and fury of the
rising political storm of the Revolution, whose first faint
rumblings were being dimly heard in the near distance by
all. Good republican as he fancied himself, Alfieri had
openly expressed his delight at the events of 1789, and
had even watched with approving eyes the destruction of
the Bastille with its evil memories of the tyranny of
French kings. As he gazed at the extraordinary spectacle
in the company of his friend Pindemonte, the poet con-

159

ceived the idea of celebrating so hopeful a sign of the re-
generation of the French people in some verses, which he
ultimately published under the title of *Parigi Sbastig-
liata*. The rapid course of the Revolution in Paris,
however, soon served to open his eyes and to change the
current of his views and sympathies. Alfieri was, indeed,
all too ready to rejoice and break into song when he
watched the power of the French monarchy crumble
away before the advance of the awakened people of
France ; but when the aforesaid great and glorious populace began to attack the privileges and property of his own
class, then the Revolution began to assume a very different
aspect in his eyes ; especially when the swiftly passing
events in Paris soon sent a far-reaching financial shock
throughout Europe, and the appearance of a paper
currency began to affect the republican count's pocket
in a most unpleasant manner. The attitude of the
Parisians towards the *ancienne noblesse* (of which class
Alfieri possessed to the full all the selfishness and pride)
began to annoy him, so that he complains bitterly of
Didot's impertinent workmen wasting their time in talking politics, instead of attending to their proper task of
producing quickly the immortal works of the great
Count Vittorio Alfieri. Nevertheless, if he were growing
dissatisfied and anxious in his mind, his concern was mild
when compared with that of the Countess, who suddenly
was brought to perceive the possibility of all her glittering fabric of social and intellectual pre-eminence that had
been built with such care being undermined and levelled
with the ground. Already Italy (whence she drew part of
her income) was feeling the financial strain ; whilst the
critical position of the French court and the rising demo-
cratic fury began to make her tremble for the safety of her
treasured pension.

Towards the close of 1789 Alfieri had the satisfaction
of receiving from Didot's press the completed edition of
his works that he had been superintending, but this
circumstance in no wise lessened his personal alarm for

the future or his blind and impotent rage against France and the French nation. "Things were ever growing worse"; so he records in the concluding pages of the first part of the *Vita* now being transcribed; "and our security and our peaceful existence in this modern Babylon were being threatened. Every day our anxiety increased, and we became more suspicious of the future actions of this race of human apes, seeing that my Lady and I myself were unfortunately in their midst, and were therefore filled with a continual sense of apprehension and helplessness." * However, Alfieri further on declares that so long as he retains possession of his Lady, all the rest is immaterial to him;—"inasmuch as I live in her and for her alone, so that truly no thought vexes or terrifies me, save the idea of losing her; nor do I pray Heaven for any boon but that of being the first of us to be taken from this world of sorrows." † Thus, of the brief period spent in the house in the Rue de Bourgogne, surrounded by all the wit and charm and luxury that Paris could afford, two years were passed in a state of serious alarm or uncertainty which sadly detracted from the happiness of both.

As the political horizon in France grew darker and more ominous, the fears of the pair were augmented, so that they both became eager to find a permanent home elsewhere. Already, even at her own table, the Countess had received a sharp lesson concerning the propriety of Alfieri and herself espousing the popular cause, when the revolutionary painter, David, suddenly one day thundered out his opinion that peace and prosperity would nevermore be restored in France till Queen Marie-Antoinette was sent to the guillotine; a remark which must have horrified the Countess and which certainly caused some of her guests there and then to leave her house. Acting on a sudden impulse caused by disgust at the present trend of affairs in France, and being most uncomfortably haunted by the prospect of the ultimate loss of her court

* *Vita*, vol. ii. p. 188.   † *Ibidem*, p. 193.

pension, the Countess, probably at Alfieri's own suggestion, decided to pay a visit to England; a visit which
might even under certain circumstances be prolonged
into a lengthy residence on these island-shores where, so
Alfieri was wont to declare, true Liberty alone could
flourish.

Having dismissed her servants and surrendered her lease
of the charming *hôtel* in the Rue de Borgogne, the
Countess of Albany prepared to quit France, of course in
Alfieri's company, in order to visit the land over which
she still claimed to be a titular queen. If we are to credit
the statements set forth in the *Vita*,* this expedition was
due solely to the disturbed state of Paris combined with
his Lady's intense desire to see England.

Both these reasons seem probable enough so far as they
go, but there was an additional though carefully concealed
incentive to this tour, which is unrecorded in the *Vita*;
and this was the hope, perhaps only a slight one, that the
Countess might obtain some financial aid from the British
Government as the widow of a grandson of King James
II. Towards the end of April 1791, therefore, Alfieri
and the Countess, with their horses and a considerable
train, first saw the white cliffs of Dover, and after landing
proceeded to London, where they remained for three
months. Here then the Countess was able to satisfy her
curiosity as to the nature of her late husband's vaunted
realms to the full; whilst she herself, either unconscious
of any incongruity or indifferent to the old familiar claims
she had once heard advanced with such spirit in her own
little court of the Santi Apostoli in Rome, actually
decided to attend the court of George III. in her capacity
of Princess of Stolberg-Gedern. This step must, of course,
have been taken with the full approval of Alfieri, that
professional hater of queens and kings; and it is, therefore, not unfair to surmise that her attendance at St. James'
must have had in view some other object than mere
curiosity. The poet himself, in the short account of this

* *Vita*, vol. ii. p. 201.

visit to England contained in the *Vita*, never mentions this episode ; but he does allude to the very precarious state of the finances both of himself and of his companion, owing to the troubled condition of France, describing themselves as being " *impiccatissimi per la parte pecuniaria.*" *
Whether the Countess did actually appeal for financial aid from the Government is unknown, but it seems unlikely that she ever did so appeal directly, though she probably made several efforts in a quiet way to obtain the good offices of such few persons of influence as showed her any attention, for it is quite a remarkable circumstance that so little notice should have been taken either of Alfieri or of the widow of that Pretender, who less than than fifty years before (as many persons then living must have remembered clearly) had shaken the Hanoverian throne to its foundations.   Whatever hopes the Countess may have originally built on this visit (and we truly believe pecuniary help to have been its first consideration), she must have been grievously disappointed, for certainly nothing substantial resulted therefrom.   It is quite evident from a letter of Lord Camelford's, of 1792 (to which we shall allude presently), that Pitt was approached on this subject by his cousin, the Lord Camelford just mentioned, but without success ; whilst the historian Lord Stanhope was distinctly of opinion that " no present aid was afforded her." † Rumours, however, of her appearance at the Usurper's court were transmitted to Rome, giving great offence to the old Cardinal-King, who was already sufficiently provoked with his sister-in-law, for during the ensuing winter Madame de Boigne, in her delightful *Memoirs*, speaks of the querulous scorn of the poor old man, who little dreamed how soon and how thankfully he himself would be accepting the bounty of King George.

" The Cardinal was at that time very indignant with

* *Vita*, vol. ii. p. 203.
† *Edinburgh Review* (1861), vol. cxiv. pp. 145–182.

his sister-in-law, the Countess of Albany, who had accepted a pension from the Court of London, and he spoke of the matter with the strong assumption of a wounded royal dignity. So true is it that in times of revolution it becomes very difficult to tell in advance whither one may oneself be led." *

This unexpected presentation at court of the Pretender's widow caused a mild flutter of excitement in the fashionable world of London, and Horace Walpole's comments thereon to his friends, the Misses Berry, though fairly well known to the general reader, cannot well be omitted here, especially in view of the comparatively small interest taken by English society as a whole in the presence of Countess with her distinguished companion, whom most persons in London for the sake of propriety affected to regard as her second husband.

"BERKELEY SQUARE, *Thursday, May* 19, 1791.

"The Countess of Albany is not only in England, in London, but at this very moment, I believe, in the palace of St. James'; not restored by as rapid a revolution as the French, but, as was observed last night at Lady Mount-Edgcumbe's, by that topsy-turvy-hood that characterises the present age. Within these two months the Pope has been burnt in Paris; Madame du Barry, mistress of Louise Quinze, has dined with the Lord Mayor of London; and the Pretender's widow is presented to the Queen of Great Britain. She is to be introduced by her great-grandfather's niece, the young Countess of Ailesbury.† That curiosity should bring her hither, I do not quite wonder; still less that she abhorred her husband; but methinks it is not very well bred to his family nor very sensible, but a new way of passing eldest.—*Apropos*, I hear there is a medal struck at Rome of her brother-in-law as Henry the Ninth. . . ." ‡

* *Memoires de la Comtesse de Boigne*, vol. i. p. 108.

† Lady Anne Rawdon, daughter of John, Earl of Moira, and wife of Thomas Brudenell, first Earl of Ailesbury.

‡ *Walpole's Letters* (R. Bentley, 1840), vol. vi. p. 429.

This account is followed almost immediately by a later and fuller description of the intruding "Queen of England," sent by the writer (who could well recall the old unpleasantly exciting days of the 'Forty-five) to his friends who were then travelling in Italy.

"Well, I have had an exact account of the interview of the two Queens, from one who stood close to them. The Dowager was announced as Princess of Stolberg. She was well dressed, and not at all embarassed. The King talked to her a good deal, but always about her passage, the sea, and general topics; the Queen in the same way but less. Then she stood between the Dukes of Gloucester and Clarence, and had a good deal of conversation with the former, who may perhaps have met her in Italy. Not a word between her and the Princesses; nor did I hear of the Prince; but he was there, and probably spoke to her. The Queen looked at her earnestly. To add to the singularity of the day, it is the Queen's birthday. Another odd accident; at the Opera at the Pantheon, Madame d'Albany was carried into the King's box and sate there. It is not of a piece with her going to court, that she seals with the royal arms. I have been told to-night, that you will not be able to get a medal of the Royal Cardinal, as very few were struck, and only for presents, so pray give yourself but little trouble about it." *

A few days later, the English arch-gossip of the eighteenth century was privileged to see the *soi-disante* queen with his own eyes, at Lady Ailesbury's small party arranged especially to meet her.

"Well, I have seen Madame d'Albany, who has not a rag of royalty about her. She has good eyes and teeth, but I think can have had no more beauty than remains,

* *Ibidem*, pp. 425, 430. The Countess invariably used the royal arms on her seal, generally impaled with those of Stolberg-Gedern, as may be seen on several of her letters in the British Museum.

except youth. She is civil and easy, but German and ordinary. Lady Ailesbury made a small assemblage for her on Monday, and my curiosity is satisfied." *

Walpole's disparaging remarks on the personal appearance of the Countess sound strange in contrast with the universal tributes to her grace and beauty which had been paid on the Continent to the enchanting princess whom the great Alfieri had especially chosen to immortalise as his "Donna Amata." Perhaps the antiquated beau and dilettante was growing blind or had not wholly cast off the slough of the old Whiggish prejudices of the Jacobite scare, when nothing connected with the exiled royal family could possibly be allowed to own the smallest scrap of worth or charm. In any case, he only appears flippant and supercilious in his remarks about the Countess of Albany, as when he mentions that at some party or other, " the late Queen of France, Madame du Barry, was there ; and the late Queen of England, Madame d'Albany, was *not*." †

The Jacobite anniversary of " White Rose Day," the honoured birthday of James the Third, inspired Walpole however, to observe that " Madame d'Albany might have found plenty of white roses on her own tenth of June (in the gardens of Strawberry Hill), but on that very day she chose to go to see the King in the House of Lords, with the crown on his head, proroguing the Parliament. What an odd *rencontre !* Was it philosophy or insensibility ? I believe it is certain that her husband was in Westminster Hall at the coronation." †

This circumstance is also described by Hannah More, who was present at the King's prorogation of Parliament in state on June 10, 1791. " The Bishop of London carried us to hear the King make his speech in the House of Lords. As it was quite new to me, I was very well entertained ; but the thing that was most amusing was to see, among the ladies, the Princes of Stolberg, Countess

* *Ibidem*, p. 436.   † *Ibidem*, p. 444

of Albany, wife to the Pretender, sitting just at the foot of the Throne, which she might once have expected to have mounted ; and what diverted the party, when I put them in mind of it, was that it happened to be the tenth of June, the [Old] Pretender's birthday. I have the honour to be very much like her, and this opinion was confirmed yesterday when we met again." *

Yes, it was evident that the fascinating Countess of Albany was at last beginning to lose her perishable gift of beauty, to the gradual passing of which Alfieri so touchingly and delicately refers in his Autobiography. In Rome, in Florence, at Colmar and in Paris all witnesses spoke of her surpassing charm and loveliness ; but the English capital, which she came to visit on the eve of her fortieth year, recognised in her naught else than an agreeable but middle-aged woman, more German than French in the judgment of so particular a critic as Horace Walpole. Now, indeed, there was drawing nigh the time, as the Countess herself observes in one of her letters to Teresa Mocenni, to begin to forget the face and to think only of the proper adornment of the soul.

Three months were thus consumed in this life of the capital, and we venture to think most unsatisfactorily to the pair, who evidently hoped to turn their visit to a more substantial account. To Alfieri (whose presence in our midst seems to have passed by almost unmarked by contemporary writers) the sojourn in a great city, which he had already seen thrice before, possessed but small interest. "Grown a little older " (so he records his fleeting impressions in the *Vita*) " since my last two visits, I was still able to admire, though not so heartily, the moral effects of the English mode of government ; but I was more than ever disgusted with the English climate and the decadent mode of life :—Always eating, and always sitting up till two or three o'clock in the morning, a life opposed wholly to literature, study, and health. We both grew speedily tired of our existence in England ;

* *Hannah More's Memoirs*, vol. ii. p. 343.

167

my Lady because she had satisfied her curiosity, and myself because I was much troubled with the gout, which seems truly indigenous to that favoured isle." *

Before their departure, however, both Alfieri and the Countess were contemplating a tour in Scotland, and it was but the continuous cold and wet of the English July that frustrated this scheme, which was at last exchanged for a short tour in the west and midlands of England itself. It would have been rather amusing to hear of the experiences in the north of the widow of the British Pretender, for there can be no question as to the reception the Countess would have met with at the hands of the many Jacobites of quality, who were still a social power in Edinburgh. But whilst on the one hand, the old Scottish families with Jacobite traditions and sympathies would perhaps have given some unpleasant proof of their opinion of the taste and hardihood of the lady who had deserted "Bonnie Prince Charlie," and was now travelling with his supplanter in the ancient realm of the Royal Stuarts; on the other hand, the Whig adherents in the great towns would probably have hastened to do her honour, provided they were willing to accept the fictitious theory of the lady's marriage with her male companion. In any case, the projected journey never was accomplished, and the pair, rather unwillingly, left our shores with Scotland still unvisited.

Before setting forth on their expedition to the midlands, the Countess paid a brief visit to Park Place, as the guest of General Conway, apparently the only English country-house she ever honoured thus with her presence. Evidently, the life led here did not greatly rouse her admiration, for she describes it as very dull and wearisome for a busy person like herself, " since we passed all our time in each other's society. We breakfasted together at ten ; we walked about together for a couple of hours ; we dined at four ; and we walked about again together ; we then sate down to tea, and worked until the supper hour—

* *Vita*, vol. ii. p. 202.

which was half-past ten ; and at midnight we went to bed. This mode of living would answer very well with people who understood each other perfectly and were all intimate friends ; but it is not suitable for strangers meeting thus for no particular purpose." *

This condemnation of the inanity of English country-house life is drawn from an account written by the Countess herself and called by her " *Souvenirs de Voyage en Angleterre*," of which the original manuscript is preserved in the Musée Fabre at Montpellier. Some writers have professed to find a good deal of valuable criticism in these memorials of her tour in England, and speak of her keen powers of observation and her original views of things English. But as a matter of fact, this little work (which is written in bad French and positively swarms with every sort of mis-spelling, for the authoress seems wholly unable to grasp the elements of any English place-name) can boast of no special value or interest except in so far as it was composed by Louise Countess of Albany. Her general observations are common-place to the last degree, and might easily have been inscribed by any intelligent and educated foreigner who was travelling for the first time in England and was keeping a journal for private amusement. A few bald speculations and aphorisms on the advantages of the form of government then prevalent in this country merely form a dull *rechauffé* of Alfieri's trite and tedious opinions on the same subject. It is the fashion to quote certain passages from this trivial journal, and as it is certainly interesting to trace from its pages the movements of the Countess and Alfieri, as they hurriedly passed through what they considered the most interesting spots in the South of England, we shall follow the movements of the pair by means of the *Souvenirs de Voyage*.

On July 22, the Countess and Alfieri arrived at Oxford, where they visited several of the colleges, including New

* Léon-G. Pélissier, *Lettres et Écrits divers de la Comtesse d'Albany*, pp. 28-37.

College, which the lady tells us dates from the seventh century, since it contains a tomb of that period. Perhaps she confuses New College with Christ Church, in the latter of which she was much struck at the arrangement whereby all the inmates of this educational foundation had their places carefully assigned according to social rank, the sons of peers even dining at a special table. From Oxford the Countess drove over to inspect Blenheim Palace, which she calls a *grand pâté de pierres*; and a few days later she visited Stowe House, near Buckingham. She complains of the melancholy and deserted air of these English country palaces, and considers the French *châteaux* brighter and more attractive in every way. On July 25, the pair travelled, by way of Northampton, to Birmingham, where they lodged in the same inn as the judges who were then engaged in trying Dr. Priestley and others for treason, and as a result of this chance incident, the Countess makes a few commonplace remarks on the ideas and position of the " Dissidenters," as she calls them, who cannot enter Parliament owing to the influence of the privileged Anglican communion, which is the dominant religion of the country :— " According to the simple light of reason, it would seem that all religions ought to be treated on an equality ; but it must be that the English have discovered that such a state of things would be injurious to their government, since they make so many distinctions. The Presbyterians are even more tyrannical than the Catholics, who have been treated like them since the Revolution of 1688."

From Birmingham the Countess went to Worcester, passing through " the most lovely country imaginable," and sleeping at Upton on the way. She found Worcester more cheerful and better built than London, as is the case, she remarks, with all the provincial towns. Next they proceeded to Gloucester, by way of Newport in Monmouthshire, through a district very rich in pastures and swarming with sheep and cattle, of which the numbers feeding in the meadows seem to have caused

170

her great surprise. At Gloucester, we are informed that "the very beautiful Gothic cathedral church was built in the ninth century, and formerly belonged to a monastery that was destroyed by Henry VIII." Here also the pair visited some prisons built on the model of Mr. Hoart (*sic*), the late philanthropist.*

On July 29, the Countess reached Bristol, "a very ancient, large and busy city, situated on two rivers leading to the sea . . . but squalid and dismal like all old towns." From Bristol she went to see Lord de Clifford's fine seat of Kingsweston, where she admired the distant views of the Welsh hills to be seen from its terraces overlooking the Bristol Channel. On August 1, Bath was reached, where the Countess was greatly struck with the regularity and elegance of the architecture; whilst the sight of this abode of wealth and fashion, then at the zenith of its reputation, caused her to inscribe some reflections in her *Souvenirs*, which we quote here.

"The town, which is the best built in England (at least in the parts I visited) is always increasing in size and beauty, so as to attract the world of fashion, for its houses are all private residences and it has no factories. In winter it is filled with visitors. The English are very fond of watering-places, in hopes of finding more amusement there, for they are ever fleeing from the *ennui* wherewith they are devoured. There is no nation so given to pursuing pleasure and distraction, or yet which carries more dullness into its pleasures and has less method in amusing itself. The women who are supposed to enjoy the quiet and the course of waters at Bath are extremely dissipated. When in London, they never pass a day in their own homes; even the old ladies with raddled and faded faces still consider themselves ornaments to a party. This attitude I attribute to the dull discomfort of their own homes; for they can only see their friends in crowds of an evening at eleven, or else they must remain at home, a prey to

* John Howard.

171

boredom. They must, therefore, perforce go where all the world meets, or otherwise they would be left severely alone. They spend four months of the year in London and are lost to sight during the other eight, unless one goes to seek them in the country, which occasionally happens, but not often ; and even there they only repeat the life of the city. For one goes to bed in the country as late as in town, and does not obtain the privilege of breathing the morning air. There is no real liberty, for all dine together, and consort together, to their mutual weariness."

The Countess next passed through Wiltshire, sleeping a night at the old coaching inn at Marlborough, "one of the best hostelries in England." She was struck by the poverty and wretchedness of the inhabitants in these rural districts, and at the rags and nakedness of the children in the villages. This sad state of things in so wealthy a country, she attributes to the chicanery practised in regard to the heavy taxes imposed. She reaches Windsor on August 7, having rested one night at Reading. Here she enjoyed seeing the pictures and works of art in the royal Castle, but did not think the view from the great terrace so fine or expansive as that from the palace of St. Germains.

Quitting Windsor on August 8, the pair set out to inspect Sir John Herschel's obervatory at Salthill, where the great astronomer and his sister received these distinguished visitors with much kindness, showing them various instruments and telling them much that was new and interesting about the moon and stars. "He is a simple, unpretentious man," remarks the Countess, "and he made me see without difficulty such objects as might interest me, as though they were the most ordinary things in the world. I have always noticed that true worth is modest, and certainly Archel (*sic*) is that."

The following day the Countess went to Hampton Court, where she admired Mantegna's cartoons, but thought the park ill-kept, and was displeased with the *grande enfillade* of endless small rooms inside the palace itself. From Hampton Court the Countess and Alfieri returned to London by way of Richmond.

This journal concludes with a series of general remarks, none of them very flattering, upon the habits, ideas, and behaviour of the English nation. After complaining of the late hours (which both she and Alfieri especially detested), of the odious climate, of the enormous taxes and consequent dearness of everything, of the universal worship of money, and of the national craving for gaiety and diversion that all vainly strive to attain, the Countess concludes with an allusion to English views of matrimony :— " The English husbands are exacting and harsh, whilst their wives are for the most part more discreet than in continental lands, since they run more risk. The very arrangement of their houses prevents them from receiving anybody at home without the knowledge of their servants or husbands. They are usually good wives and good mothers. But they love the gaming-table, and the great ladies are much too fond of gadding. London is wholly ignorant of intimate society, or of its peculiar charm. It is a case of family life with husband and children, for the claims of parents are absolutely ignored, at least in the circles that I have frequented." The Countess ends her *Souvenirs* with a fling at the national ignorance concerning works of art, although Englishmen are much given to buying pictures of whose merits they have little understanding.

We repeat, it is solely as an account written by Louise, Countess of Albany, that this ill-written and ill-constructed essay or journal possesses any value, although the description of the rapid journey of three weeks is curious as a specimen of the tours then made in England by distinguished foreigners in order to gain a closer acquaintance with the life, scenery, and people of our island.

On August 20, after four months spent in England, the pair were ready to leave for Dover, so as to return to the

Continent, with the intention of making a short tour in Holland before re-incarcerating themselves (as Alfieri expresses it) in Paris. They duly reached Dover, where an unexpected incident befel the poet, which it is difficult to know whether to call comical or pathetic. At the very moment when Alfieri, who had gone ahead, was superintending matters connected with the passage to Calais, he caught the eye of his former charmer (whose very existence he had apparently well-nigh forgotten), Penelope Pitt, the divorced wife of Lord Ligonier and now married to a person in humble life. The lady was standing among the small crowd of idle sight-seers that always collects on the pier to witness the comings and goings of the packet-boats, and Alfieri noted at once that her beauty seemed in no wise impaired by the lapse of nearly twenty years. "At first," he relates, "I thought I must be dreaming, but I gazed steadily, and then she smiled significantly, so that I was reassured. I cannot describe all the varied emotions and feelings that this apparition caused me. But I said not a word, and only entered the ship to await my Lady's arrival."

Alfieri, haunted by the face and smile of poor Penelope, could not resist sending her a letter full of kind messages and good advice from Calais, to which the lady duly sent a reply, that reached him at Brussels. In this letter Penelope thanked him for his warm sympathy and his well-meant but wholly superfluous advice to mend her ways. She was happy, so she declared, in her present husband, and was rather inclined to bless Alfieri for having been the cause of her removal years ago from a sphere of artificial and fashionable life, which she had never regretted. The writer concluded with the following allusion to himself and the Countess, which is not without a spice of gentle irony.

" . . . Allow me in my turn to assure you of the real pleasure that the news of your present happiness causes me, a happiness that I am sure you deserve. During the last two years I have often been pleased to hear you spoken of both in Paris and London, where your writings (which I have not yet been able to procure) are admired and appreciated. It is said you are attached to the Princess with whom you travel, and judging from her agreeable and intelligent face, she seems well fitted to satisfy a heart so sensitive and fastidious as your own. They say, too, that she is afraid of you (and there I clearly recognise your power !) for without desiring it, or even perhaps without perceiving it, you inspire this feeling in all who love you. . . .

"DOVER, *August* 26. PENELOPE." *

Although the tone of her letter is generous and friendly, in spite of its excusable under-current of mild irony, Alfieri was deeply offended by this reply, and in his Autobiography he speaks with extreme annoyance of Penelope's "strange, obstinate and evil-disposed character, which is happily rare in her class of life, especially in her own sex."

* *Vita,* vol. ii. pp. 204-208. As to the fear inspired by Alfieri, the sonnet beginning

> Che feci ? Obimè ! da que' begli occhi un fiume
> Uscia di pianti, e la cagion' io n'era ?
> —*Poesie Amorose,* p. 133.

clearly proves that this harsh and hot-tempered egotist occasionally bullied his " Donna Amata " till she shed tears.

CHAPTER X

CASA ALFIERI

'Twas yesterday, but there have passed me over
Almost three lustres, Lady, since the day
I paced these streets a solitary rover,
Wending a dreary and indifferent way.
Whilst thou, in convent garth, far from thy lover,
Obtained'st such balm of restfulness as lay
In thinking that thy spouse could ne'er discover
Thy sad retreat, nor cruel force display.
Thou hadst indeed some jot of consolation,
When naught but tumult filled my lonely breast ;
And Florence saw my tears and agitation.
—Now all is changed ; the city's self is blest ;
And we, united after separation,
Can smile and make of ancient ills our jest.*

> *Sonnet of V. Alfieri addressed to the Countess of Albany
> on their return to Florence in the autumn of* 1792

LANDING at Ostend the Countess and Alfieri made a short tour in the Netherlands, visiting Antwerp, The Hague, Amsterdam and other places of interest. At the first-mentioned town the sight of the many fine paintings by Rubens seems to have inspired the brief monograph on that artist, which ranks amongst the Countess' few original compositions.† Some weeks were then spent (apparently without the presence of her cavalier) at Brussels in order to see her mother and her unmarried sister Gustavine, to whom the Countess was warmly attached ; and towards the end of October the pair were once more in that " Cloaca maxima " of Paris, which in spite of all drawbacks they must have

---

* *E mi par ieri, e al terza or manca (Poesie Amorose,* p. 239).

† Pélissier, *Lettres et Écrits Divers de la Comtesse d'Albany,* pp. 37-40.

176

preferred as a place of residence to London, for a new and " very handsome and convenient " house in the Rue de Provence was rented and furnished by them early in the year 1792, the old existence of social and intellectual amusement being resumed.

The death of Alfieri's mother in April 1792, put an end for the time being to the poet's expressed intention of returning soon to Italy ; but the violent events of that fateful summer, which saw the utter downfall of the French monarchy, were finally sufficient to drive the pair from the city, which they had apparently still decided to inhabit for an indefinite period. The terrible event of the storming of the Tuileries, on the night of August 10, was what ultimately decided both the Countess and Alfieri to beat as hasty a retreat as possible from the devoted city. "August 10th," writes Alfieri to Mario Bianchi, " is a day most fatal to Liberty, for therein France has by a second revolution passed from tolerable anarchy (if ever such a thing can be) to the monstrous tyranny of the vilest and most bloodthirsty of mobs." *
Their one thought was now to remove from Paris ere it might become too late, and frantic efforts were made to obtain the necessary passports, which was in itself no easy task. The account of the departure from Paris, then in the throes of revolution, affords one of the most graphic incidents in the whole of Alfieri's Autobiography ; and we think it best to let the poet tell in his own words the story of the deadly risks both he and the Countess ran, before escaping from the midst of the horrors that were beginning to accumulate daily to end in the indiscriminate massacres of September.†

" After the raid on the Tuileries, I thought of nought except how to save my Friend from the perils that threatened us both. I would not delay a single day,

* *Lettere Inedite*, p. 215.

† *Vita*, vol. ii. pp. 213-221. A letter to the Abbé di Caluso, describing the events of August 10, is included in the Appendix to the *Vita*, pp. 212-217.

and on the 12th of August all our preparations were completed. There was, however, one great obstacle to overcome, that of obtaining passports to leave Paris and the kingdom. I moved heaven and earth for two or three days, and at last on the 15th we secured them as foreigners; I from the Venetian Envoy, and my Friend from the Minister of Denmark, the only envoys of Louis XVI. still remaining, for the King had long been no more than a shadow. We had still more difficulty in obtaining passports for our servants, whose height, colour of hair, age, sex, and I know not what, had all to be described. Furnished with all these symbols of slavery, we fixed our departure for Monday, August 20th; but when all was ready, a natural sense of fear made us hasten our exit by two days, and so we started on the evening of Saturday, the 18th.

"We had scarcely reached the Barrière Blanche, the nearest gate for us to take the St. Denis road towards Calais, whither we were bound so as to fly with all speed out of this unhappy land, than we were accosted by three or four of the National Guards with an officer. After examining our passports, they were inclined to open to us the barrier of this vast prison, when we saw issue from a foul inn near the gate some cut-throats and rascals, all tipsy, savage and ragged. When these creatures perceived our two carriages loaded with boxes and trunks, with two maids and three men-servants, they set to exclaiming that all the rich nobles wanted to desert Paris and to carry away their hoards, whilst leaving the people in misery and misfortune. Then there arose an argument between our handful of National Guards and this mob of rascals, the former being for letting us pass and the latter for our detention. I leaped out of the carriage into the middle of the road, and with my seven passports in my hand began to gesticulate, shout and make more noise than the Frenchmen themselves (the only way to deal effectually with Frenchmen). They read the papers one after another, or rather, listened

178

to those of their number who could read. Furious and boiling with rage, I either ignored or despised my imminent danger at this moment. Thrice I snatched my papers from their hands, crying aloud at the top of my voice : 'Listen ! Listen ! My name is Alfieri. I am an Italian and not a Frenchman. Tall, thin, pale, red-haired. Look well at me, and see it is I. I have a passport, and it is genuine. I obtained it from those who were authorised to supply it. I have permission to pass, and, by God, I will pass ! '

" All this time a crowd of persons surrounded our two carriages, some of them crying out : 'We ought to set fire to the coaches ! ' and others, 'We'll stone them ! ' Most of them exclaimed, 'They are rich fugitive nobles, so we must bring them to the Hôtel de Ville for trial.'

" Finally, the feeble assistance of the four National Guards, who from time to time let fall a word or two in our favour, the noise I made with my stentorian voice, my waving aloft the passports, and especially the half-hour consumed in these arguments served to weary these tiger-monkeys (*scimio-tigri*), whose opposition began to flag. The Guards now signed to me to re-enter the coach, where I had left my Friend in a state of mind that can be imagined. I mounted the step, the postillions leaped on the horses, the gate was thrown wide open, and we emerged at full gallop, pursued by the yells, insults and curses of the mob.

" It was a mercy for us that the suggestion to take us to the Hôtel de Ville was not acted upon. Arriving there with our two coaches and baggage, and with all the appearance of escaping nobles, we should have run imminent risk. Once brought before those rascals of the Municipality, we should nevermore have quitted Paris, for we should have been sent to prison, and a fortnight later to the guillotine.

" Escaping thus from that Hell, on the third day we reached Calais, after producing our papers more than

forty times on the road. I have since learnt that we
were the first foreigners to fly from Paris and from France
after the catastrophe of August 10th. Wherever we
had to present our passports, all who perused them
seemed petrified at the first glance, for they had been
printed in the King's name, which had later been erased.
All the officials were either ignorant or ill-informed
of the late events in Paris and were consequently much
agitated at the sight of these papers.

"See then under what auspices I finally quitted
France, with the sincere hope and resolve nevermore
to set foot in that country!"*

This sudden and rapid flight from the French capital
was, as Alfieri avers, only undertaken in the nick of time,
for two days later, on the exact date for which their
departure had been originally fixed, the representatives
of the very people, who had lately granted them leave
to quit Paris, appeared at the deserted house in the Rue
de Provence with an order for the detention of the
Countess of Albany; and it needs little speculation
to imagine what the fate of the Stuart Queen would have
been, had she once fallen into the blood-stained hands
of the Jacobins. Finding both Alfieri and the Countess
already flown, the officials of the new Republic seized
upon the furniture, the horses and the libraries of the
absent pair; nor could any amount of application made
later from time to time ever succeed in obtaining their
return or any sum in compensation for the property
thus forcibly taken. As it was, the loss of their belongings, and especially that of Alfieri's valuable library,
seemed trivial in the eyes of the owners, who were only
too thankful to have escaped with whole skins, especially
when they learned a little later of the fate which befel
the Comte de Flahault and many another of their friends
who perished in the September massacres.

It seems to have been Alfieri's first intention to make

* *Vita*, vol. ii. pp. 213–221.

his way from Calais to England, but finding war already declared between France and Britain, he and the Countess proceeded to Brussels, whence Madame d'Albany, greatly unnerved by her late experiences, subsequently retired to a *château* near Ath, where there resided her third sister, Françoise-Claudia, the wife of Count d'Arberg and later the faithful friend and companion of the Empress Joséphine.* The month of September was spent in this pleasant country retreat, which was situated not far from Mons and the scenes of her childhood, whilst by the beginning of October she was sufficiently recovered from her late alarms and fatigue to start on the proposed journey back to Italy. This step had been urged by Alfieri, who had been busily employed during his Belgian residence in writing the most violent diatribes in verse against France, Frenchmen, and the French Revolution, that were subsequently included in his celebrated medley known as the *Miso-Gallo*. Travelling by way of Spa, Frankfort, and Innspruck the pair at last were delighted to find themselves once more on Italian soil, with the barrier of the Alps placed between themselves and a nation in the torturing throes of revolution ; and whilst at Verona, Alfieri met with his old friend Ippolito Pindemonte, to whom he expressed his deep regret at having composed his approving ode on the fall of the Bastille. At this point Alfieri and the Countess had to make up their minds as to their future plans, which was no easy matter, seeing that their income had been already reduced by one half since the late troubles in France, and that there was every prospect of its diminishing yet more rapidly in the face of a possible French invasion of Italy. From the following letter to Bianchi it will be seen that the return to Florence and their decision to settle in that city were the results of chance rather than of desire or sentiment, as has sometimes been supposed.

* For some account of this lady the reader is referred to Madame Ducrest's *Memoirs of the Empress Joséphine*. (London, 1894.)

"DEAREST FRIEND,—Here I am since yesterday. I received your very welcome letter at Verona. We set out thence straight for Tuscany, on account of the vast number of foreigners who are crowding into Italy, a circumstance that has urged us forward to look out for a house. But we are already too late to get one at Pisa, where my Lady wanted to settle, for every house there is let, and at ridiculously high rents. So we came on here direct from Pistoja, and are now searching for a place to lay our heads. Were I alone, I should quickly find something, for a single man always lights upon a lodging, but it is not so with my Lady, who is accustomed to be housed suitably. Much time and patience are being expended, before we can get properly accommodated, nor do I know if we shall ever find what we require here. . . .

"My Lady thanks both yourself and Teresa Mocenni warmly for your kind messages, and is longing to make your acquaintance." *

Meanwhile, Alfieri and the Countess were remaining in great discomfort at the inn of the *Acquila*, where the poet complains to his friend, Mario Bianchi, of the bitter cold of the Tuscan winter, which was in those days untempered by the appliances used in northern countries. Later, they seem to have left the inn, and to have taken a small furnished apartment by the month, where they were equally uncomfortable.

"We have five servants who cannot speak a word of Italian to add to our troubles," writes Alfieri to his crony at Siena. "We have been obliged to buy everything, and to provide ourselves with linen, wherever we may go eventually, for as fugitives from Paris we are, so to speak, half-naked, for all our furniture, our books and our belongings are left behind there." †

* *Lettere Inedite*, pp. 216, 217.   † *Ibidem.*

The physical discomfort of the Countess, in a town which it would seem she was not over-anxious to inhabit, was increased by the reports, perhaps exaggerated, of the terrible plight of her relatives in France and Flanders, the Comtesse d'Arberg being forced to take refuge in the kingdom of Holland. In this state of agitation and uncertainty the winter of 1792–1793 ebbed away, still leaving the pair without a home of their own. Alfieri himself passed the time in composing more diatribes against the French to add to his collection of the *Miso-Gallo*, and the Countess in writing lengthy letters to her many absent friends. The former suffered a good deal from attacks of gout, brought on largely by his own imprudence in spite of the warnings of his lady, " who scolds me, because I am ill, as if I were to blame for it ! " In June, the poet writes to Bianchi saying, " I am fairly well in body, but very ill in spirit. Uncertainty is one of the worst torments a man can experience, and especially in my own case, for I am so impatient. I am uncertain as to where I shall settle ; whether I shall ever see my books again, which have all been seized in Paris ; whether I shall have bread to eat ; or a head on my shoulders ; or a roof or place where I can consider myself free, secure and independent." *

It was at this point, soon after their return to Florence, that the Countess made yet another indirect appeal to the British Government for financial support, to fill the void left by the fall of the French monarchy, whereby she had definitely and for ever lost her annuity of 60,000 *livres*. There happened to be staying in Florence at this moment Thomas Pitt of Boconnoc, Lord Camelford, cousin of the Prime Minister William Pitt, who had himself, if we may so conclude from the terms of his cousin's letter quoted below, expressed some sympathy in the affairs of the Countess of Albany during her visit to London in the previous year. To Lord Camelford,

* *Ibidem.*

therefore, the distressed lady now applied, giving him a most pitiful, but also (it must be admitted) a somewhat exaggerated account of the straitness of her circumstances. Her appeal was instantly championed by the good-natured Cornish peer, who composed the following letter to his less susceptible relation :

"FLORENCE, *December* 14, 1792.

"MY DEAR SIR,—I write to acquit myself of a commission I have received from the Comtesse Albany, who desires to assure you that the kind part you were so good to take in her business, both when she left England and since, lays her under obligations that she shall never forget.*

"After what is past, I conclude it is in vain to hope the subject can be renewed in any shape hereafter. It is impossible for me, however, to be witness to the situation of that unfortunate lady without reflecting upon the effect her present distress must produce upon every feeling mind in Europe. By her flight from France (where, had she remained two days longer, her certain imprisonment had been the consequence, and she would have been included in the general massacre) she has lost every resource from that country. Driven afterwards from her family at Brussels, from the apprehensions of what has actually taken place immediately after, she has taken refuge here as the only asylum that could afford her any promise of safety ; and here she lives upon the *débris* of what she could save out of her fortune at a sequin a day. I need make no comments. Your generous mind will supply them. If she had a pension of £1000, she would be happy. Pardon me, my dear Sir, if I cannot resist the impulse that has made me state this to you, having no means of laying it before the Person whose good heart would, I am sure, be not insensible to it, if he could be witness to it as I am. It is a strange world,

* *See* chapter ix.

184

and the vicissitudes of it are striking in a manner never before experienced.

> " Ever most affectionately yours,
> " CAMELFORD." *

The writer of this letter died himself a few weeks later of the gout at Pisa, apparently before ever he dispatched his appeal on behalf of the Countess of Albany, and it seems to have been forwarded eventually to Pitt through the Earl of Bristol.   No notice appears to have been taken of its contents, perhaps from sheer forgetfulness or indifference on the part of Pitt ; or possibly because that shrewd politician was already aware that the financial position of the Countess was not quite so desperate as she declared, seeing that for the present at all events her annuity from the Cardinal of York was being paid to her regularly.   In any case, it is clear that, despite her continual efforts, the Countess signally failed during these years to obtain any pension out of the Privy Purse of George III.

It was whilst Alfieri and the Countess were remaining on at Florence, homeless and disturbed both by private and political cares, that there stepped into their joint existence a certain young man, whose advent was destined to prove of the first importance to both.   This was none other than the French painter, François-Xavier-Pascal Fabre, of Montpellier, who was first introduced to the notice of Alfieri by that curious English dilettante and wanderer on the Continent, Frederick-Augustus Hervey, Earl of Bristol and Bishop of Derry, whom the poet had pithily described as " a lunatic, but a lunatic of genius and education."   Fabre, of whose work the Earl-Bishop was an enthusiastic admirer, had barely reached his twenty-seventh year, having been born at Montpellier in 1766.   The son of a drawing-master, the young François-Xavier had studied his art with

* Earl Stanhope, *Life of William Pitt*, vol. ii. pp. 181, 182.   The " Person " with the good heart is, of course, King George III.

marked success under the great painter, David, gaining the *Prix de Rome* at the age of twenty-one ; a circumstance which necessitated his residence in Rome itself. Here his course of study was most unpleasantly interrupted by the tumults, in the spring of 1793, that arose out of the attempt of the new minister of the French Republic, Ugo Basseville, to spread abroad revolutionary ideas amongst the subjects of Pope Pius VI. As a result of these riots and the assaults of the Roman populace upon the French Academy, its pupils had to flee ; whilst so strongly Royalist were the views held by this young plebeian artist, that later he refused to return to the city, where his native country was now represented by another envoy of the detested Republic. He therefore drifted to Florence, supporting himself by his paintings, and especially by his excellent portraits, which are far superior to his rather cold, pedantic, mannered compositions, conceived in the pseudo-classical style of his master, David. As a rising painter of undoubted genius, but chiefly as a young Frenchman who abhorred and abused the new government of his native land in terms of unmeasured bitterness, Fabre was at once received warmly by the author of the *Miso-Gallo*, now consumed with his fury of fear and hatred against the present rulers of France. A commission to paint his portrait, and also that of the Countess of Albany, must have speedily followed the first introduction of the artist to the poet, for as early as July 12, 1793, Bianchi is informed in a letter that " a painter of considerable reputation, an exile from Rome during the late troubles, is now painting my portrait." The picture here mentioned is evidently that now preserved in the French Room of the Uffizi Gallery in Florence, which represents Alfieri with his flowing reddish hair, his wide prominent blue eyes, his delicate fingers adorned with the great cameo ring with Dante's bust that he always wore, and the queer picturesque blue cloak lined with scarlet that the poet was wont to affect. It is a speaking portrait of a great and

186

interesting, if not an estimable personality; and though this likeness was made when the original was in his forty-fifth year, there still lingers some of the fire and charm of youth about the handsome, selfish proud face, which gives us a clue to the extraordinary fascination the great Italian tragedian was wont to exercise over so many adoring women, of whom the Countess of Albany was the last and the most celebrated.

That the illustrious sitter was satisfied with this portrait becomes clear from the fine sonnet, which Alfieri himself addressed to his counterfeit, describing closely his own personal appearance.

> O perfect mirror of all speech veracious,
> Show me what soul and substance are mine own!
> —Scant ruddy locks upon a forehead spacious,
> Of stature tall, but glances earthward prone;
> A supple form on spindle-shanks supported;
> White skin, blue eyes with kindly aspect shown,
> Straight nose and well-formed mouth, with teeth most gracious;
> Pallid in face as tyrant on his throne.
> Now harsh and bitter, mild anon and pleading;
> Ever irascible yet ne'er malign;
> With heart and brain some strife for ever kneading,
> The serious and the gay but ill combine.
> Hero or knave thyself by turns esteeming,
> Art great or vile?—O Death, the answer's thine! *

The natural answer that suggests itself to the direct query in the last line of this famous sonnet is as usual to be found midway between the alternatives mentioned by the writer.

A little later, the painter, now held in the highest esteem both by Alfieri and the Countess, set to work on a portrait of the latter, which to-day hangs in the Uffizi Gallery beside that of Alfieri. It is an able delineation of the Countess of Albany at the age of forty or a little

---

* *Sublime specchio di veraci detti* (Reumont, *Appendix*, p. 350). It is remarkable that Ugo Foscolo, whose portrait was executed later by Fabre, in this instance imitated Alfieri by composing the sonnet *Solcata ho fronte, occhi incavati intenti*; so that two of Fabre's portraits thus gave birth to two descriptive sonnets of the first rank.

187

over, but it has been accepted as a likeness with the most varied verdicts by its critics. "A cook with the hands of a fine lady," is one very severe comment, and certainly the artist has not stooped in this instance to flatter the last Stuart Queen. All the charm and vivacity of the former *Regina dei Cuori*, that Bontetten and the gay world of Rome had applauded some thirteen or fourteen years before, have evidently been omitted by Fabre's candid brush, which presents us with a quiet, rather phlegmatic-looking middle-aged lady, somewhat answering to the recent criticism of Horace Walpole as "German and ordinary." Only the beautiful hands and arms go to redeem the commonplace nature of the portrait, which exhibits to us plainly the fact that the Countess had already ceased to take much interest in her personal appearance, being wholly content to rest on her past reputation for loveliness and brilliance. The picture bears pasted on its reverse side a sonnet by Alfieri, headed, *"Altro ritratto della Signora Comtessa d'Albania, Firenze,* 1794."

> Of all the gifts within my Dame's possessing,
> So long experienced yet so hard to tell,
> I rank the first, as my peculiar blessing,
> Her Heart, which only lofty thoughts impel.
> It was her virtue mine own heart addressing,
> And not her beauty, that first cast its spell;
> And now thereon, with year on year progressing,
> I know my happiness is founded well.
> And though her life is clogged with many a burden,
> Ever she bears each cross right cheerfully;
> Though slow to anger, she is swift to pardon;
> Harbours that heart no spice of jealousy.
> For kindness she returns a double guerdon,
> Nor does her mind recall past injury.*

Here then, side by side in the famous Florentine Gallery, are to be seen the twin portraits of the poet and his "Donna Amata," painted in middle life by the skilful hand of their friend Monsieur Fabre, who in later

---

* *Di quanti ha pregi la mia Donna eccelsi (Poesie Amorose,* p. 210).

LOUISE, COUNTESS OF ALBANY
From the portrait by F. X. Fabre

Alinari

days presented these two pictures to the city of Florence at the special request of the Countess.

From the first it is easy to see that Fabre became almost immediately a dear and honoured guest at Casa Alfieri, the house on the Lung' Arno which the poet was finally able to purchase in the last months of 1793, after vainly searching for a suitable residence for himself and his lady for nearly a twelvemonth. This house, which to-day bears a tablet commemorating one, and one only, of the illustrious pair that once dwelt therein,* faces full south towards the river and the ancient quarter of Oltr' Arno, distinguished by the tall tower of Santo Spirito and the prodigious mass of the Pitti Palace beyond. It stands at right angles to the graceful bridge of Santa Trinità, built by the Renaissance architect Ammannati, and forms one of a small group of ancient palaces formerly belonging to the powerful republican family of Gianfigliazzi, extolled by Dante, whose heraldic emblem, a ramping lion, is still to be seen sculptured on the walls. At the back of these houses, to northward, lies the form of the pretty gothic church of Santa Trinità, beloved of the great Michelangelo, who named it *mia dama*. Casa Alfieri, as the house chosen by the poet as a home for himself and the Countess of Albany, was, and is still, commonly called, is a mediæval mansion, though modernised externally in the middle of the past century. It consists of a ground floor with heavily barred windows and a lofty rounded portal in the usual Florentine style of architecture, and of three storeys with seven round-headed windows facing full south and enjoying a good view of the jade-green river, the red roofs and towers of Oltr' Arno, with distant glimpses of the olive-clad hills beyond the city walls. The topmost storey of all, once a *loggia* or open pillared balcony, was added by Alfieri himself, who declared this goodsized mansion to be inconveniently small for the needs

---

* " *Vittorio Alfieri, principe della Tragedia, qui con magnanimi sensi molti anni detto, è qui morì.*"

189

of himself and his companion. Here the great tragedian
possessed his library on the second floor, whilst the
Countess occupied the fine sunny chambers on the
piano nobile overlooking the river and the bridge, which
still to-day affords an ever-moving picture of Florentine
life with the passing crowds, the carts and carriages,
the processions of priests, the soldiers marching to martial
music ; whilst in those distant days the Grand-Ducal
court was wont to drive along this quay of an afternoon
in full state for the usual airing in the park of the Cascinè.
Here then, in the old Gianfigliazzi palace, began that
quiet orderly life of daily exercise, studious reading,
writing and social entertainment, which the Countess
was destined to enjoy, with one interruption only, for
over thirty years, and which was shared by her companion
for a third of that period.

Already Alfieri, on returning from Italy, had felt
again the old eagerness to see his tragedies acted, and
even before settling in the new home on the Lung' Arno
he had gone to Siena, apparently alone, to take part
in the representation of his favourite play of *Saul,* by
the students of the University, which was then being
governed by his old friend, the Arch-priest Luti. No
sooner were he and the Countess established in Casa
Alfieri, than one of the rooms was fitted up as a temporary
theatre, wherein occasional performances were given
to which personal friends were invited. A few of these
curious cards of invitation are still preserved among the
papers of Alfieri in the Museum at Montpellier, of which
the following is a specimen : *

> 1794. Di 20 Febbraio, Giovedi.
>
> A Ore Sette.
>
> Recita Privata. In Casa Gianfigliazzi.
>
> No. 11.   (Name of Guest invited.)

---

* Mazzatinti, *Le Carte Alfieriane.* (*Giornale Storico,* vol. iii. p. 51.)

At these performances in his own house, the poet himself usually took a leading part, as indeed he had already acted in the case of the *Antigone*, presented in the Spanish Envoy's palace in Rome years before ; but, as may easily be imagined, his acting and theatrical attitudes left much to be desired, for he ranted and mouthed in a grotesque manner. Nevertheless, invitations to these dramatic receptions were much sought after by Florentine society and by the various foreigners of distinction that the city constantly attracted. Indeed, the first two or three years in the new home passed pleasantly enough, for Alfieri had not as yet given way to the intense despair and misanthropy, which were later caused by the French invasions of Italy ; nor were the pair, though their income had been much diminished, as yet reduced to actual straits, for Alfieri was receiving the usual payments from his sister at Turin, whilst the Countess continued to draw regularly her 6000 crowns from her brother-in-law's secretary, Monsignore Cesarini, with whom she always remained on friendly terms. With the constant society of chosen friends (amongst whom their newly discovered visitor, Fabre, was already beginning to be ranked foremost), with vigorous application to literary work, with daily rides or drives for the sake of health, and with the giving of dramatic performances, the poet found life fairly agreeable in the Tuscan capital; whilst the Countess was also busily employed in her daily occupations of reading, of painting, and of writing long letters to her many friends, of commenting on Alfieri's latest works, and of taking solitary walks each morning along the quay of the Lung' Arno, and thence by way of the crowded Borgo Ogni Santi and the market gardens round Porta Prato into the beautiful sylvan park of the Cascinè. Florence was, of course, a place absolutely familiar to her with its memories, both pleasant and unpleasant, of her married life, and she seems to have borne little real attachment to the city; provided, however, Alfieri were only

191

happy there, she was perfectly content to reside in this spot.

The haunting dread of a French invasion and a further loss of income were, of course, always hanging over the heads of both, bringing an element of uncertainty and even of alarm into their daily life. Already French troops were preparing to cross the Alps, an event which would mean the occupation of Turin and the consequent diminution of Alfieri's annuity, as is hinted at in the following friendly and facetious letter from the eccentric Lord Bristol.

"SIENA, THE ATHENS OF TUSCANY.

". . . I have devoured *Saul,* and am now digesting him. It gives me a still higher opinion of your talents. You must suffer me to see it acted, so as to augment my esteem for your genius. You will afford me this boon, will you not, my friend ?

"And the adorable Countess ? How is she ? If those French devils get so far as Turin, I offer you my purse, my place and my park. My cellar would be useless to you, for not content with Pindar's genius, you also possess his taste. *Ariston men hudor.* . . .

"Among all the admirers you have gained, none is more devoted to you than the Earl of Bristol and Bishop of Derry." *

Whilst the political horizon was growing darker and darker in Italy each month, and even each week, as the new French Republic's despised forces under a rising young Corsican officer of artillery called Napoleon Buonaparte, were slowly but surely overmastering the vaunted legions of the Emperor in the Lombard plains, a terrible grief overtook Alfieri in the midst of his many anxieties. This was no less than the death, long threatened but long delayed, of his intimate friend Mario Bianchi, with whom he had kept up a constant

* *Lettere Inedite, Appendix,* pp. 278, 279.

correspondence for the last twelve years, but who had at last succumbed to his ever threatening malady of consumption, the symptoms of which had been growing more pronounced for some years past. He died in the autumn of 1796, at the early age of forty, the event being announced to Alfieri by his mistress, the Teresa Mocenni of the *crocchietto saporito* which had years before extended so hearty a welcome to the poet on his arrival at Siena. The deceased Chevalier Bianchi had apparently never been seen by the Countess; nevertheless, she took a genuine interest in his affairs and in those of his Teresa, whose merits she was destined later to appreciate. To the ill tidings sent by the now heart-broken Madame Mocenni, Alfieri replied in a letter of sympathy, with a characteristic undercurrent of egotistic alarm for the fate of himself and his lady.

" SIGNORA TERESA, PADRONA STIMATISSIMA,—Your long silence has made me tremble instead of hope, so that I was in no wise anxious to hear news, knowing there was no hope. I have only learned the fatal news through your letter of this morning. Otherwise, I should have hastened to write to you, not to console you (which is impossible), but to participate in your grief, which is all one can do in such a case as yours. Signora Teresa, you deserve my pity far more than our dead Friend, whose sufferings are finished. Your letter lacerates my heart. I experience all the horrors of a situation which I begin to shudder at in thought; seeing that it will be my own some day. And oh, what can be worse for me than to live on in isolation, in a foreign and inhospitable city, shut in myself alone! O God, I hope I shall not be the survivor! Yet, on the other hand, how can I desire for the Better Part of Myself a fate I should never have the courage to endure? These are terrible reflections, and I often meditate on them. Sometimes I compose verses on them for my mind's relief, but I can never reconcile myself to the idea of being left solitary nor to leaving my Lady in a similar plight, since for the same reason she would fare worse than you yourself, Signora Teresa, at the present terrible moment. To you, I can say, 'You have other ties in this world; you have your own city; you have a family; you have mutual friends with whom to discuss and bewail the beloved Friend; and above all, you are a mother, and that of itself ought to supply you with courage in your distress.' So you see, we shall be more bereaved than yourself under similar circumstances. But what does that help? I know it does not help, nor can anything help save for you to talk of Mario and to give free vent to your grief. If you care to do either of these things by letter, unburden your heart and have no fear of wearying me thereby, but write pages many and full. If I should be poor in words of reply, I shall certainly be rich in tears whilst I am reading through your letters (as I am at this moment with your present letter before me). Oppressed by your loss and by our own chance of a similar calamity to ourselves, I now make an end. But remember you have friends and children." *

A second letter from Alfieri to the despairing Madame Mocenni contains the beautiful sonnet † which includes the exquisite lines :

Teco, O Donna, piangendo assai piu dico.
Il pianto è in dolce favellar che tace.

(Full clear my tears express my words to thee,
For this my grief seems silent eloquence.)

That Alfieri was deeply grieved both by his friend's death and by the consequent misery of the unhappy Teresa Mocenni is quite obvious and patent; yet one cannot help noticing with a smile the intense egotism and selfishness of the man, who in spite of his genuine

* *Lettere Inedite. Op. Cit.*
† *Sollievo al duol del dianzi estinto amico.*

sympathy with another's grief is still moved to self-compassion, as he is suddenly struck with the alarming thought of a like blow descending upon the inmates of Casa Alfieri. This remarkable, and in some ways fine, letter affords us therefore an insight into the radically selfish nature of the Italian "Prince of the Tragic Drama," which is extremely helpful towards estimating the value he placed upon his present union with the Countess of Albany. It was indeed the sad fate of poor ailing Mario Bianchi, which inspired him to address the sonnet "*Donna, s'io sol di mi cura prendessi*" to the Countess herself, with its final line "*Sola un' anima siam, sola una salma,*" which expresses the fervent wish that he and his Lady, being perfectly united in life, may not be divided in death. This strong statement of undying devotion ought therefore to be compared with the sentiments addressed to the Abbé di Caluso (since Bianchi's death his sole surviving intimate correspondent) and to his sister, the Countess Giulia Alfieri di Cumiana, on his death-bed, which will be mentioned in the next chapter but one.

The grief of the bereaved Teresa Mocenni produced one important result. She herself visited Florence a little later in order to seek sympathy in her loss from Alfieri, who naturally recommended his unhappy friend for further consolation to the Countess of Albany. Before Madame Mocenni's return to Siena, the two women seem to have sworn a friendship that was only terminated by the death of Teresa, in the autumn of 1802, during which period a large number of letters passed regularly between the pair. Those written by the Countess to her new-found Sienese friend have happily been preserved almost intact, and for various reasons they are of sufficient interest and value to require the following chapter to themselves.

CHAPTER XI

TERESA MOCENNI

"My dear Teresa, . . . you are the only Italian woman I
have ever grown fond of, or has proved sympathetic to me. Tell
me about yourself, and your affairs always and often, and be
assured that in myself you will find a friend who never changes."
—*Opening Letter of the Countess of Albany to Signora Teresa Regoli-
Mocenni of Siena.**

THE intimate correspondence between the Countess
of Albany and her two Sienese friends, Signora Teresa
Regoli-Mocenni and the Arch-priest Ansano Luti,
opens in November 1797, with a warm invitation from
the former to write to her constantly on terms of frankness
and affection. As has been explained already, Teresa
Mocenni was an old acquaintance of Alfieri, who used
to frequent her house in the far-away days of the *crocchietto saporito*; whilst the Countess herself had only
once met this Madame Mocenni, shortly after the death
of her devoted *cavaliere servente*, Mario Bianchi, Alfieri's
old friend and constant correspondent, in the winter of
1796. The Countess, Alfieri, Teresa Mocenni and the
Arch-priest Luti were moreover all united by a mutual
bond of admiration for the long-dead Francesco Gori,
whom Madame d'Albany in one of her letters describes
as " one of the most estimable men I have ever known,
and also the kindest of creatures, with the heart of an
angel and the mind of one of those heroes of the antique

* L. G. Pélissier, *Lettres Inédites de la Comtesse d'Albany à Ses Amis de
Sienne*. (Tome I. Paris, Fontemoing, 1904.)

(Unless stated otherwise, all references in this chapter are to the above-
mentioned work.)

196

world whom we all revere." Teresa Mocenni herself, a woman of no small learning and refinement, had formerly by her charm and tact contrived to draw around her in Siena a circle of the most cultured and agreeable persons in the place; but her pleasure in life itself had always been sadly marred by the existence of a husband, Ansano Mocenni, a Sienese merchant, who was evidently a Philistine with strong commercial instincts and (what was infinitely worse in the writer's eyes) with a decided leaning towards liberal or " Jacobin " views in politics. Teresa seems to have detested her spouse cordially, whilst Madame d'Albany never alludes to this man (whom in spite of his alleged iniquities one cannot help pitying) by his name, but invariably by some epithet of disgust or contempt, calling him *zanzaro perpetuel, il Brontolone* (the Grumbler), *imbécile de mari* and other insulting terms. And besides the unwelcome presence of the " Brontolone," poor Teresa was ever deploring the loss of her *cavaliere servente*, Mario Bianchi, who had died a twelvemonth before the opening of this correspondence at the early age of forty. Nor were the persecutions of a living husband and the sad memories of a lost lover the only afflictions the unhappy lady was forced to bear, for she was likewise much beset by domestic difficulties in finding suitable matches for her daughters and in rearing and educating her large family, for she was already the mother of several children; whilst the expected birth of yet another infant to the " Brontolone " at this very time causes considerable amusement to the childless mistress of Casa Alfieri, who never ceases to congratulate herself on her failure to become a mother. To this undesired baby, the Countess, not over-graciously, consents to stand godmother, provided the child be a girl, in which event the names of Luisa-Vittoria are to be bestowed on it. To another of her Teresa's children, a boy born in 1784, Alfieri himself had become sponsor and given his own name of Vittorio, in consequence of

197

which Madame d'Albany takes a special interest in this youth, maintaining with him a pleasant correspondence, undertaken with the two-fold object of teaching him French and of inspiring his unformed mind with choice sentiments carefully selected from the works of Cicero or Seneca.[*]

Of the Arch-priest Luti, a scholar and an old friend of Alfieri, but little is known beyond what comes to the surface in these letters, and that little, to speak frankly, reflects ill on his moral character. Moreover, during a time of political repression in Siena, Luti showed himself distinctly ungenerous or cowardly in ostentatiously avoiding the *salon* of his old friend, Teresa Mocenni, much to the indignation of her champion in Florence, who speaks her mind very freely on his conduct in this and in sundry other matters. For throughout these letters the financial complications caused by the folly of Luti's mistress, a person in humble life (for this literary priest did not exist without female consolation), are often discussed with perfect *sang-froid* by Madame d'Albany. The substance of these letters is mostly intended for Teresa, but all are directed to the Arch-priest, who is sometimes styled on the subscription for safety's sake " il Cittadino Luti."

In spite of her wit and learning, Teresa Mocenni was but the wife of a Sienese merchant, who kept the Casa Alfieri well supplied with various groceries, notably with the chocolate and gingerbread that figure in so many of the letters, and this circumstance in a manner gives a higher value to her connection with so important a personage as the Countess of Albany. Her beloved Teresa not being a great lady, the Countess' letters to her are in consequence fairly free from that tedious element, which the author of *Vanity Fair* would perhaps have characterised as " fashionable slip-slop." On the contrary, they deal with matters of immediate private concern, great or small, and are not stuffed with weari-

* Pélissier, *Lettres Inédites, &c. Appendix* II. pp. 439-457.

some accounts of modish balls and assemblies, followed by strings of aristocratic names, or seasoned with faded scandals in high life and with *bon-mots* that have long lost all their point and savour. Indeed, in one letter this high and mighty widow of a *de jure* king proceeds to read her provincial friend a full lecture concerning her ignorance as to the great social world of Rome.

Nevertheless, we gain not a few entertaining sketches of persons of some celebrity in these pages. We are afforded glimpses of the Tuscan diplomatists, Lucchesini and Carletti, the latter being labelled as "a mass of conceit and selfishness, and Heaven knows why!"— of the Cardinals Consalvi, Antonelli, Zondadari and York ("*qui me deteste comme Lucifer!*"), the last-named being held up to merciless ridicule; of the severe General Miollis; of the pious but silly old King Charles-Emmanuel of Sardinia; of the eccentric Lord Bristol, Bishop of Derry; and of other persons of note, all of whom are delineated for us in the sharp unfeeling language wherein Madame d'Albany was a proficient. We breathe, as it were, a natural atmosphere of intimate humanity in this correspondence, which is couched throughout in rather slovenly French, well-peppered with Italian idioms, for the writer's cosmopolitan training does not seem to have permitted her to acquire a complete mastery over any one tongue. It is, however, pleasant for us to play the harmless part of eavesdropper in these feminine confidences of more than a century ago, which passed between the widow of Prince Charles-Edward Stuart and the superior wife of the ill-tempered merchant of Siena; between the "Donna Amata" of the Italian tragic poet and the bereaved mistress of the late Chevalier Mario Bianchi. Throughout the volume containing the one hundred and seventy-six letters, which the industry and learning of Monsieur Pélissier have collected and edited for us, we are presented with many shrewd remarks on a variety of subjects from the most lofty to

199

the most trivial ; a mass of homely but not uninteresting details about Casa Alfieri, and several pages of a scarcely serious pessimism wherein the Countess is ever prone to indulge. We have also many comments of no special value on the political topics of these stirring days, coupled with an unreasoning and unreasonable abuse of the French armies and the French nation. Possibly, Madame d'Albany's invective is made the fiercer by reason of the fact that her two friends in Siena, especially the Arch-priest Luti, did not wholly share the writer's reactionary ideals. Criticisms of books, new and old, constantly occur ; whilst good advice on the preservation of health, on political deportment, on education of children, on marrying of daughters, and a host of other subjects is liberally showered both on Teresa and the Arch-priest, without a thought of future publication on the part of the famous woman who indited these letters.

We begin by quoting the first letter *in toto* ; for though it is not of special interest, it will afford a useful specimen of the epistolary style of Madame d'Albany to the friend chosen to be the special confidant of her fears, her hopes, her views, and her doubts.

" MY DEAR TERESA,—I deeply regret you did not remain longer in Florence, also that I have not known you earlier, for you are the only Italian woman I have ever grown fond of, or that has ever proved sympathetic to me. I greatly hope you will love me always, and that we shall remain friends for life, and of this hope your excellent disposition, which hitherto I know better by report than by experience, seems a sure guarantee. Be assured that all which concerns yourself will prove of interest to me, so tell me about your affairs always and often, and believe that in myself you will find a friend who never changes. How could you fancy we should never meet again, when we are living [at each others' gates, as it were ? If you cannot find your way to me, well then, I shall go to see you. But I am in hopes you will still be able to come and spend the month of October in Florence ; do not despair of this, I beg you. The most impossible things sometimes come to pass in this world, whilst the most likely often fail to occur. Courage, my dear, do not let yourself fall a prey to melancholy. Well indeed do I realise that your heart is lacerated ; nevertheless sustain yourself with reason, or rather trust yourself to Time, that destroying tyrant who swallows up even the deepest-rooted affections. Yet he never obliterates true friendship ; he only blunts the sharp arrows of grief. And yet, despite my fine phrases that are easier to supply than to follow, I shudder in thinking on the loss you have sustained. My heart bleeds for you. Carletti, our minister in disgrace, writes to me that he will endeavour to talk with you about me, since we are such friends. Receive him, for he will divert your thoughts.

"I do not yet send you [Alfieri's] sonnets, because the Count Vittorio, who is your true friend, has begun to have his portrait painted, and at eleven o'clock we go for him to sit to Monsieur Fabre, who sends you the homage of respect. We often talk over you together. You shall have the sonnets presently.

"If you want any article dyed in Florence, my dear Teresa, pray send without scruple ; and I say this because I love to employ myself on your behalf, and because you know I do not make this offer out of empty compliment.

"You will have seen the terms of the Peace [of Campo Formio]. Italy is sacrificed and is made tributary to the French. What a crime to have allowed these brigands to force the barrier of the Alps !

"I am well, and so is the Poet. I trust your slight malady will have left no ill effects behind. Take care of yourself and arm yourself with patience against your Perpetual Mosquito, and take the line of acting as you please and paying no attention to him. Keep well employed to distract your thoughts, and read books

201

which fortify the heart and refresh the brain. I will
try to procure you a copy of the Essays of Montaigne,
who is our breviary, for he teaches one to think and he
invigorates the soul.

"Farewell, my dear Teresa. Send me news of yourself, and give kind messages to the Arch-priest both
from myself and from Count Alfieri. You may rely
for ever on my tender and unchanging devotion throughout life. I embrace you with my whole heart a thousand
times over. Love me, for I am not undeserving of your
love, since no one pays more deference to your many
virtues.

"What are your children doing? Was Vittorio
right or wrong? Tell me of every interest you have,
and believe that you have no better friend in the world
than myself." *

The allusion herein to the Poet's picture by Fabre,
leads us to remark that Madame d'Albany was at this
period occupying her leisure hours with painting ; † and
what more natural than that under the influence of this
new-sprung friendship, she would wish to accomplish
a likeness of her Teresa? It is an agreeable picture of
domestic culture and industry in Casa Alfieri that is
presented to us ; the Poet, now approaching fifty,
burying himself in a deep study of the classical authors,
toujours enseveli sous les in-folios grecs et latins ; whilst
the equally energetic Countess continues to paint with
all the enthusiasm of an amateur, whose achievements
were far from contemptible. In succeeding letters
there is frequent mention of a portrait of her dear Teresa,
which the illustrious artist hopes from the serious expression bestowed on the face "will frighten the 'Brontolone' on looking at it. Perhaps it will even bring

---

* pp. 3, 4.

† In January 1910, there was being offered for sale in a Florentine *bric-à-
brac* shop the portrait of a gentleman in blue coat and white cravat, signed
on the canvas "Louise de Stolberg, Comtesse d'Albany, 1795." The painting was certainly not without merit.

you some welcome peace by making him go early to bed every evening, so that you yourself can converse at your ease with the Arch-priest."

A letter dated February 27, 1798, contains a fair example of the Countess' habitual strain of melancholy over the political situation after the recent peace of Campo Formio, since both she and Alfieri were ever deploring their expected fate at the hands of the victorious French, who were pretty certain sooner or later to occupy Florence. The author of the *Miso-Gallo* had perhaps some real cause for alarm, but his gloomy views were shared in a double degree by his companion, who never ceases to lament the evil in store and to abuse (so long as she dared) the French Government and its agents in Italy.

"You are correct, my dear Teresa, in saying that plenty of people would envy my lot, and if so on account of the Friend I possess, they are right, for I, too, estimate myself a happy woman on that score. But the world does not know what I feel, and the Friend too ; or what I suffer myself from seeing him suffer from the late events, and from seeing the wicked triumphant on all sides, with ourselves on the eve of flight we know not whither, and in a state of terrible uncertainty. Who can say he is safe from undeserved imprisonment ? Who can declare with assurance at this moment, ' I shall not die in fetters '? For the more noble the man, the more reason has he to fear these wretches.

"Do you really think life itself would be supportable, when every principle of public religion and morality has been swept away ? Ah, happy he who neither thinks of nor beholds the results in Italy. And hard it is to have to spend the residue of one's days wandering hither and thither, with no sense of security anywhere. I find that at forty-five life no longer worth the struggle, and if it were not for our Friend, I should welcome death with all my heart. For I am not like the majority of persons who believe in the supreme joy of living; I am disgusted with everything, and see the realities of life more clearly since the Revolution. I have therefore an overwhelming contempt for the human race, and even my heart has grown hardened, for the good or ill of the multitude affects me no more. Only fools and knaves do I see in this world. And if I lost our Friend, I should have lost my all; yet how can one count on anything for certain in this world, wherein at the very moment we imagine we have seized firmly upon happiness, it eludes our grasp?

"Believe me, my dear Teresa, that I am expressing my true and well-weighed sentiments. I thought that after my husband's death I should continue in peace and happiness, when lo, the Revolution, which has turned my life into a perpetual state of anxiety as to my safety and my means of existence. So you see there is no hope of a real state of peace.

"If I had children, I should go mad, but mercifully in that respect I have been fortunate. I shall be told, 'Think of the Pope's position!' True, but he has the good luck to be eighty-two and tottering on the verge of the grave, whilst I am only forty-five. My good time is past and gone, and there only awaits me now a vista of sickness and old age. But I am dwelling on a theme, which will not tend to cheer you, for you have experienced troubles of every kind, and more numerous even than my own. . . .

"Alas, poor humanity! What a mockery it is! Since the proclamation of the Rights of Man, never have men been so treated like sheep. They are sold like hogs to the highest bidder, after being weighed. *Basta!* Farewell, my dear Arch-priest. We are all sick, for we are all living in the midst of a moral plague, and who knows but that we may not catch its infection ourselves? The Poet salutes you. . . ."*

* pp. 46-48.

204

We get, of course, numerous glimpses of Alfieri, generally called the Poet, who usually sends greeting to his old Sienese friends by means of the letters of the Countess. In July 1798, we learn of his intention to renounce poetry, in answer to a request for some sonnets from Signora Mocenni.

" The Poet charges me with a thousand kind messages to you. He writes nothing more nowadays that he can send you, and when once he has attained his fiftieth birthday, he has made a resolution beforehand of renouncing his *bella madonna*, Poesy, so as not to sink into the absurd number of those superannuated swans, his brother bards, who go on composing verses with hoary heads. At present he is studying Greek, and is revising his former satires, and for some time past I have seen nothing fresh to send you. Have you had his sonnet written for Fabre ? If not, I shall get it for you." *

To Teresa Mocenni's melancholy and disconsolate outpourings concerning her departed lover, the Countess replies in the following strain, which is evidently intended to console her friend.

" . . . I always envy the lot of those deeply religious persons who lay all their burdens at the foot of the Cross, and thereby acquire merit in the sight of Heaven. It is an awful crime to deprive any one of religion, but especially a woman. How much less unhappy you would feel, my dear Teresa, if only you were *dévote*, or if you hoped to see your Mario again ! But I do not conceive how you could see him again, even if he is really calling to you to deliver him, for if you *do* believe in a future life, he has committed no crime to make him unhappy ; and if you do *not* believe, he is non-existent. Thus in neither case is he suffering. Yet he is more fortunate than yourself, for he enjoys peace and cessation from fears. I never pity the Dead ; it is the living who

* p. 112.

are left behind that I commiserate on account of their separation from those they love. Consider then your friend as happy and freed from the anxieties of this world. Mourn for him, because you have lost him, but not because he is wretched or suffering, for he endures less than you do yourself, since he feels nothing. Then calm your imagination, and above all things do not encourage such agitating notions, my dear Teresa. Reason must enforce her sway at the end of a certain interval. So do as I tell you ; mourn for your friend as lost but not unhappy." *

And again, in a letter of a week later (March 20), Madame d'Albany makes a further attempt to cheer and advise her disconsolate Teresa, still brooding over the lost Mario Bianchi in her waking and sleeping hours.

" You ought to try to avoid the very spots that recall your Friend and the happy hours you passed together. You must allow the wound to become cicatrized, and not seek to reopen it continually, otherwise it will never heal. It is only Time that can soften grief, and change it into a tender memory of happy moments past and gone ; but the waiting for Time's healing is a terribly tedious process. I pity you with all my soul, and I did pity you already before I actually knew you. You may rest assured that I share your troubles, and I feel them all the more, because I am constantly trembling lest the same fate overtake myself. The Poet keeps well, but at the least sign of suffering, my heart grows alarmed, as you may well imagine, especially at this crisis. What shall I do without him ? I only hold on to life for his sake, whilst you have children with whom to share your affection. Vittorio deserves your loving attention ; and if you occupy yourself with him, he will love you in return, whilst he can bear grateful witness to your love by consecrating himself to your service. Tell him so from me." *

* pp. 50, 51.   * p. 54.

The following confidential complaints and expressions of uneasiness were written on July 9, 1798.

" . . . For myself, I have from my earliest years been familiar with misfortune. I was born the eldest of the children of my mother, who wanted a boy and in consequence received and treated me ill all my youthful days. She shut me in a convent where I learned nothing, in order to pay a smaller sum for my education and thus to have more money for her own amusement, for my mother has never thought of aught else but to play, enjoy life and dress herself up to her present age of sixty-five. She affianced me (so as to get rid of me) to the most insupportable man that ever lived, a man uniting in himself every possible fault and prejudice in addition to the lackey's vice of drunkenness.

" I hoped then after his death to live peaceably and happily, had not these political upheavals plunged me once more into alarm for my very means of existence. The only happiness I have enjoyed (and indeed it is no small one) is in having a Friend such as the Poet. Yet even he causes me uneasiness at this moment, for I suffer on his behalf, and if ever some change took place in this country under a French occupation, I should be terrified about him, since his detestation of their rule is well known, because he loathes tyranny under whatsoever form it may present itself. You see, my dear Teresa, how I love you, and with what confidence I address you, feeling sure of your heart and of your feelings towards myself. I should love to live in the same town with you, to open my heart to you every instant of the day, and to share in your own troubles, for you are even more wretched than I, and this thought torments me." *

In October 1798, Madame d'Albany accepts the post of sponsor to Teresa's new-born baby, the little Luisa-Vittoria Mocenni.

* pp. 104, 105.

"My very dear Teresa," she writes on October 16, "I have never yet been a godmother in my life, and I understand nothing about the matter, so arrange everything as you wish, for it is only my affection for yourself that has induced me to accede to your request. I do not know a cat in Siena, so I should be under great difficulty in asking any one to act for me, but it seems to me that your daughter [Quirina] could easily represent me. Besides, I understand nothing of this church ceremony. I remember that once in London a friend of mine asked me to act sponsor together with General de Paoli, and that I agreed, but nobody appeared for me on that occasion. . . ."*

Eventually the Countess appeals to Luti for his services : "As I comprehend nothing about this affair of standing sponsor and still less about the fees to the priests, I beg you to pay out whatever is necessary to have Teresa's child sprinkled, and I will repay you promptly, for I know the Church gives nothing without payment, not even a drop of water !"

The writer is not very complimentary to her Teresa as a mother, though she makes many suggestions for the education of her numerous progeny, concerning whose future prospects she always takes the most gloomy views. ". . . Really, I do not know where one is to place children to prevent their growing up wicked. It seems to me you have a great number of these *marmousets*, and they must be a terrible anxiety to you."

We obtain some rather curious accounts of the humble household of the Fabres in the course of these letters. The painter was now inhabiting a house together with an aged father and mother and his brother Edouard, a doctor, who was rapidly obtaining a good practice in Florence, where amongst other patients he soon reckoned the great Alfieri, now growing more feeble with each succeeding year. Madame Fabre was appa-

* pp. 148, 150.

rently the first of the family to arrive, namely, in August 1798.—" Fabre sends you his respectful homage. His mother arrived in Florence about twelve days ago from Marseilles. She is a little old woman of fifty-eight, lively as gunpowder, who cleans the house from cellar to garret. It will be an economical move for him, since she will take charge of his linen and all his household affairs, and he won't have to pay her any wages, whilst an extra woman in the house costs very little." *

Dr. Edouard Fabre was the last to appear, and in a letter of July 28, 1801, Madame d'Albany writes :

" Fabre works on, but with a sad heart. He is painting a picture of *Socrates drinking the hemlock*. He sends you his respectful homage. He sees nothing of his countrymen, whose occupation of Florence keeps aloof all strangers, which means an empty purse. His brother, the Doctor, is doing very well with his profession, being specially clever at treating the *maladie française*, which keeps him in constant practice. Thus money flows into Casa Fabre from a tainted source ! They are worthy people, well deserving of happiness, all four living on terms of perfect unity." †

The fourth member of the Fabre household was, of course, the father, a drawing-master and the original instructor of his talented son, whose works were far more appreciated in his own generation than they are at the present day. All four members of this humble family of *emigrés* from Montpellier were staunch Legitimists and keen haters of the Republic, a circumstance that certainly helped to endear them in a special degree to the supercilious master and mistress of Casa Alfieri. Of François-Xavier's position and influence with Alfieri and the Countess we have already spoken ; but the esteem wherein the artist was held was subsequently extended, though in a less degree, to Doctor Edouard Fabre, who was credited with an unusual knowledge of the poet's

* p. 134.   † p. 402.

constitution. The homely parents are only mentioned in terms of gracious condescension by the Countess, who merely approves of them as being of some assistance to their gifted sons : " the father, who gives lessons in drawing, makes a little money thereby. The mother manages the housekeeping, and pays for her sustenance by her hard work. They are all deeply attached to one another, and live contentedly and without quarrelling. But for *circumstances*, the Painter would already have amassed a fair fortune, for at the time of the Revolution he had more than fourteen big pictures commissioned for France, where he would have obtained some high post. But we must never think on the past, save to regret it."

In a later letter, the Countess mentions a visit of the French general of occupation, Miollis, to Fabre's studio, where, however, he made no purchase. " Doubtless he is accustomed to get his pictures for nothing!" * is her spiteful comment thereon.

Meanwhile, Teresa Mocenni had retired to her small property of Piano, near Siena, where the Countess professes to envy her this rural retreat.

" I have read with delight, my dear Teresa, the description of your country-home, which must be quite charming, and raises a desire in me to see it myself some day. What would you say on seeing me appear *chez vous*, like a bombshell ? How I should love to see and embrace you once again ! I strongly approve of the life you are leading, but take plenty of exercise both for mind and body. Quiet is an excellent tonic for our mental faculties, and the country can give us a fresh supply of vitality.

" But will you believe me when I tell you that I do not care to live in the country ? Not, however, because it bores me, for I know too well how to pass my time to advantage. But never having been brought up in the

* p 367.

country, I possess no real affection for it. The time soon comes when I begin to long for society of an evening, and as I cannot have it, I grow discontented. After being busy all day long, I require some distraction at night, and that is a want the country cannot supply." *

And again she writes to her "Saint of Piano" on April 19, 1800 : ". . . I am delighted to learn you are happy in the country with your books and your peasants. To have a contented mind and an easy conscience is a real boon. Both of these I myself also enjoy. Even in the midst of a crowded room I always feel solitary, and sometimes in regarding other people I form a higher estimate of myself; not that I am really good, but that I sometimes gain by comparison with others." †

There are a good many allusions, all contemptuous, to that queer creature, Frederick-Augustus Hervey, Earl of Bristol and Bishop of Derry, who spent many years of his life wandering aimlessly about Italy, buying works of art, and indeed (to quote Madame d'Albany's own words) committing every species of folly. This ornament of the English peerage and the Irish episcopate reckoned one virtue at least in his critic's eyes, for he was a warm patron of Fabre and a sincere admirer of his genius. On August 2, 1800, the Countess relates to Luti how she has just seen *ce fou Bristol* passing beneath her window, clad presumably in the red plush breeches and broad-brimmed white hat that he generally affected to the amazement of his Italian friends, who came to consider this costume as the official garb of a heretic bishop.

" That idiot, Bristol, my dear Arch-priest, has already returned from Siena, and as I was reading your letter he passed beneath my window. I cannot imagine for what purpose he went to Siena ? Tell me, I entreat you, if he has not found some woman there that he has

* p. 257.　　　　　† p. 265.

brought back here with him, for we have seen him driving about with a pretty creature, and he told us before he left he was going to see *une de ses amies*. It's an eccentric, who has an ample fortune to sustain his extravagances." *

Other confidences concerning the *amours*, the servants and the follies of this crazy peer-prelate follow at intervals, but they are far from edifying and had better lie imbedded in their writer's original French.

Amongst the various persons of less importance who cross the stage of this correspondence, mention ought to be made of the Cicciaporci family; a father, wife and daughter. Signor Antonio Cicciaporci was the natural son of Donna Anna Cicciaporci, a noble Roman lady of easy virtue and the acknowledged mistress of the dissipated Venetian Cardinal Cornaro, Governor of Rome, in consequence of which the lady had been nick-named the "Abbé Anna." † Their son Antonio had contrived to marry an English lady of position, and was the possessor of a miniature of the Countess of Albany painted at the time of her first residence in Rome as the bride of Prince Charles Edward—a work of art that was presumably one of the spoils extracted by the so-called Abbé Anna from her Cardinal-lover. To this miniature the Countess alludes in a letter of October 10, 1800.

"A thousand messages to the Cicciaporci. I hope the head of the family will take care of himself for the sake of his wife and daughter. I did not know before that he had a miniature of myself. It cannot any longer bear any resemblance to me, for it must be at least a quarter of a century old, and that lapse of time leaves marks on the face that change its expression and blot out its freshness. Now I must think of beautifying the soul, so that it may be tolerated in its old age." ‡

* p. 305.   † Silvagni, *Corte di Roma*.
‡ p. 327.

On the arrival of this family in Florence, Madame d'Albany presents her friend with a very candid criticism of the trio: "... Madame Cicciaporci * is a good woman who speaks all languages equally ill, and yet talks a great deal. ... She always amazes me with her chatter, and is apt to become intensely wearisome. She has seen everything, and she knows everything. That pose fatigues me, and occasionally her husband also. He is a man of sense, and I believe he is patient. English-women have many good qualities, but they are so restless by nature, that they must sometimes make their husbands regret their extreme chastity ! *But this is quite between ourselves.*"

And again, in a letter of somewhat later date, the Countess returns to this Anglo-Italian household. " The Cicciaporci family are all of them well. The husband has had an attack of the gout, but is better. The wife has her usual slight ailments. She is a good creature but a hopeless chatterbox. The girl is nice, and worth ten of her mother."

In December Madame d'Albany receives a letter from Teresa complaining of the insipid conversation and crass ignorance of the people of Siena, which annoy her so much that she has decided to abjure in future such society as the town offered. That easy-going and tolerant ecclesiastic, the Arch-priest Luti, by no means shared the Mocenni's views on this subject, and his opinion is strongly upheld by the Countess in the following letter, dated December 28, 1799, which contains what is on the whole the best piece of advice yet bestowed on her absent friend.

" I fully agree, my dear Teresa, with the Arch-priest in condemning your intolerance of fools. I am far from counselling any self-abasement, which is an idea quite

* She was a daughter of Sir John Stuart, Bart., of Allanbank, and sister to the wife of Sir J. C. Hippisley. (*Journal of Elizabeth, Lady Holland*, vol. i. p. 31.)

alien to my disposition. But in this world it is always necessary to apologise for any superior qualities we may possess, and particularly for originality of mind and education in a small town (like Siena), where all are ignorant, especially the women, and where a common impression prevails that study itself is a crime. They are punishing you too, my dear Teresa, for the delightful group of interesting people you collected around you some years ago,* for envy and jealousy do not easily forgive. So it is bad policy for you to make yourself enemies of all these fools, whose number is inexhaustible. An apt remark or a compliment can be of use, but above all things never discuss either with them or in their hearing any subject they do not understand. You must descend to their level, and not expect them to mount to your heights. If you had studied your Montaigne's Essays carefully, you would have gathered how one can learn something from everybody, even from the silliest. One never ought to cite oneself as an example, but— since our letters constitute a sort of confession, to which the Arch-priest gives absolution, for we are worthy to be his penitents—for my own part I take society in the evening as a relaxation, wherein I get amusement out of the fools who abound here in Florence, as though they were persons of real interest. I play my part, and never do I speak to them either of my studies or of my know- ledge, so that no woman can accuse me of so much as hinting to her that I even opened a book. We often laugh together, the Poet and I, over the absurdities we have heard, and yourself and the Arch-priest might act in the same manner. . . . My years have made me very indulgent, and my experience of the world has taught me to be tolerant of all. But there are so few people who are in the position of being able to act as they ought. Your own philosophy, my dear Teresa, ought to serve you to the same end ; namely, to be severe to yourself and indulgent towards others. Do not raise

* An allusion to the *crocchiette saporito* of Alfieri's youth.

up enemies, if only in the interests of your children; and enemies are commonly made so easily out of the merest remark or trifle, for all fools are so sensitive." [*]

We have already mentioned Madame d'Albany's occupation of painting, and it seems that after sending Teresa her own portrait, she decides to make her a present of a picture by her own hand of St. Teresa of Spain, Signora Mocenni's own tutelar saint. In an amusing letter of October 4, 1800, the despatch of this gift is announced with an account of Fabre's professional alterations and improvements on the canvas, which in a postscript the French artist modestly deprecates. Other matters not without some interest are also touched upon in this letter.

" To-day, my dear Teresa, your patron saint will set off on her travels ! I hope she will reach you by next Tuesday, so that I may hear of her safe arrival, and of your own opinion of her. I promised you to resort to Monsieur Fabre's brush so as to correct my mistakes ; and he has lent himself to my plan, partly out of his usual kindness towards myself, and partly because he wants you to possess a better picture of your celestial guardian in your oratory. I trust you will have cause to be satisfied with his saintly efforts. I never blow my own trumpet, and you yourself are well aware that I am not capable of bestowing so sweet an expression on any face. However, provided you are pleased with the result, Monsieur Fabre and I will be equally contented, and you can recall us both to your mind whenever you look on your picture. It was, however, rather effrontery on my part to mingle my painting with his. Happily, however, the touches of his brush help to hide my own efforts.

" I am very sorry to hear of Monsieur Cicciaporci's illness, for it is of a kind that increases with years. I am afraid when he comes to Florence, he will drink too much

* pp. 227-229.

215

at the dinner-parties given by English visitors here. In Italy one cannot drink overmuch wine with impunity, especially the Tuscan vintages. I beg you to make my compliments both to him and his family. I pity his poor wife for her anxiety, since it is an awful thing to feel that in a moment one may be deprived of the person who is absolutely essential to one's happiness. But one cannot, and ought not, to count for certain on anything in this world; and thus it was that St. Teresa only thought of Heaven and loved no one but God. Happy are those who can imitate her example and detach themselves entirely from every earthly tie ! But I am still far from this attitude of perfection.

" You will have heard of our armistice of forty-five days, which is due to expire on November 9th, when it will be too late in the season to recommence hostilities, and consequently the French will continue in Italy to devour what little remains to be eaten. I have always called this truce a state of neither peace nor war, but one eternal round of plunder.

" I do not know who can have informed you of the recapture of Peschiera, for there have been no actual engagements on either side since the battle of Marengo. I suspect Madame Santa-Maria prefers Siena to Florence, because she is made more of there; and as this lady has been a prominent personage all her life, she is in no hurry to be lost once more in the general crowd, where men think of nothing but amorous intrigue, and care nothing about strangers in their midst, unless they can suck some advantage out of them. If your pretty women in Siena are as insipid as are ours here, I am not surprised to learn that your boy from Denmark cannot find much pleasure in their society. Our women have no sort of conversation, but they are at least quite good enough for the men who frequent their houses.

" I salute the Arch-priest and I implore him not to give way to despair. I have no doubt his prayers will prove very efficacious, but personally I prefer to trust to our armies, which are not quite so vanquished as he seems to think.

" I should like you to find a husband (not for myself !), but for a young girl, who is not pretty, but full of talent, of very good birth, and with a fair dowry. This young person has been excellently educated ; she has a professor's knowledge of music, plays on the harpsichord, writes well, knows how to cast accounts and speaks several languages. It is likely, too, that one day she may become rich. I beg you to see if there exists at Siena a suitable *parti* for this young lady. It is difficult to marry her here, since she is plain, though without any physical defect, for she is tall and well formed.

" Farewell, my dear Teresa, I embrace you a thousand times over with all my heart. Rely ever on my tender affection. I now yield the pen, not the brush to Monsieur Fabre ! "

(Postscript in Monsieur Fabre's handwriting)

" I came to visit Madame la Comtesse at the moment of her shutting down her letter, and I have asked her permission to use the remainder of her sheet of paper so as to rectify a mistake in her letter. For I have not contributed so much to the value of your picture of St. Teresa as Madame la Comtesse has been generous enough to declare. The composition is wholly her own, as are the attitude of the Saint, the original sketch and the whole idea. My only claim to merit is that from time to time I have corrected some technical faults, which is far from having made the poem ! I have the honour, Madame, to be with respect, your very humble and very obedient servant,

" F.-X. FABRE." *

The following pessimistic letter contains an early example of the Countess' favourite description of herself

* pp. 323–326.

as " sitting at the window, to watch the magic-lantern of the world without " :

" . . . The Revolution has disillusioned me concerning all things. It is not that formerly I failed to realise that nothing is certain in this world, but to have had the actual experience of this before my very eyes has wrought an indescribable effect on me. I care no longer for anything, nor count upon anything. I exist from day to day, since I can no longer depend on a settled abode. I say ever to myself, ' *If I am here a month hence !* ' But I find that what I have lost in one way, I have gained in another, for I have discovered in myself a force of character of which I never imagined myself capable. I do not fear Death, but regard it with calmness ; and instead of clinging the more to life as I grow older, I find myself growing each day more detached from it. The world is to me no more than a magic-lantern. I watch it pass, as I sit at the window. Only one thing do I fear, and if I did not fear that, I should fear nothing : it is the loss of the Friend for whose sake alone I live. I could, however, prefer to see him dead rather than unhappy, because I love him for himself, although his loss to me would be an overwhelming blow."

Of Madame d'Albany's constant comments on the much-abused, and no doubt very provoking Signore Mocenni, one passage, taken from a letter of April 11, 1801, to Luti, must suffice here.

" Our Saint Teresa is very good to receive the ' Brontolone ' in her country-house at Piano, but I pity her with all my heart. Her patience surpasses that of all the Saints who ever existed. I admire her for it, but at the same time I could wish that he who exercises her virtue would himself depart to Paradise to weary some other Saint ! But nuisances like the ' Brontolone ' never die, and if the Grumbler had been the least necessary to our Teresa,

218

he would have passed away ages ago. Indeed, it is
absolutely certain that those human beings who are
useless and mischievous are also indestructible. I believe
their own selfishness supplies them with an endless
fund of vitality." *

The last letter included in Monsieur Pélissier's collection bears the date of February 27, 1802, and is chiefly
concerned with the betrothal of Teresa's daughter,
Quirina, to Signore Ferdinando Magiotti, son of Major
Magiotti, of Montevarchi, and herein the Countess
alludes in the most disparaging terms to the bridegroom-
elect.

" I still know nothing of your marriage scheme, which
interests me much and which I recommend every Sunday
to the person who is negociating it. I could hope for
success, since you desire it, although I should never have
disposed of any daughter of mine to a fool of that type,
whose face would make me fly a hundred paces !
" What would afford me pleasure in this arrangement
is that I should have the good fortune of seeing you in
Florence; and I believe your daughter also would get
to like me on a closer acquaintance, provided she has
the same qualities as her mother. But you are totally
mistaken, my dear Teresa, allow me to tell you, as to
Rome and as to society in general. In Rome, as in all
other cities, a woman, whether she be noble or *bourgeoise*,
has no need of a protector, so long as she will remain
content with her own station, will stay at home and not
go gadding outside her own set. You were mistaken
in telling your daughter that the only difference in this
world is one between vice and virtue, for unhappily
this is a fallacy. . . . If your daughter nurses any real
attachment of the heart, it is foolish for you to marry
her off thus, and rend her miserable. So long as the
old Magiotti father lives, he will remain master of the

* p. 368.

219

house, and an absolute and tiresome master into the bargain. . . ."

This same letter contains a dissertation on priests, which is not without the writer's usual common-sense.

" . . . Priests are not so black as they are painted, and one must not judge them all by some of the country parish-priests, who are ignorant and odious, leaders of bigoted women and of silly men. From my own experience I have never yet met with one priest who has given me other than excellent advice, since they all know their duties thoroughly. The most narrow-minded I have ever met are the Irish Dominicans, who come out here straight from their native bogs and have not a grain of common-sense. The English priests and bigots are unendurable, and a thousand times more fanatical than the Italian, who have the knack of accommodating human weakness with celestial virtue.

" My brother-in-law has had a stroke of apoplexy, but two cuppings in succession soon put him on his legs again, so that he was off the next day to St. Peter's to receive the coffin of Pius VI., which was attended with unusual pomp. All the Frenchmen present were in deep mourning, as an act of reparation for the late Pope's treatment by their nation. Farewell, my Teresa, I embrace you, and I cordially salute the Arch-priest; also the Poet and Fabre both salute you." *

That which is evidently the latest letter in this correspondence is dated only " *le* 21," but from the allusions contained therein as to Quirina Mocenni's imminent marriage, it was probably written on July 21st, of the year 1802.†

" I thank our Quirina, my dear Teresa, for sending me news of yourself during the time you were nursing

---

* pp. 428–431.

† Unpublished MSS. in Biblioteca Marucelliana, Florence (A. 146–536) *See* Appendix of this work.

your husband, who will probably be sufficiently recovered to start on Wednesday. You will suffer terribly from the heat. The bridegroom awaits his bride with eager impatience, like the bridegroom in the Song of Songs, and they say he is in such a state of excitement that he has to be kept calm with doses of melon-seeds ! . . ."

The Countess continues to make more contemptuous, and indeed untranslatable, remarks about poor Quirina's intended spouse, saying he is exactly like a donkey and practically idiotic, remarks that own, however, some value in affording further proof, if any such were needed, of her personal disapproval of this particular match for her friend's daughter, although some Italian writers still persist in holding the Countess of Albany more or less responsible for this unhappy marriage.

The letter concludes with an allusion to Fabre's father, who was then at the point of death.

"We are stewing as usual in the heat, which shows no sign of abating. You will find Fabre somewhat depressed. His father, who was suffering from dropsy, had a stroke of paralysis last Tuesday, and has lost the power of speech and all feeling on one side. He is alive, but as he was desperately ill last night, he may be dead this morning, which will be a mercy both for himself and for his sons ; for an invalid in such a condition is miserable himself and renders those around him miserable also. His wife is in despair, for her husband was her only resource, since she has no friends here, and women of her class hate to spend solitary evenings. Farewell, my dear Teresa, till we have the pleasure of seeing you here. Keep well. A thousand kind messages to Quirina.

"P.S.—I salute the Arch-priest, who (I hear) has given his benediction on this extraordinary marriage ! "

This letter, poking constant fun at the matrimonial prospects of her friend's daughter, is apparently the last of the series. Teresa and her husband duly attended their daughter's wedding on August 20, but soon after the ceremony Madame Mocenni, whose health had long been failing with dropsical symptoms, fell ill and finally died on September 20, being buried in the family chapel of Sant' Ansano, on the River Arbia. Her loss naturally came as a severe blow to the Countess, whose succeeding letters to the Arch-priest are filled with laments for her late friend.

" It is some consolation to me, my dear Arch-priest, to talk with you of my loved Teresa, who has been the victim of a brutal husband. This dear friend of mine was to have reached Florence on my *festa*, and she actually died on my birthday, always a melancholy anniversary for me. I shall mourn all my life for this excellent friend, whom I was so looking forward to seeing again.

" I cannot grow accustomed to the thought that we have lost our friend. I expect all the women of Siena are condoling with you over her loss. She was a woman above all prejudices, with certain qualities beyond her own station and standard. She had a sound judgment, and she only required a little more knowledge of the world and a wider acquaintance with the great theatre of life. . . .

" I cannot reconcile myself, my dear Arch-priest, to the thought that our Teresa is no more. I suppose Providence always acts for the best, yet it is awful to observe how it leaves the evil in this world, and carries off the necessary and the good. By ever punishing and harassing the innocent, it renders the guilty prosperous. . . .

" I do not think our Teresa ever wrote anything, nor was she highly cultivated. She had wonderful natural gifts, and was marvellous considering her defective education ; but her learning was mediocre, and she had not much time for self-instruction on account of her many household duties. But she was a rare woman, both in heart and mind." *

It may be mentioned here that after Teresa's death, the Countess continued to correspond with the Arch-priest Luti for more than four years, although the poor old priest had become half-paralysed, and so helpless that he was cruelly nicknamed "*il mezzo-prete*" by his acquaintances. He died in February 1807, when the Chevalier Alessandro Cerretani took his place as her chief correspondent at Siena. To this new friend the Countess therefore expresses her hope that Luti died in full faith and without any doubts as to the future : " Tell me, I beg you, if the Arch-priest expired in peace ? He seemed to me not very firm in his belief. Was he convinced ? For myself, I do not see how one can doubt for a moment."

This question was apparently answered by Cerretani to the satisfaction of the Countess, who observes in her next letter of March 24 : " I am delighted to learn that the Arch-priest was not tormented by useless fears in his dying hours. He has evidently made the edifying end, that is a duty incumbent on us all." †

In another letter, the Countess again reverts to the loss of her Teresa, who would have comforted her at Luti's death. " My ill-luck is persistent, for had my Teresa been alive, she would have shared my tears. How tenderly I loved her ! . . ." ‡

.   .   .   .

The sequel to Madame d'Albany's professed devotion to Teresa and her children, which has been set forth endlessly in her letters, must be briefly given here. In spite of her loud and apparently sincere lamentations over " that poor woman, who was truly unique," it is strange to record that the intimate affection towards

* *Lettere Inedite di V. Alfieri. Appendix*, pp. 283, 284.
† C. Milanesi, *Alfieri in Siena.*
‡ *Ibidem.*

the mother was only in a very limited degree extended to the children, whom Teresa had especially commended to her influential friend, and in whose welfare the Countess had always hitherto expressed a warm concern. The subsequent attitude of the Countess of Albany towards Vittorio and Quirina Mocenni makes a mean and ungracious story, which it is regrettable that we are compelled to notice here, though in an endeavour to obtain a fair and full estimate of the character and career of the Stuart *Reine d'Angleterre*, it must in duty be transcribed in this place.

After her Teresa's death, her old confidant in Florence continued to direct letters to Vittorio Mocenni, a promising lad with a pronounced taste for science and literature. The kindly and encouraging tone of these letters not unnaturally induced the young fellow to assume that so prominent and wealthy a personage as the Countess would be willing to do all that was possible in aiding his future prospects. In such an expectation, however, Vittorio Mocenni soon found himself grievously mistaken, when a special request of his to the Countess to use her influence for the obtaining of a certain official post was met with a reply so cold, grudging and indifferent as practically to amount to a downright refusal of his plea.

" My dear Sir," she writes to her Teresa's favourite son and Alfieri's godson, " surely you do not mean to ask me to apply to persons I do not know, when I can barely obtain interest with my own friends? You are fully aware there are some people I do not care to approach. Besides, the man who bestows the kind of place you require is unknown to me. I have spoken to Puccini on your behalf, and he tells me that, since it is the *Commune* which is concerned with this type of post, it will be very hard to obtain one. Believe me, you must try to make your own way without applying to others. You have a good career before you, and one that ought to render you independent of assistance. Keep well, and count on my interest." *

A month later the Countess in a cold brief note gives the importunate youth the same unfeeling and unsympathetic advice, telling him she can be of no further help to him. Disappointed and disillusioned in his dead mother's chosen friend, Vittorio Mocenni ceased to apply ; duly took his medical degree at Pisa in 1809 ; and died a year later at Milan at the early age of twenty-six.

What could have been the true cause of this cold and callous conduct towards poor Vittorio, whom she had so constantly instructed and lectured in his mother's life-time ? Was the high-born queen of a brilliant Florentine *salon*, the widow of a *de jure* king, tired of her connection —though a connection of her own choosing—with these *bourgeois* people of Siena ? Was her loudly expressed affection for Teresa Mocenni limited solely to the woman whilst she was still living and able to afford distraction to the great lady, who had invited her friendship and her confidence ? Had the young Vittorio unwittingly committed some unpardonable offence, some serious breach of etiquette, that had suddenly caused the Countess thus to veer round and to turn a deaf ear to the entreaties of her friend's favourite son ? It is impossible to tell the cause of her conduct, but we have some means to enable us to form our judgment in this matter from the Countess' treatment of the sister, of whose ill-starred marriage we have lately spoken. With a semi-idiotic husband and a hard forbidding and avaricious father-in-law, poor Quirina Mocenni-Magiotti was already leading a life of mingled misery and monotony, but instead of seeking to console her or to alleviate the hardness of her lot in a thousand ways such as the Countess well understood, Madame d'Albany seems actually to find a pleasure

* R. Tomei-Finamore, *La Comtesse d'Albany, &c.* Rivista Abruzzese, 1892, p. 326.

that is almost malicious in enlarging to Luti upon the domestic troubles of Quirina and her squalid household, prying into and commenting on the miserable married life of her friend's favourite daughter, and that in spite of the apparently affectionate letters she occasionally wrote to young Madame Magiotti herself.* For Quirina was indeed, even on the Countess' own showing, far from unworthy of the care and affection which the dead Teresa had evidently hoped the Countess would lavish on her child.

"I have just seen our Quirina," she writes on December 11, 1802, to Luti, less than three months after Teresa's death. "I am pleased with her. She has agreeable manners. She talks well, and seems to feel her mother's loss deeply. She is a little like her mother ; not pretty, but with a good figure." Naturally, her young married daughter could not be expected to fill the void caused by Teresa's death, yet for that dead friend's sake surely the Countess might, and should have made some strong effort to lighten her sad lot, to sympathise with her, and to assist her in certain delicate matters, wherein Madame d'Albany's long experience would have been of the greatest value.

But on March 19, 1803, the Countess slyly hints to Luti : "I believe Quirina yearns desperately for a *cavaliere servente!* But such creatures are rare, and she herself is not pretty. Her complexion in particular is bad, and she owns no charm save her youth. . . .

"The loss of her mother has been a great misfortune for her. Her presence here would have been most useful in establishing her, and in helping her to make pleasant acquaintances. As for myself, I cannot undertake this task for her, since I no longer go into society, and having renounced social worries, I have no intention of troubling myself. I am too elderly."

Alas, one can only attribute this open confession of neglect and indifference to a cold and selfish nature,

* For these letters, *see* Vitelleschi, pp. 599–602.

which declines to take the least trouble on behalf of an unhappy young woman, even though she happen to be the dearest daughter of her dearest friend.

Yet if Quirina's difficult position failed to draw any mark of practical sympathy from the Countess, the poor creature's domestic afflictions afforded her an endless source of satirical comment in her letters to Luti. Much as she had formerly nicknamed her Teresa's husband the " Brontolone," so now she took to calling Quirina's stern parent-in-law the " Cerberus ";—" A busy spy and tell-tale of other peoples' affairs, especially those of women," such is the biting stricture of one Italian writer who hated the Countess ; and certainly her obvious satisfaction in discussing the miseries of Madame Magiotti helps one to understand such a remark, even if it were grossly exaggerated. In later years Quirina returned the Countess' secret malevolence with interest, warning her lover, Ugo Foscolo, against Madame d'Albany's specious professions of friendship. " She is a spiteful, gossiping, heartless woman. I warned you against her a thousand times when you were at Milan, and I had a thousand good reasons for so doing." *

But the story of the relations between the Countess of Albany, Quirina Mocenni and Ugo Foscolo will be fully related and commented on in another chapter.

* R. Tomei-Finamore. *Op cit.* Reumont remarks that " there is some exaggeration but also some truth in this statement."

CHAPTER XII

LAST DAYS OF ALFIERI

" Truly, if the great poet of Asti could visit the marble of the sepulchre, that his Friend with royal munificence erected to him in Santa Croce by the hand of Antonio Canova, and could realise the indifference, if not actual oblivion, wherewith his countrymen have surrounded the memory of Her for whom he hoped an immortality, such as befel Bice Portinari or Laura de Noves, he would be grievously disappointed ! "—E. del Cerro *L'Amica di Alfieri*, (*Conversazione della Domenica*, July 1886.)

THE letters of the Countess to her friend Teresa Mocenni quoted in the last chapter have already afforded us a glimpse into the domestic life of Casa Alfieri during the evil years of the French invasion of Italy, and from them we can easily realise the fierce resentment and anxiety experienced by the pair, but especially by Alfieri, whose hatred of the French had grown into a perfect obsession. Throughout the years 1797 and 1798 he was vainly looking for a victory, whether on Italian soil or on the Mediterranean, which would serve to crush the Republic, now firmly seated in Italy by the terms of the Treaty of Campo Formio. But despite the hopes aroused by the departure of the dreaded and detested Napoleon Buonaparte to Egypt in May, 1798, affairs in Italy seemed to go from bad to worse, when in March of the following year, 1799, General Scherer from Mantua issued his proclamation to the people of Tuscany, condemning the inaction of the vacillating Grand-Duke Ferdinand III. (in spite of the latter's warm professions of devotion to the French Government), and announcing a forthcoming invasion of Tuscany in a peaceful spirit for the

228

true advantage of that country. This news fell like a thunderbolt on the Grand-Duke, who in fear and trembling at once published a manifesto calling on his subjects to admit the expected French troops with every mark of respect. Accordingly, on March 25, the republican army under Generals Gauthier and Miollis arrived at the Porta San Gallo, escorted by the rabble of Florence crying out " Morte ai codini ! " (Death to the aristocrats !), made a prisoner of the Grand-Duke, who was allowed twenty-four hours wherein to evacuate his capital for ever ; and set up the tree of liberty in the Piazza della Signoria, the historic square before the great Palazzo Vecchio. A number of sweeping decrees of a revolutionary nature were now promulgated by the conquering force, and as each of these began with the formula " Nous voulons " (we will), the sharp-witted Florentines promptly christened these invaders and also their sympathisers in the city as the *Nuvoloni*, a name that clung and was used in opposition to the term *Codini*, or old-fashioned aristocrats.[*]

With the loathed nation thus in practical possession of his place of residence, the indignation and disgust of Alfieri may be imagined. To remain in Florence under such circumstances seemed insupportable to him, and he had accordingly made beforehand all arrangements for his retirement in such an event, rather than to be called on to endure the odious chance of having officers of the French army, or officials of the new provisional government of Tuscany quartered in his house. A few hours before the actual appearance of the invaders therefore, Alfieri and the Countess, having packed or hidden all their belongings, left Casa Alfieri to take up their abode in a villa at Montughi, a spot about a mile and a half to the north-east of the Porta San Gallo, whereby the French entered Florence amid the acclamations of the mob on Lady Day, 1799. Here, vainly trying to turn a deaf ear to the alarming reports of the revolutionary doings in the

[*] G. Conti, *Firenze Vecchia*, p. 10.

city, the pair sought to distract and console themselves
by a severe and well-defined course of study, the poet
working with a pathetic ardour at his Greek and the
Countess occupying herself with her habitual reading
and writing. In this manner then they endeavoured to
meet their troubles and chagrin in the true spirit of philosophy. "Oppressed, but not subdued, by the universal
tyranny," says Alfieri, "we settled in our villa with only
a few servants, I and the sweet Half of Myself; and we
both set ourselves resolutely to study, for she is fairly
cognisant of English and German; knows both French
and Italian equally well; is fully versed in the literature
of these four races; and has some acquaintance through
translations with the classics." * Of her friend's occupation, Madame d'Albany, who evidently found his
latest craze to acquire Greek, somewhat trying, writes
thus in a humorous vein, to the Abbé di Caluso :—"Our
Friend has no need of witnesses to assure you of his genuine
application to Greek, for I notice it every moment of
the day ! All is become Greek for us now, at table and
out driving; everything possesses its Greek name, and
he has nothing in his mouth but Greek declensions
and conjugations. Now, at last being better versed
in the tongue, he grows calmer; and I feel sure he
will acquire all the Greek that is possible for a man
who has begun to learn that language at so mature an
age." †

Of her own quiet and studious existence in the villa at
Montughi, the Countess gives a brief description to
Teresa Mocenni in a letter written during this period of
retreat.

* *Vita*, vol. ii. p. 265. This passage concerning the linguistic abilities
of the Countess of Albany has given rise to many satirical witticisms on the
attainments of that lady, seeing how imperfectly she wrote both in French
and Italian. Says Bertana : "One can judge of her proficiency in English
and German from her skill in French and Italian ! "

† Mazzatinti, p. 331. *Note.*—This quotation is a postscript by the
Countess to a letter from Alfieri himself to Caluso, describing his progress
in the study of Greek.

230

" My health is good, and we are living quietly in the country. I have seen no further sign of military preparations, for I have not set foot in Florence since the twenty-fifth of March, the day of our departure, and I have never walked beyond our own *podere* or that of our neighbours. I pass from my writing-table to the garden, and from the garden to meals, after which I return again to the garden. I go to bed at half-past nine and rise at half-past four in the morning. I almost lead the life of a nun, except that instead of singing the praises of God I admire his handiwork, and follow in books, step by step, those who have admired it before me with a deeper knowledge. Milton was thoroughly permeated with the sublime nature of the Deity, and magnifies it with enthusiasm in his poem of *Paradise Lost*, which I am reading with intense pleasure. The operations of mankind appear of such slight significance when one considers the immensity of the globe and of the stars ; a fact that we now see proved in the mischief wrought by men's hands during the past ten years. All that is quickly made, is quickly destroyed ; such is the law of Nature." *

As to the daily course of reading in which the Countess indulges, we are enlightened yet further by her account in a letter to Teresa Mocenni, written a few months before the retirement to the Florentine villa.

" As soon as I get my remittance from Rome, I shall set to again and purchase a second library. I have already collected five or six hundred volumes, but I want to see once more my three thousand books, which was the extent of my library in Paris. I shall send you a catalogue of my books to make your choice from, but if you will entrust yourself to my supervision, I shall prescribe a course of reading for you which will enable you to classify your studies in your head. As for myself, I began with the Bible and all works appertaining to it, such as the *History*

* Pélissier, pp. 176, 177.

of the Jews, by Josephus ; the *History of the Jews and their Relations with foreign Nations*, by Prideaux, a very interesting work ; but this little Palestine, the home of the Jewish people, was tormented by its neighbours and yet showed great powers of resistance. Josephus' description of the siege of Jerusalem under Titus is a piece of history well worth reading. I have also read other books dealing with the Jews, including the *Moeurs des Israelites*, by Fleury. Having completed my studies in this direction, I began upon ecclesiastical history, so as to understand our own religion and the origin of ecclesiastical laws. Moscherni's treatise on this subject particularly interested me. I have also skimmed through Fleury, a Roman Catholic, for the former writer is a Lutheran. Having finished this great undertaking, I approached Herodotus, with a full history of Greece, by Gillies, that I am now reading ; after which I shall take Thucydides, Xenophon, &c. I always, however, read prose and poetry on alternate days, so as to undergo a course of epic poetry, starting with Homer, Vergil, *the Thebaid, the Argonauts*, and then the modern poets according to their dates—Camoens, Tasso, Milton, *the Henriade* of Voltaire and the like. Last week, I have begun to read Greek drama, using French, English and Italian translations of the plays. There, my Teresa, is the order of my studies ! Early in the morning, before rising from bed and during odd moments in the day, I also read some works of the present time."

Early in July, 1799, military reverses in Lombardy, due to the absence of Buonaparte in the Orient, rather unexpectedly compelled the French troops to evacuate Florence, to the delight and exultation of the recluse sulking at Montughi, who joyfully announces the welcome departure of the invaders to the Abbé di Caluso, (who, it may be remarked, had lately submitted to the new Republican Government at Turin, and had freely surrendered all his benefices).

232

" . . . I have spent the 102 days of the French tyranny over Florence entirely in a villa near the Capuchim convent at Montughi, in fine air ; nor did I once set foot in the city till July 6th, which was the day of its purification. At present I still live at the villa, but sometimes I descend into Florence, and especially on every occasion when Austrian troops arrive, so as to witness the transports, the jubilee and the genuine delight of the whole people in their liberators, although the men of Arezzo have done even more than the Austrians. Tuscany is now wholly free from the invader, and the sun once more turns his face in splendour upon us." *

Alfieri's content was fated to be of short duration. In the spring of the following year, 1800, Buonaparte returned from Egypt, again crossed the Alps, and by the decisive victory of Marengo on June 14, laid the whole of Italy prostrate before him. Once more the French troops under General Miollis were in command of Florence, whither the deposed Grand-Duke Ferdinand had most prudently not yet ventured to return, whilst the ultimate fate of Tuscany and of its capital was left hanging in the political balance to await the pleasure and decision of the victor. This most trying state of uncertainty, to which the Countess makes such frequent allusion in her letters to Teresa Mocenni, lasted for nearly two years, and the constant suspense induced thereby helped greatly to shorten the life of Alfieri, already harassed by cares of money, and by fears perhaps not wholly ungrounded of some political act of revenge upon himself. It is evident from her letters that the Countess of Albany must have passed through a most anxious and troublesome period during these last few years of her companion's existence. The natural violence and irritability of the poet grew more marked with his rapidly declining health, so that acquaintances, friends, and even his beloved lady were

* Mazzatinti, p. 345.

sometimes made to feel the weight of his savage and capricious temper. For reasons of economy forced to put down his saddle horses, he was wont to wander in all weathers outside the gates of Florence, or in the dank chilly churches filled with monuments of illustrious Italians dead and gone. In these solitary rambles his embittered soul found some degree of consolation in composing satirical verse, as when he watched the droves of swine wallowing in the mire outside Porta Pinti, and in one of his sonnets compared the Tuscan porkers with the "tiger-monkeys" of France, to the disadvantage of the latter. Hating to be accompanied in these lonely walks, even by his lady, people would watch the patriot-poet muttering to himself his wayward fancies, and smile or sigh according to their disposition ; or else some enthusiastic reader of his tragedies, such us Ugo Foscolo, would follow the roving bard in secret to note his gestures of anger or despair. And if abroad he appeared a solitary and a misanthrope, in his own house he often must have been regarded as a veritable ogre by any luckless wight who was bold enough to seek an interview or a favour. The poor actor Antonio Morrochesi, in some theatrical reminiscences,* gives a ludicrous account of Alfieri's refusal to see him concerning a proposed performance of his own tragedy of *Saul*. The sound of the infuriated Count's voice, within his library, promptly consigning him to the devil, was enough to scare the expectant actor outside the door and to send him flying in haste down the richly carpeted stairway (which seems to have greatly impressed the poor suppliant as a curious fad in so great a genius), without daring to show himself in person. For the same reason, too, Melchiorre Delfino, the learned historian of San Marino, positively declined an introduction to Alfieri on seeing him abuse and belabour some boy for accidentally splashing his silk stock-

---

* *V. Alfieri in Firenze.* This little work contains an amusing account of the poet's violence, and also of his generosity, one of his redeeming virtues.

ALFIERI IN HIS LAST DAYS
From the portrait by F. X. Fabre

ings with water from a puddle. The poet continually
cuffed and reviled his servants on the smallest provocation, and merely expressed his regret for his brutality
towards them by leaving stray coins in conspicuous
places of his rooms for them to pocket. That he showed
himself rude and inconsiderate to his lady goes without
saying, and this attitude was sometimes even extended
to her guests in Casa Alfieri, as in the case of the great
linguist Mezzofanti. His eccentricity kept pace with his
uncontrollable violence, for, always sensitive to the
effects of heat and cold, he had his clothes specially
arranged with tapes and ribbons, so that portions of
them could be removed by his servants from any part of
his body, should a particular member feel too warm or to
chilly.* He became in short a human fiend of egotism,
selfishness and bad temper ; a veritable Eastern potentate
whose every wish was law ; and whose constant outbursts of passion made the whole house suffer from the
poor Countess of Albany down to the meanest servant in
his employment. That Alfieri had genuine good qualities
none will deny. He was honourable in all his dealings,
and never made his reduced finances an excuse for running
into debt. He was generous in the extreme to the
Countess, who from the time of Cardinal York's flight
from Rome, in 1798, must have been left for a short period
absolutely penniless ; a catastrophe which Lady Holland,
who knew her well at this time, says she bore cheerfully
and without complaint. Yet in spite of all, the Countess
in her confidential correspondence with her Sienese
friends continually harps on her ever-present fear of the
death of Alfieri, for whose sake alone (so she solemnly
avers) she desires to cling to an existence that the present
political troubles had made odious to her. Although
scarcely past fifty years of age, the poet was evidently
failing, and his constitution, already somewhat enfeebled,
was being heavily over-taxed by his constant and unreasonable devotion to study, by his financial cares, by

* G. Biagi, *Aneddotti Letterari* (*Alfieriana*, p. 180).

his political hatreds and disappointments, and by his exhausting fits of anger and resentment

In the autumn of 1801, Alfieri was seized with his first severe attack, which was partly, at least, due to his over-zealous study of the classics. The skill and attention of Doctor Édouard Fabre managed to save the patient on this occasion, but there can be little doubt that from this time onward he was a doomed man, who was hastening his end by his own restlessness and imprudence.

"The Poet," writes Madame d'Albany to Theresa Mocenni on September 12, 1801, "has been ill. His gout has flown to his chest, and he has had a bad cough followed by loss of blood, which has troubled him greatly. He has also suffered much from his head, all the result of over-working during the last month. So foolish of him ! The craving to write and to study is the only passion that is increased by its use, and one carries it to excess ; that is what our Poet has done. And therefore for the last week he has not been allowed so much as to open a book, as the result of having opened too many of them."

Again, a week later, Madame d'Albany cannot give a much improved account to her friend at Siena. "The Poet is a little better, but his illness has greatly alarmed me. He has lost a little blood, and the gout has again flown to his chest, the result of a movement of his head, which has brought the blood to the upper regions."

It was Doctor Fabre, as we have said, who contrived to restore Alfieri on this occasion ; and on October 3, the Countess is able to report his convalescence.

"The Poet is quite well. Dr. Fabre has cured him, by giving him some pills, which have greatly benefited his digestion, which was his weak spot, because he worked too much and rested too little, like so many men of letters."

It is needless to state again that the political views of

236

the once-ardent republican poet had undergone a complete revulsion under stress of the events following upon the French Revolution. The hater of kings and courts, who had once expressed his contempt of poor old Metastasio for making too obsequious a bow to the great Empress Maria-Teresa and who had expatriated himself from his own native land of Piedmont on account of the humiliating restrictions imposed by the Sardinian monarchy, had absolutely turned his political coat. He was now one of the first to hasten and pay his homage to the amiable but bigoted old King Charles-Emmanuel, who had sought asylum in Florence after his expulsion from his capital of Turin. " Voici votre tyran ! " were the words wherewith the fallen monarch, once the butt of Alfieri's hatred and contempt, greeted with good-natured irony his ex-subject, as he saw the poet approach to salute him at the villa of Poggio Imperiale. So altered were his views and so bitter his detestation of the French, that Alfieri absolutely refused to make the acquaintance of General Miollis, the new commandant of Florence, a man of most upright and ascetic life, an ideal republican, who spurned all the luxury that Italy could offer, and moreover a man of letters and knowledge, who had expressed himself as anxious to make Alfieri's acquaintance. The incident is described at some length in the pages of the *Vita*, where the writer speaks of his attitude of stern refusal with intense satisfaction.

Miollis, having vainly called at Casa Alfieri, finally wrote a polite note to the author of the *Miso-Gallo*, begging him to name an hour when it would be convenient to receive him privately as a guest eager to make the personal acquaintance of so great a genius. To this Alfieri replied, that if Miollis, as military master of the vanquished city of Florence, were to *command* his presence, he would be compelled to attend at the Citadel ; but if on the other hand the General's request had only been made for private reasons, then the poet begged to be excused the honour of the proposed interview. In case the General might be led to call again at the house on the Lung' Arno, Alfieri had caused to be suspended near the entrance a large placard printed and signed by himself, stating that " Vittorio Alfieri, not being a public character and presuming himself to be his own master, at least in his own house, gives notice to all comers that he does not receive persons he does not know ; nor messages, parcels, and letters, save from those who are his friends." *

This piece of gratuitous rudeness was met with quiet dignity on the part of the soldier insulted, who will in the opinion of all fair-minded people probably be admitted as the victor in this curious passage of arms between an Italian poet and a French general.

" In reading the tragedies of Vittorio Alfieri," was Miollis' reply to Alfieri's note ; " I thought him a different sort of man, and I therefore desired his acquaintance. Realising now his true nature, I have no longer that desire.—MIOLLIS, GENERAL COMMANDING IN TUSCANY. Brumaire 30, An IX."

Alfieri's own version of this ridiculous and not very creditable incident is styled by himself to his own complete satisfaction, " *Dialogue between a Lion in a Cage (Alfieri) and his Keeper, a Crocodile (Miollis).*" †

The year 1801 saw further troubles piling themselves up to add to the mingled alarm and irritation of Casa Alfieri. Before the close of this year the poet learned to his deep distress of the sudden death of his young nephew, the Count of Cumiana, his sister's only son, and consequently the heir-male of the ancient family of Alfieri of Cortemilia. This sad event greatly affected him, for he was now suffering much, partly as the result of bad health and partly from the lowness of spirits induced by the passing events in the political world. The treaty of Lunéville, to which the exhausted Emperor had been thankful to accede in February, finally settled the fate

* *Vita II.*, pp. 280, 281. Teza, *Vita, Lettere e Giornali*, p. 447.
† Mazzatinti, *Le Carte Alfieriane*.

238

of Tuscany, that had so long remained unsolved.   By this compact all hope of a restoration of the exiled Ferdinand III. was dissipated, for the omnipotent Napoleon now declared the former Grand-Duchy a kingdom under the name of the Kingdom of Etruria, with Louis de Bourbon, Prince of Parma, for its first nominal sovereign, who would in reality be merely a puppet of French policy.   The news was received with deep misgiving and vexation in Casa Alfieri, whereof the Countess relieves her mind to her friend Teresa Mocenni in the following dismal epistle.

" . . . The Peace has satisfied nobody here.   They have sung *Te Deums* and given assemblies, but nobody attended them.   We have no cause for congratulation at this fresh treaty, which is as hateful as every other act of the conquerors.   It is but a truce, which will only last until some favourable event can deliver us, or until the House of Austria is grown sufficiently powerful again to re-commence the war.   The French have never succeeded in remaining long in Italy, and though at this moment they are its absolute masters, they will only pillage it and devour it hastily, so as to get more money to spend in France without taxing Buonaparte's subjects.   Our Arch-priest (whom I salute) will be truly glad to see a reduction in the garrison of occupation at Siena.   We have just seen a number of the soldiers of the Cisalpine Republic pass by on their way to their homes.   They have notified their presence here by looting some shops during the only night they stopped in Florence.   One cannot imagine how so undisciplined an army can last intact.

"*Tiriamo avanti con coraggio.* We have our moments of despair, the Poet and I.   Right am I in saying, ' the world has ever been the same ' ; but I could well have been spared the spectacle of these late and repeated scenes.   We have spent thirty (*sic*) years of our life so happily, that Fate might indeed have left us to end our career in the same state.   The Grand-Duke's lot is much to be pitied in having to surrender so fair a realm, the heritage of his ancestors, simply because it suited Consul Buonaparte's whim, after he had invaded the country during an armistice ! Ah, what injustice from above and below ! If I had been *dévote*, the experiences of the past ten years would have turned me into an infidel ! Adieu, Arch-priest, the world is a vile thing. . . .

" Our poor Grand-Duke is in despair at the idea of never returning to Tuscany, whilst the Grand-Duchess weeps night and day. Torregiani, who has returned here, told me this. That poor prince keeps on saying, ' *I was prepared for everything save that !* ' "

The following year was rendered less melancholy to the master and mistress of Casa Alfieri by the welcome presence of their beloved friend and faithful correspondent, the Abbé di Caluso, who paid a special visit to Florence in order to be with the poet, now slowly sinking into the grave, as was evident to all around him. Yet the indomitable nature of the man triumphed over physical weakness. He led the same life as of old; walking, riding and driving; spent hours daily in his library writing a series of comedies, revising former works, and studying the Greek authors with an almost childish delight in the latest accomplishment of his tireless industry. So pleased was he with his prowess in this dead language, and so elated with the discriminating praise bestowed upon his labours by the Abbé di Caluso, that one of the last acts of his life, and indeed, the very last incident mentioned by him in the Autobiography he was inditing, was his playful invention of a mock Order—" the Order of Homer "—which he bestowed upon himself as a reward for his application in mastering Greek at the age of fifty. The collar of this novel decoration, which the poet occasionally wore round his neck, was of gold set with gems and engraved with the names of twenty-four poets of various nations and periods, whilst on its pendant was a cameo portrait of Homer. With his habitual infantile conceit, Alfieri composed a Greek elegiac couplet extolling his new invention, which may roughly be rendered thus :

> To call me a genuine knight were no great misnomer,
> When I vested myself with the Order of Homer.*

This description of the Order of Homer concludes the self-told story of Alfieri's life as inscribed and explained by himself, and it bears the date " May 14, 1803." The sands were now indeed running out fast, and the poet was growing daily more feeble and irritable, and leaving unheeded the entreaties of his lady, who did what was possible to urge her companion to a more reasonable mode of living. To the last he was engaged upon his Autobiography, and scarcely had he completed this work to the point already mentioned than, whilst out driving on the afternoon of October 3, he caught a severe chill in the stomach, which at last compelled him to keep his bed. All that the devotion of the Countess and the skill of Dr. Edouard Fabre could compass was done ; but Alfieri was quick to perceive that this illness of his was mortal, whereupon he prepared to meet death with something of the old Roman fortitude he had so extolled in his dramas. Perhaps he was really pleased that the boon he had so often prayed for, at least on paper, that his own death might precede that of his lady, was now likely to be realised. On his sick-bed, whilst he was being tenderly nursed by the Countess, his thoughts went out to the dearly beloved Abbé di Caluso, his oldest surviving friend, and though suffering and feeble he was able to compose an affectionate letter of farewell with a certain most particular request to the Abbé.

" As I am expecting almost daily to succumb to the desperate illness that is now consuming me, I have thought it well to leave these few lines to be given to you in proof that to my very last moment on earth you were present in my mind and were very dear to my heart.

* *Vita*, vol. ii. pp. 301–303.

"The Personage, whom above everything else in this world I have venerated and loved, can some day tell you the details of my illness. I implore and conjure you to do all in your power to visit and console her, and to arrange with her concerning the various requests I have made with regard to my writings.

"At this moment I do not want to give you further pain by telling you more. In yourself I have known a man without parallel for goodness in every relation of life. I depart loving and esteeming you, and priding myself on the possession of your friendship, even if I have not deserved it. Farewell. Farewell." *

A last letter was also written to his sister, the Comtessa Giulia Alfieri di Cumiana, telling her of his impending death, and recommending to her the Countess of Albany, who would be rendered inconsolable thereby. He likewise informs his sister that he has left the Countess heiress to all his property which was not comprised in the *Donation* made to herself in 1778, adding that " the straitness of circumstances wherein this most estimable Personage finds herself, like all others, has urged me to this step." †

Vittorio Alfieri expired not in his bed, but in an easy chair beside the fire, early on the morning of October 8. According to the account, not necessarily a credible one, of the old Marchesa di Priè, a former flame of Alfieri's,‡ efforts were made by herself to introduce a priest into the dying man's chamber, since of late his softened attitude towards the old *régime* upset by the French Revolution had led many well-meaning persons to suppose he was anxious to become reconciled to the Church, whose ministers he had always professed to despise. But in any case, the patient was too far gone to be conscious of any such attempts, and the great poet finally passed away, as

* Teza, *Vita, Lettere e Giornali*, pp. 467, 468.
† *Ibidem*, p. 468.
‡ Reumont, *Gino Capponi e il suo Secolo*, pp. 32, 33.

the Countess herself relates, "like a bird without a struggle, like a lamp whose oil had all escaped." According to custom, the body was hastily placed in its coffin, and was exposed to the gaze of his comparatively few acquaintances or admirers in Florence, amongst the latter, however, being the poet Châteaubriand, who was gravely impressed with the tall commanding figure, the fine haughty features and the lofty intelligent forehead of "*il grande Astigiano*," as Vittorio Alfieri is constantly called in Italian history and literature.

The private character of Alfieri has so often been criticised in the course of this biography of the Countess of Albany, that perhaps a short but shrewd outside estimate of the man may be conveniently added here, in case our own judgment should be regarded as too severe or too prejudiced.

"Alfieri's character was exceedingly peculiar, and notwithstanding some fine and elevated points, cannot but be pronounced unamiable. Its most prominent features were an indomitable energy of will, which was shown by the whole of his literary career ; a ceaseless craving for celebrity ; and a boundless self-esteem, which exhibited itself in a reserved haughtiness of manner, and made him really a bigoted aristocrat at heart, while professing and supposing himself a violent democrat."—In commenting therefore on his relations with the Countess of Albany, it is as well to bear in mind the extraordinary nature of the man, and to consider the extreme difficulties and trials of the lady's life-long attachment to and connection with so erratic, selfish, violent and wilful a genius. That the Countess must have endured much is obvious ; yet her placid nature, combined with her deep and unalterable affection, was able to support her throughout her long and difficult task of ministering to so troublesome and often so thankless a companion. With his death however, all her past trials and crosses were forgotten, and there was only remembered the real loyalty the poet owned to herself, his "*amante ed amica*." His fits of temper, his frequent abuse of herself and of her friends, his numerous infidelities, were all forgiven and forgotten in the absorbing contemplation of their mutual affection, and of Alfieri's stupendous genius, which it now became her chief duty and her sole consolation to exhibit and explain to the world at large. That the Countess of Albany was overwhelmed with grief at her companion's death, even her most remorseless critic, Signore Bertana, is fain to admit; although he has the hardness of heart to declare that " the tears of the Stolberg woman prove but little. Indifferent to the death of her Friend, she could not be, but it seems to me that Death possesses a special virtue in arousing old and spent affections." * In confutation of this unkind statement, it is only necessary to peruse the letter which the Countess wrote in reply to the condolences of Alfieri's old friend in Paris, the Hellenist scholar, Monsieur D'Anse de Villoison, two months after her friend's death, for there is a ring of genuine despair and tenderness in this communication, which ought to disarm all suspicion of insincerity in the writer.

"FLORENCE, *December* 9, 1803.

"I was quite sure, my dear Sir, you would be deeply affected by the terrible loss I have sustained. You know by experience how deadly a blow it is for me to lose One with whom I have lived for twenty-six years, and who has never caused me a moment's annoyance; One whom I have ever loved, respected and adored. I am the most unhappy creature alive. By this cruel blow I have lost my consolation, my companion, and almost my very mind. I am alone now in a world that has grown odious to me. The greatest happiness, and indeed, the only happiness I can look for, will be to go and join this Incomparable Friend. . . .

"He was quite well on the morning of the 3rd of October, and did his work as usual; but on my return to the house at four o'clock, I found him feverish. The gout then

* Bertana, p. 276.

244

settled in his stomach, which has long been weak, so that he could scarcely eat anything for fear of indigestion which was brought on by every morsel he swallowed at meals. Finally, on Saturday the 8th, after spending rather a better night than he had lately experienced, he grew very faint, his sight became dimmed, and he died quietly, like a bird, without a struggle, quite unconscious of death. Ah Monsieur! What a blow! I have lost my all. I feel as if my heart had been torn away. Even now I cannot realise I shall never see him again. Remember that for the last ten years I have scarcely ever left his side; that we have spent our days together. I used to sit near him when he was at work, and I used vainly to implore him not to over-tax his powers; but his craving for study increased daily, as he sought to drive from his mind the passing events of the time by constant occupation. His mind was always bent on what was serious, and Florence afforded him no relaxation. I keep on reproaching myself for not having urged him to make a tour, so as to distract his mind. His burning soul could no longer dwell in a body that it constantly threatened to consume. He is happy, in that he has ceased to behold our disasters. His fame will surely spread. The loss is mine alone, for he made the joy of my life. I am too restless now to busy myself. Formerly the days were ever too short, and I used to read for seven or eight hours; but now I cannot open any of my books, which appear hateful to me." *

As soon as the violence of her grief had abated somewhat, the Countess prepared to carry out the wishes of her dead Friend with regard to his numerous manuscripts; and with the help of the sympathetic Abbé di Caluso, who had come to Florence for this purpose, and also with the assistance of the attentive Fabre, the work of preparing a full edition of Alfieri's writings, both pub-

* Letter included in the Appendix to the *Vita*. Also Del Cerro, pp. 246–248.

lished and unpublished, for the press, was being slowly pushed forward for the next four years. The Abbé, to whom Alfieri had bequeathed his favourite red cornelian signet ring with the portrait of Dante, was busily employed in sorting through the papers in the library of Casa Alfieri, which henceforward was kept by the Countess as a sort of shrine sacred to the memory of its departed occupant, nothing being disturbed or touched save by the hands of herself or of some devoted friend, such as Fabre or the Abbé di Caluso. But the intense devotion to the Friend and the engrossing desire to see his writings and name made famous throughout Italy and Europe, were urging the Countess to take measures beyond that of merely producing his literary works, for she was contemplating a monument to be erected in the great church of Santa Croce, the Pantheon of the illustrious dead of Florence, where Alfieri's corpse had already been buried. By his will, the poet had left the Countess any money he may have possessed, and though probably this was little enough, yet since the return of her brother-in-law to Rome and the recent grant of an annual pension to him of £4000 from the Privy Purse of George III., the Stuart annuity of 6000 *scudi* was once again being paid her fully and punctually.*
Though far from wealthy therefore, the Countess, who always showed herself a capable and frugal manager, was prepared to expend a substantial sum upon a monument worthy at once of Alfieri's genius and of her own undying affection. For this purpose she now approached the great sculptor, Antonio Canova, with the suggestion that he would undertake the task that was equally dear to her heart and her ambition, and the sculptor immediately assured her of his willingness to carry out her request.

The proposal to erect a colossal cenotaph to the late Vittorio Alfieri, who during his lifetime had railed at

* For the Royal Pension to the Cardinal of York, see *The Last of the Royal Stuarts*, pp. 227–241.

priests and popes, and had expired without becoming definitely reconciled to the Church, was not favourably regarded in clerical circles in Florence. The Franciscan friars of Santa Croce, perhaps egged on by Archbishop Martini and some of the higher clergy, affected to demur at the idea of the Countess of Albany utilising their church to glorify an alleged sceptic. A certain learned Chevalier Angelo d'Elci, a deep student of the classics and a composer of long-forgotten satires, also used his influence to prevent the erection of the monument, possibly out of some secret grudge against the memory of Alfieri.* This attempt of d'Elci's was most warmly resented by the Countess, who later in a letter to the poet Ugo Foscolo expresses her undying detestation of the man, who sought to thwart her aims and to diminish the fame of her friend.

" I have known this old pedant from the age of eighteen. Although a handsome boy, he was the laughing-stock of all young people on account of his clumsiness and eccentricity. As an older man, he has grown jealous, malevolent, precise and pedantic without genius or imagination. . . . I hate him, and after Buonaparte he is the man I most abhor in the whole world. Nor am I unreasonable in this, for it was he who made every effort to induce the friars of Santa Croce to stop the erection of the mausoleum to Count Alfieri, telling them he had been a scoffer at religion." †

For some little time, this unexpected opposition on the part of the Florentine clergy seemed likely to meet with success, so much so that the Countess was meditating to erect her mausoleum elsewhere. " For myself," so she writes to her friend the Chevalier Cerretani;

* A fine collection of first editions of the classics, presented by the Chevalier d'Elci to the city of Florence, is preserved in the Rotunda of the Laurentian Library, together with the donor's bust.

† Del Cerro, *Epistolario . . . di Ugo Foscolo, &c.*, p. 31.

" it is all the same. I shall place the monument either
in the Duomo of Florence, or in the Pantheon in Rome,
or in the cathedral of Milan, or in Ste. Geneviève in
Paris ; somebody will be glad to accept it." *

Meanwhile, the model for the mausoleum was being
constructed in Rome, and the necessary estimates were
being prepared, most of this correspondence being entrusted to Fabre, who wrote numerous letters on the
subject both to Canova himself and to his brother, the
Abbé Gian-Battista Canova ; the Countess herself
having already written to thank the sculptor for his
willingness to undertake the commission.

" I thank you, my dear Canova, for agreeing to design
the tribute I wish to render to this Incomparable Friend,
who admired you as much as I do. I should have preferred one or two complete figures, but I defer to your
judgment, for I feel sure you will achieve something
worthy of your own reputation, of the Person for whom
you are employed, and of the intended site of the monument. I therefore await your design with impatience,
and flatter myself you will furnish it with all despatch.
I am the more grateful to you, since I am well aware of
the immense number of works awaiting your attention ;
but I should like your own name that confers honour on
Italy, to be united with that of so celebrated a man ;
whilst my own name will obtain a reflected glory from its
association with yours and his. I find no consolation
save in immortalising my attachment for twenty-six
years to such a genius, and in mourning for him all the
remainder of my days. Accept again, my dear Canova,
the token of gratitude and esteem.

"*March* 12.   LOUISE DE STOLBERG, C. D'ALBANY." †

During the autumn of the same year the Countess, in

* L. G. Pélissier, *Canova, la Comtesse d'Albany et le Tombeau d'Alfieri*
(*Nuovo Archivio Veneto*, 1902, vol. iii. p. 147. Note i.).
† *Ibidem*, p. 154.

company with Fabre, made a hasty journey to Rome to visit the sculptor's studio, and to inspect the working-model of the mausoleum, which had just been completed. The cost had already been settled between the pair, and was in the opinion of Madame d'Albany most reasonable.

" I pledge myself to pay M. le Chevalier Antonio Canova 8000 Roman *scudi* for the execution in marble of the model he has already made of the monument of Count Vittorio Alfieri. All expenses of the work are to be included in this sum, excepting the socle of grey marble which will be furnished in Florence.

" I also charge my heirs to consider this present contract as sacred, and to execute it with all speed, in the event of my death before the completion of the mausoleum. . . .

" Signed in Rome, October 23rd, 1804.

" LOUISE DE STOLBERG, COMTESSE D'ALBANY." *

For six years the hard-worked Canova was occupied with the commission, so that the mausoleum was only finally set up in Santa Croce so late as the autumn of 1810, at a time when the Countess and Fabre were both absent in Paris, the final arrangements being left to Dr. Edouard Fabre. In the last month of the same year Madame d'Albany remitted the final instalment of the total sum of 10,000 *scudi* for the completed monument, the oval base of grey marble costing apparently the extra 2000 *scudi*. Early in January 1811, the Countess, on receiving Canova's final acknowledgment of payment, again expresses her satisfaction with his efforts : " I cannot thank you sufficiently for the Monument, with which I am perfectly satisfied ; it is worthy of yourself and of Him for whom it was intended. I have a double pleasure in thus seeing your two names united. Certainly, Italy can boast of the production in this century of two men equal to her antique heroes." †

* *Ibidem*, p. 156.   † *Ibidem*, p. 241.

The monument itself, which is well known to, though not greatly admired by the many persons to whom the famous Florentine church of Santa Croce is familiar, offers a ponderous example of the classical style, whereof Canova in Italy and Flaxman in England were the principal exponents ; nor is Alfieri's tomb usually regarded as a favourable specimen of Canova's taste or skill. It represents the Genius of Italy, a tall graceful female figure robed and crowned, mourning over an altar adorned with tragic masks and wreaths, and bearing a medallion with a good profile portrait of the deceased poet. On the oval base below is a brief but prominent inscription cut in the solid marble—*Vittorio Alfierio Astensi Aloisia e Principibus Stolbergis Albanie Comitissa M.P. Ann. MDCCCX* — (To Vittorio Alfieri of Asti, Louise Countess of Albany and Princess of Stolberg placed this monument, 1810) ;—" In the union of these two names inscribed thus for all eternity," says the Countess' leading modern biographer, " there is a serene piece of audacity that amounts to a superior definition of morality." *

On beholding her monument on returning to Florence, in 1811, the Countess in no wise altered her first favourable opinion, telling one correspondent, the Baron de Castille, that " it is magnificent, eclipsing all the other monuments in the church, so that they appear mean by comparison. I send you a sketch of it. It cost 10,000 *scudi*. . . . What particularly pleases me is that it has been all paid for, even to the last hundred *livres*. We people of method do not care for debts ! " †

Other friends of the Countess were less inclined to share her complacent sense of satisfaction in Canova's production ; and Sismondi, always frank and critical, who saw the recently unveiled monument whilst passing through Florence in November 1810, wrote his candid impressions at once to the Countess, then in Paris.

* *Ibidem*, p. 243.
† *Ibidem*, p. 239.

MONUMENT TO ALFIERI, BY CANOVA,
IN SANTA CROCE, FLORENCE

Alinari

"GENEVA, *November* 19, 1810.

". . . In passing through Florence lately I inspected with admiration the splendid monument you have lately had erected. I am a very poor judge of works of art owing to my defective sight, so that I have never been able to form my taste properly, if I can aspire to taste at all. However, there seemed to me an imposing grandeur and simplicity in Canova's work. The figure of Italy is most pathetic, lovely and dignified ; she looks a queen in mourning. I miss—but perhaps I am mistaken—a certain symmetry that one expects to find in sculptured tombs of this class. The colossal figure of Italy at one side of the mausoleum seems rather to require a pendant, as in Michelangelo's Tombs of the Medici, where all the corners of the monuments are occupied. There they form a true part of the design ; whilst here, in Canova's work, Italy appears rather as an outside spectator, and belongs really to the crowd who mourn for the hero and not to the tomb itself." *

This shrewd piece of criticism on the monument's lack of symmetry may well be applied to the Alfieri Tomb to-day, although few persons visiting Santa Croce nowadays pause long before the great mass of marble with its weeping Genius, since modern taste requires a different type of art for its satisfaction, so that Alfieri's costly monument and sonorous tragedies which delighted his own generation are alike neglected or despised in this.

According to the usual Florentine custom, sonnets, odes, and epigrams on the newly erected mausoleum were showered upon the famous sculptor. These proved mostly complimentary, though a few expressed dissatisfaction with this new addition to the glories of Santa Croce, which dwarfed so many of the older historic monuments of Donatello and Rossellino. One of these scribblers is at least sharp enough to have a fling at Canova for represent-

* St. Réné Taillandier, *Lettres Inédites de J. C. L. de Sismondi, &c.* pp. 128, 129.

251

ing Italy clothed and crowned, after the late invasions of the French and the ruthless plundering of her choicest treasures of art from Florence, Venice, and Rome.

Canova questa volta l' has bagliata,
Fè l'Italia vestita, ed è spogliata !

(In the well-draped Italia our sculptor has blundered,
Since her raiment and jewels have long since been plundered !)

It was doubtless Alfieri's original intention that the ashes of himself and his " Donna Amata " should ulti-mately rest in the same tomb ; but Canova's great monu-ment in the nave of Santa Croce stands alone in memory of the poet, whilst the lady who erected it reposes in a corner of the distant Chapel of the Sacrament in the south transept of the vast church.

CHAPTER XIII

FRANÇOIS-XAVIER FABRE

" If grief does not slay—and very rarely has it such power—
then after the tears, after the wringing of the heart, after the
days of mute despair, they who are struck by a great irreparable
loss must of necessity return to their usual life, and do no more
than obtain sweet ointment for the unhealed wounds from their
past memories, together with the purifying force of every past
mistake, and even of every thought. This Louise Countess of
Albany ought, and was able to do, and this she did."

A. SASSI, *La Vedovanza dell Amica dell' Alfieri*

As time gradually began to blunt the sharp arrows of
her grief, and as the self-set task of editing Alfieri's
complete works, with the aid of Fabre and the Abbé di
Caluso, gave her constant occupation, the Countess of
Albany slowly resumed her normal course of life, preparing to settle indefinitely in the city and in the very house
where her Friend had so lately passed away. She showed
no sign of following Alfieri to the tomb, for though her
sorrow was genuine, deep and lasting, her health seems
to have been in no wise affected by the shock, or by the
loss of one whose personality undoubtedly filled the
greatest part in her existence. From the even tenor
of her past daily life, always somewhat mechanically
arranged in accordance with Alfieri's fixed principles,
the Countess found no great difficulty in falling into
a monotonous but not unpleasant routine, which included
early rising, several hours of study or of painting, a
regular morning walk, and the habit of receiving a few
persons daily at dinner, and a goodly number of acquaintances at her nightly receptions. Hitherto the presence
of the morose and soured poet had proved a considerable

253

obstacle to that life. of entertainment and intellectual
society which the Countess especially loved, and had
carried out with such success in her Parisian *hôtel*. So
far as she was able, therefore, she assumed once more
her favourite part as a social hostess, though on a smaller
scale, in a smaller city, and with a smaller income. One
word as to her financial position may not come amiss
here. By Alfieri's death she had certainly lost a considerable portion of their joint income, whilst her commission
to Canova for the monument in Santa Croce, with its
cost of 10,000 Roman *scudi* (about £3000 sterling at
least), must naturally have made a large inroad on her
already diminished fortune. Certainly, the lady was
hard pressed at this moment, and with her thoughts
always turning longingly to the comfortable French
pension which that odious Revolution had filched from
her, she began to hope that possibly the new master of
France might be inclined to regard a claim coming from
herself with a favourable eye.

The Countess had already known the Empress of the
French as the Vicomtesse Beauharnais in her Parisian
days, and she had even written to her with congratula-
tions upon the escape of herself and her husband (whom
she was constantly abusing in her private letters to
Madame Mocenni) upon their escape from the recent
attempt at assassination in 1801. Her letter on this
occasion was evidently conceived in the warmest terms
of apparent joy and sincerity, as the following reply
from the future Empress will show.

"PARIS, 1801.

"How deeply grateful I am to you, dear Friend, for
the affectionate and sympathetic interest you display
in Buonaparte and myself. A friendship so distinguished as yours brings some consolation amid the
terrible alarms and continual dangers to which we are
exposed, so that we regret them less when they arouse

254

evidence of an esteem as genuine as that which you express.

"JOSÉPHINE BONAPARTE (*née* LAPAGERIE)." *

This communication, with its gracious and warm reply from Joséphine, seemed a propitious beginning to her projected scheme, though the Countess evidently did not dare pursue the idea of obtaining a pension from the First Consul during the few remaining years of Alfieri's life. Yet she probably nursed the idea in strict secrecy, for no doubt she also built upon the ultimate success of such an attempt, seeing that her sister, Françoise-Claudia Comtesse d'Arberg, later became the trusted and valued lady-in-waiting to the new Empress. For this purpose, the Countess selected as her intermediary a certain Chevalier Luigi Angiolini, in the diplomatic service, who loved to spend his spare time in serving persons of quality and importance, and had already assisted Alfieri and herself in some financial matters a few years before. To this willing acquaintance therefore Madame d'Albany now applied in May 1804, a few months after Alfieri's death. Her demand for the lost French pension is curiously, but perhaps purposely, mixed up with a suggestion for Angiolini to arrange a marriage between the old Spanish Ambassador in Paris, Admiral Gravina, and her own youngest and unmarried sister, the Princess Gustavine of Stolberg-Gedern. After recapitulating the mutual advantages to both parties that would accrue from such an union, the Countess proceeds to make her own request in the moving terms which she knew well how to employ, appealing at once to Angiolini's personal vanity (which was doubtless great) and to the high esteem wherein he was held by herself and Alfieri; and also painting her own position of bereavement and poverty in the most dismal colours. To both these demands the sympathetic Angiolini replied that he would attempt his utmost,

* Reumont, *Appendix*, p. 174.

255

and no doubt he did all that was possible, although in the end neither was the desired match between the mature Gustavine de Stolberg and the elderly Admiral arranged, nor was the lost pension ever restored by Napoleon Buonaparte. The curious Memorandum, drawn up on this occasion for the guidance of the Buonapartes and of Talleyrand, contains some very strange statements, including the admission that in the spring of 1802 the Countess of Albany had declined to avail herself of Napoleon's apparent offer to restore her own books as well as Alfieri's library, which had been confiscated during the Reign of Terror. So decided a step the Countess would never have dared to take without the knowledge and consent of Alfieri, and it is indeed mystifying to read that she declared herself willing to surrender up her " Incomparable Friend's " most treasured possession to Napoleon, provided he would grant her the coveted pension. The Memorandum proceeds to state that nobody had higher claims on the Emperor's generosity than the sister-in-law of the last heir of the Royal Stuarts and the widow of the late Pretender. Finally, a conviction is expressed that Napoleon himself, on persuing this paper with its list of the lady's claims, will promptly order the restoration of the suspended annuity to so worthy and exalted an applicant.*

Whether or no this amazing document was ever perused by Napoleon's own eyes is unknown; but it is certain that the Countess' claim was never admitted by him, though when, why, or where refused, it is impossible to say. We shrewdly suspect that the failure to obtain the annuity claimed, for which object the Countess had most certainly humbled herself considerably before a person for whom in private she ever evinced (most truthfully) her cordial detestation, is largely responsible for the undying hatred she ever afterwards bore to the Emperor, and for the almost indecent

* G. Sforza, *La Vedova di Un Pretendente e Napoleone I*. Vitelleschi, vol. ii. pp. 561–566.

delight wherewith she gloated later over his humiliation and fall. And yet she must have had personal interviews with the Emperor in Paris during her honourable but enforced residence there in 1809–1810, so that it is therefore not unreasonable to presume that there must have been an element of personal as well as political dislike in her hostile attitude towards him. In this connection a curious but well-authenticated and characteristic anecdote is related of this visit of hers to Paris. Vague rumours having reached Napoleon's ears concerning the birth of a son and heir to Prince Charles-Edward Stuart a year or so after his marriage to the Stolberg princess, the Emperor was sufficiently interested or impressed by the story as to command the immediate presence of the Countess of Albany at the Tuileries. Here, the lady, much to her disgust, was left alone waiting in a room for some length of time, until Napoleon himself suddenly burst in, and with the brusque and tactless manner he so often assumed, suddenly demanded of the inwardly enraged but outwardly placid Countess, whether she had ever borne children. " *Mais jamais, Sire !* " replied she, with a most emphatic denial to a question so unexpected. " Then it's a pity ! " was Napoleon's sole comment, whereupon he immediately left the Stuart Queen alone in the room to find her way out of the palace as best she might.* A sharp refusal to grant her petition for the desired annuity, combined with a series of petty slights and with his abrupt command to reside for a year in Paris willy-nilly, were perhaps all-sufficient to account for her fierce loathing of the Emperor ; but in any case the relations between the Countess of Albany and Napoleon remain still very obscure, and indeed the contradictory Angiolini correspondence throws darkness rather than light upon this curious and not uninteresting side-issue in history.

With the death of the Cardinal of York in July 1807,

---

* Anecdote from a private source, communicated to me by the kindness and courtesy of the Honble Henry S. Littleton.

the indefatigable Countess made a further application, this time to the British king, by whom her request was actually granted, mainly at the instigation of the good-natured Sir John Hippisley. Early in the New Year of 1808, therefore, she had the intense satisfaction of reading the following welcome letter from Lord Hawkesbury, to Sir John, which set at rest all her fears as to the lack of a comfortable income for the evening of her life.

"WHITEHALL, *December* 22, 1807.

"SIR,—I had the honour of laying before the King the letter of the Countess of Albany to His Majesty, together with the letter I received from you upon the same subject.

"I have great satisfaction in informing you that I have received His Majesty's command to acquaint the Countess of Albany, through you, that the King has given directions that the sum of Sixteen Hundred Pounds a year should be paid to her, to commence from the period of the death of the late Cardinal of York, and to be paid in the same manner as the pension to the Cardinal was paid.

"His Majesty has at the same time commanded me to express his regret that the demands unavoidably made upon him in consequence of the distressing, calamitous situation of so many of the Sovereign Houses of Europe, so nearly connected with His Majesty, should preclude him from extending the allowance solicited by the Countess of Albany beyond the sum above stated.

"I have the honour to be, &c. &c.,

"HAWKESBURY." *

It might have been thought that Madame d'Albany, now in the receipt of a considerable and assured income both from the British Crown and from the estate of the late Cardinal of York, would have been content to allow the matter of her lost French pension to drop. But with

* Reumont, *Appendix*, pp. 371, 372.

the restoration of the Bourbons, in 1814, once again we find her petitioning for " the 60,000 *livres* or an equivalent," although the annuity was originally granted under Louis XV. on the sole consideration of her consent to become the wife of the hereditary foe of the House of Guelph, who happened at that moment to be a political asset of some slight value to French diplomacy and ambition. It seems very strange therefore that she should not have recognised the illogicality, to say nothing of the bad taste, of her appeal under such circumstances, seeing she was now in enjoyment of a substantial income from the very nation and Royal House that her marriage with the Stuart prince was primarily intended to hurt and annoy; but despite this anomaly the Countess continued to implore her friends in Paris to assist her in the attempt. Amongst those who particularly busied themselves with this commission was the good-natured Madame de Stael, herself sinking fast into the grave in the years after Waterloo. "From the depths of my bed, my dear Queen, I have never ceased to keep up my interest in the matter which touches you so closely," so she writes from her house in the Rue Royale on April 9, 1817; and again, a week later, she suggests, by means of her second husband, the youthful Monsieur Albert Rocca, that her *chère souveraine* should stoop to declare herself an English subject in order to improve her chances of obtaining the desired pension !

In any case this attempt to induce the recently restored Bourbon king to grant what had evidently been refused some ten years before by Napoleon, ended likewise in failure. For the rest of her days Madame d'Albany had to remain content with her annuity from the Royal Stuarts and the pension from the bounty of George III.; but the income accruing from these two sources was in reality ample to maintain her in comfort and in proper surroundings, though it would appear she never ceased to hanker after the pension she lost in the detested French Revolution, or to consider herself aggrieved alternately with Napoleon and Louis XVIII. for not admitting her professed claims to it.

•   •   •   •   •

" The elegant painter " (as Ugo Foscolo styles him), François-Xavier Fabre, has so often been mentioned in the course of this narrative that no further description of him is necessary here. For ten years he had been an intimate and an obsequious friend of Count Alfieri, to whom he looked up with awe and admiration as much for his aristocratic birth and position as for his acknowledged genius. His brother, Dr. Edouard Fabre, had been Alfieri's physician, so that both the brothers were held in high favour at Casa Alfieri long before the death of the master of the house. Alfieri's esteem both for the painter and for the doctor is undeniable, and to the former on completing his portrait he had addressed the sonnet

O tu nella sublime opra d'Apelle,
Di mano e in un di nome egregio Fabro

wherein he makes a playful pun on the words Fabre and *fabro*. This is certain and undeniable ;. but what is most difficult and disputed is the degree of intimacy that existed in these comparatively early days between the Countess of Albany and the painter. Much time has been wasted, or at least unprofitably spent, in trying to prove that long ere Alfieri's death, an intrigue of a most discreditable nature had arisen between Fabre and the Countess. Assuming the existence of this *liaison*, some have declared that Alfieri himself was ignorant of this incident ; whilst others equally assert that, though cognisant of it, he was too proud or too generous to notice such a thing, or to upbraid the lady whom in the past he had extolled as his " Degno Amore," his " Donna Amata," the "metà di stesso," and had lauded in other endearing terms. It is perhaps needless to state that on such a point the evidence is both scanty and obscure. The general opinion in Italy, however, notably as proclaimed in the various biographical sketches and treatises which appeared about the time of the Alfieri Centenary in October 1903, seems to be that the Countess of Albany was certainly guilty ; that she deceived Alfieri ; and that her conduct made the last few years of his life miserable. It is only fair also to note that a few Italian writers of distinction, notably Signore Adolfo Sassi, have taken up the cudgels in defence of the maligned Countess.

It is a delicate and a very far from agreeable task to touch upon such a matter in these pages, but it is nevertheless necessary for us to give some definite opinion thereon. We are firmly convinced of the intense devotion, and of the undeviating fidelity of the Countess to her Incomparable Friend to the very last, though we are willing to admit that it is impossible at this distance of time to discover the whole truth, though all existing evidence points to the innocence and steadfast affection of the Countess of Albany. Indeed, it is for these latter-day detractors of the Countess to prove their case against her, and it is for us who uphold her character to pronounce upon the validity of any arguments they can adduce. Now what are these arguments ? The chief is, that she was a light woman by instinct, and was ready to change one lover for another according to her fancy ; yet that she fell into an overwhelming passion for Alfieri is obviously no proof of her desertion of him later. The fact is, there is throughout the whole range of the information at our disposal connected with their life at Casa Alfieri between the years 1793–1803, only one piece of definite assertion of an intrigue between Fabre and the Countess, and that is to be found in the racy reminiscences of Massimo d'Azeglio, who with scandalous ingratitude inserted in his book some very disagreeable stories about both Alfieri and the Countess, although she had frequently shown him kindness as a boy. Even here, only one anecdote deals positively with the so-called Fabre intrigue, and that is supplied from the recollections

of an aunt of d'Azeglio's, a certain old Marchesa di
Priè, a former flame of Alfieri's,* who bore a special
grudge against the Countess of Albany, in the first
instance for usurping her own place in the poet's affections; and in the second, for having thwarted (so she
alleged) her attempted introduction of a priest into his
sick-room. The story of the Marchesa di Priè is that
one evening, whilst she and other ladies were watching
one of the theatrical representations which the poet
often gave in Casa Alfieri, she observed young Fabre
unmistakably ogling the mistress of the house. The
Marchesa related this experience in after years to her
nephew, who cruelly and ungratefully gave to the world
this malicious story. Says Bertana, the leader of the
present ungallant attack on the " Donna Amata " of
Alfieri : " That d'Azeglio had really learnt this tale
from his aunt, who can doubt ? And who can with
certainty affirm that the Marchesa di Priè invented
it ? "† But surely it is the first duty of those who
regard this nasty and posthumous slander as a piece of
true evidence to show that the remarks of d'Azeglio's
old aunt were *primâ facie* correct, and not actuated by
malice, nor the result of a possible mistake on her part ?
In the first place, the *salon* of Casa Alfieri, filled with
a crowd of her friends and with Alfieri himself either
on the stage or in the room, seems a most unsuitable
and unlikely place for the unguarded display of what
all agree in describing as a disreputable intrigue. If
the Countess and Fabre were indeed secret lovers, then
it seems strange they should exhibit in so public and
therefore in so unbefitting a place, the understanding
which it was obviously to the interests of both to keep
as dark as possible. No one else, except this old Madame
de Priè, seems to have noticed either on this or on any
other occasion the slightest familiarity between the

* Reumont, *Gino Capponi e il Suo Secolo*, pp. 32, 33. Also chapter iv.
of this work.

† Bertana, p. 270.

painter and the Countess, though the natural inference from this spiteful tale would lead one to suppose their relations were scandalously open and patent to all their circle. On the contrary, realising that the Marchesa bore a grudge against her hostess, was she not safe in inventing a malevolent lie in after years, and was not the nephew safe in publishing it abroad, when the poor Countess had long been dead and therefore unable to refute so vile a slander ? On the face of things, to put the case very gently, the anecdote rests on exceedingly doubtful grounds ; and when we bear in mind that it is the only definite charge of light conduct brought against the Countess of Albany, it becomes all the more important that such a scandalous tale, published nearly half a century after her death, should be regarded with the deepest mistrust. For, apart from this anecdote in d'Azeglio's volumes, there exists no direct evidence, however slight or ill-authenticated, of the misbehaviour of the Countess of Albany, so it would seem that on this tale, and on this tale alone, rests the whole charge of her infidelity towards Alfieri during his lifetime.

On the other hand, it would be easy to point to the letters full of expressions of genuine grief and regret, which even the most ardent of Madame d'Albany's detractors dare not explain away as insincere or hypocritical. The messages sent by the dying poet to the Abbé di Caluso, and the Countess' letters to her many friends, afford endless proofs of her undoubted affection, and we think of her fidelity also. It is therefore perhaps unnecessary to argue at length against charges so false, so futile, and so belated ; but we should like to point out that a possible clue to her true relations with Fabre is to be found in the protracted course of her correspondence with Madame Mocenni. In these letters the Countess was opening her mind and her heart to her chosen friend and confidant, Teresa Mocenni, so that we may well look for some enlightenment upon this point in their contents. Now, if during the course of this corre-

263

spondence the Countess had (as she is accused) been
flirting with the young painter, she might have reasonably
been expected to pursue one of two courses. Either
she would have taken her beloved Teresa into her confidence about Fabre, and told her of her new-born passion ;
or she would, in order to allay her friend's suspicion,
have kept Fabre's name as much as possible out of her
letters. But neither of these courses does she adopt.
On the contrary, she talks most freely about Fabre, and
talks, too, in a tone of patronage that seems most unsuitable towards a lover, even a secret lover. She pokes
fun at the man's plebeian parents or at his brother's
pills ; and throughout one cannot but be struck with the
feeling that, though Fabre is quite the favourite in Casa
Alfieri, yet that he always stands on a lower plane than
that of the master and mistress of this aristocratic and
supercilious household. Signore Sassi speaks with acute
discrimination of the painter as " one of those men,
especially those humbly-born men of genius who frequent
the houses of the great and noble, having a commonplace
and unsympathetic personality, like all those men who
set themselves to obtain secure and comfortable leisure
out of women, and especially elderly women." * Such
a person as Fabre, however appreciated, could never,
Signore Sassi opines, have usurped the place in the heart
of the Countess once occupied by Alfieri. That Fabre
was useful, tactful, kind, sympathetic, agreeable, discreet,
and in short indispensable, none will deny ; but a man
may be all these things to a great lady of fifty and more,
and yet not be her lover. Of course we may be wholly
mistaken in this view, for time has obliterated our chances
of real knowledge ; but we affirm that all probability
points to the perfect innocence of the Countess ; whilst
except for the unproved story of the Marchesa di Priè,
the traducers of the lady have not apparently a tittle
of direct evidence tending to exhibit the alleged infidelity of the Countess of Albany towards her Friend.

* La Vedovanza dell' Amica dell' Alfieri, p. 638.

They may prove, and with success, that Alfieri himself grew weary in one sense of his companion, and that he ranged elsewhere outside the walls of Casa Alfieri; but it is hard to see how this revived love of intrigue in the man should of necessity be aroused also in the woman. In a word, these detractors and calumniators ought either to cease from making such charges, or else to seek for and bring forward some new and better-authenticated testimony in support of their theory.

It would seem that Fabre did not take up his abode at Casa Alfieri for some years after the poet's death, and that his arrival there was partly at least the result of accident rather than of choice or invitation. His wretched health, which required constant attention, and the death of his brother Edouard were probably the ultimate causes of his settling permanently in Casa Alfieri itself, though he visited it daily and was constantly in the company of the Countess. Bonstetten, the old admirer of the young Stuart " Queen of Hearts," writing four years after Alfieri's death, distinctly states that " she lived with the painter Fabre, who did not dwell in her house but had his meals with her. This third husband had the air of a subordinate rather than of a spouse, and only appeared occasionally ";* the word *husband* being of course used here in a facetious sense. As in Alfieri's case certain persons had persisted in speaking of a marriage-tie between the pair, so [now the old idea was mooted of a secret union between herself and Fabre, although there is not a shadow of probability in such a suggestion. Yet the report of their actual marriage found its way into the volumes of the *Biographie Universelle* during the life-time of Fabre himself, who notes the statement in his own copy preserved in the Musée Fabre, at Montpellier, with the significant denial *C'est faux !* which ought surely to be conclusive evidence on this point.† It seems that the painter was always

* Ste. Beuve, *Nouveaux Lundis*, vol. v. p. 431.
† Del Cerro, *V. Alfieri e la Comtessa d'Albany, &c.* p. 311.

willing to play the part of inferior companion to a great lady whom he had perhaps begun by toadying, but for whom he preserved to the last a discreet and unvarying devotion of service. To somebody or other, after Alfieri's death, the Countess felt herself bound to turn, and perhaps the painter had long waited for this expected opportunity. She wanted somebody who could carry on the old Alfieri traditions and rules of the house, and for this purpose none could have served better than her friend of ten years' standing, who was both eager and capable to fill this post. Between this pair Alfieri was still a living being ; his library was kept as a shrine or a museum ; both spoke of the dead poet with bated breath to the guests of the house ; and both lived in the shadow, as it were, of the departed but still prevading genius. As to his own merits, François-Xavier Fabre, though plain and homely in outward appearance, was a painter of note ; he was an excellent connoisseur and collector of all works of art, and he had a most remarkable gift of conversation. " He spoke well on all subjects," remarks Paul-Louis Courier ; " and when he spoke of art itself, it was an education to listen to him." Of the many friends of the Countess, several of them persons not only of high rank but also of strict morality, such as the Duchess of Devonshire, Miss Cornelia Knight, Lady Davey and others, not one ever seems to have taken exception to the *ménage* of Casa Alfieri, and all invariably allude to Fabre in a friendly spirit or send him polite messages of recognition. Of all her host of friends and acquaintances, surely some would have declined to visit the Countess' *salon*, had there been any suspicion of an illicit intimacy between the elderly mistress of the house and her chosen middle-aged companion. As to conventional appearances, the Countess, with her exalted notions of her own importance, cared nothing for idle gossip or speculation ; nor indeed was there occasion for her to listen to it, since all that was not only brilliant, but also most respectable, crowded eagerly to her receptions.

Such events as occurred during the peaceful remnant of her life were therefore invariably shared with this chosen help-meet of her declining years. It was with Fabre as her companion that, in 1809, she prepared to go into exile in France, when Napoleon, jealous of the social influence of the Countess among the Florentines, and suspicious of her political ideals, commanded the presence of the mistress of Casa Alfieri in Paris. This imperial and imperious summons (which constituted in reality a decided compliment to her own influential personality) had perforce to be obeyed, and most unwillingly the Countess of Albany, attended by Fabre, set out for the " Cloaca Maxima " that Alfieri had always so cordially detested.

The circumstances of the Countess' actual summons and her departure are wrapped in some mystery. Two years previously, the Queen Regent of the mushroom kingdom of Etruria and her infant son had been unceremoniously told to quit their realm, in order that Tuscany might be united with the swelling French Empire, and its inhabitants Frenchified in a civil, military and ecclesiastical sense. For this purpose the former Grand-Duchy was now divided into the three departments of the Arno, the Ombrone and the Mediterranean ; whilst the Pitti Palace, in Florence, was occupied by the court of Élise Buonaparte, eldest sister of the Emperor and the wife of Felice Baciocchi, recently created by his all-powerful brother-in-law, Prince of Piombino and Duke of Lucca. The new Governor-General (for that title seems best fitted to describe the position held by the Grand-Duchess Élise in Florence) and her court naturally did not meet with an enthusiastic welcome from the mass of the Florentines of all classes ; whilst to the Countess this new annexation to France seemed even more hateful and humiliating than the late Bourbon monarchy set up as an experiment in Tuscany and now capriciously destroyed by its creator. Élise, however, did all that was possible to conciliate the

267

unwilling and reluctant citizens of Florence, nor was she wholly unsuccessful in her well-meant efforts. Even Madame d'Albany gradually modified her dislike towards her, and Élise herself was wont to pay informal visits of a morning at Casa Alfieri, for the Countess, as the widow of a titular king, would never condescend to enter the Pitti Palace, except on the forbidden footing of a queen. Élise has sometime been accused of jealousy of the social influence and prestige of the Countess and her *salon*, and she is even represented as having secretly advised the terrible Fouché to remove this cause of annoyance, though always pretending regret for the step which she had herself suggested. But it seems far more likely that Napoleon acted thus on his own initiative, in according to the Countess a treatment similar to that already meted out to Mesdames de Stael and Récamier. Fabre, too, frequented the Palazzo Pitti to offer Élise occasional advice on matters artistic, and he even figures in a large picture by Pietro Benvenuti, the fashionable Italian painter of the day, wherein he is made to appear as discussing the merits of a bust with Felice Baciocchi in the presence of Napoleon's sister and her court. Certainly, the Countess of Albany never suspected Élise of treachery or personal dislike, for it was to her that she now appealed to obtain the recall of Napoleon's offensive and satirical order for her to quit Florence and reside in Paris, where (so he sneeringly observed) she might indulge her artistic tastes with better profit. General Menon, to whom Élise had expressed her regret at her brother's action,[*] deeming his mistress sincere, had undertaken to arrange a formal

---

[*] That Élise really endeavoured to prevent the Countess' enforced visit to Paris becomes evident from the following passage in a letter of Napoleon to Fouché himself.

"SCHÖNBRUNN, June 20, 1809.

"The Grand Duchess (Élise) did wrong to prevent the execution of the measures I ordered. I do not wish Madame d'Albany to live in Florence. . . ."—*New Letters of Napoleon I.*, translated by Lady Mary Loyd. London, 1898.

meeting between these two intellectual and semi-regal ladies of Florence, with the result that Madame d'Albany described herself as ready to pay a visit in state to the Pitti Palace, provided that on her arrival she were duly treated as a reigning sovereign. With this stipulation Buonaparte's sister affected to agree, whereupon on the day appointed the gala coach of the Stuart Queen, which had not been seen rolling in the memory of man, appeared at the portal of Casa Alfieri with its full complement of footmen in splendid scarlet liveries, white cockades, three-cornered hats and powdered wigs. Amid a crowd attracted by so unusual a spectacle, the widow of Charles-Edward Stuart drove in full panoply across the bridge of Santa Trinità and up the narrow Sdrucciolo dei Pitti to the palace. Here she was received by the officials, who led the Countess from hall to hall, and along gallery after gallery, till finally she was ushered into a small room which turned out to be Élise's bedchamber. The bed itself was occupied by Napoleon's cunning sister, who in this manner, on an obviously feigned plea of sickness, excused herself from returning the three sweeping curtseys which the entering " Reine d'Angleterre " had already performed, so that a slight bob from the lace-wrapped head on the pillow was all that the astonished and discomfited Countess could obtain in return for her obeisances of ceremony! Smothering her indignation, however, the Countess launched forth into the long tale of her grievances and of the inconvenience of her recent summons to Paris, when suddenly Élise, who was in reality not greatly interested in the story, called out, " What on earth, my dear Countess, made Alfieri so bitter an enemy of the French ? "

" You show me yourself he was quite right to hate them ! " was the retort of her now infuriated visitor, who thereupon flung out of the room without saying good-bye, and made her way back to the entrance where her carriage was drawn up. Two days later she quitted

Florence, according to the order of Napoleon, who thereby considered he was removing a social obstacle to the desired growth of union between the French Empire and its newly included Tuscan subjects.*

The year's residence in Paris, which is the sole incident of importance that serves to break the regular routine of the twenty years of Italian life after the death of Alfieri, calls for no special notice. Although annoyed at her banishment from her home, the Countess found Paris and Parisian life agreeable enough for the time being, as may be ascertained from the lively and affectionate letters addressed to her after her departure in the following year by Madame de Souza, the widow of the unfortunate Comte de Flahault, and now the wife of a Portuguese diplomatist and scholar. Owing to her sister's official position with the ex-Empress Joséphine, the Countess was an occasional visitor to Malmaison, and she also admitted a deep admiration for Hortense de Beauharnais, Queen of Holland. Another old friend was also seen during this compulsory sojourn in Paris, and that was Madame de Maltzam, now seventy-four years of age and living quietly on a tiny income at Soissons, quite reconciled to the new change of government. Naturally, Madame de Maltzam was delighted at the prospect of beholding once more the mistress whom she had served in the old days at Florence, Rome and Colmar, and longed to clasp her dear pupil to her breast. She writes to the Countess in Paris, on February 2, 1810, begging her to stay at her little house at Soissons and have a talk over old times, or else she declares herself willing to make an effort to meet her in Paris.

" . . . I have two small rooms to offer you, as well as a servant's room, all very simple but beautifully clean, for I don't suppose you will be travelling unaccompanied on so long a journey. There, my dear Countess, is what I shall have the happiness to place at your disposal !

* E. Rodocanachi, *Élise Baciocchi en Italie*, pp. 200–202.

" Are you afraid of this tiny town, for fear of being too conspicuous in it ? If so, warn me well beforehand of the date of your departure from Paris. Try to remain a week longer, if you can do so without inconvenience, and I shall then hasten my arrival by a week. I shall fly to my little *entresol*, and thence I shall run off straight into your arms, wherein I shall find sincere happiness. . . . I am ready to endure any trouble in order to be with you once again. Alas, perhaps it will be our last meeting, for at my present age, no matter how well I feel, I always seem to see the end of all things near at hand, and I face death with calmness.

" I beg you, my dear Countess, to reciprocate my warm devotion in a heart that flies out to you and longs to join you, despite all weathers.

" I have read with the deepest interest of your interview with the Emperor. He evidently showed you more deference and gentleness than he shows to most persons. . . .

" Certainly, whatever be the weather, whatever be the date of your departure, nothing shall interfere with my flying to greet you, a fortnight before you leave. Our meeting will probably be the last pleasure on earth for my old heart, but how intense a pleasure will it be ! "*

In the autumn of 1810, after a twelvemonth of honourable exile, the Countess of Albany was permitted to leave Paris amid the lamentations of her charming friend, Madame de Souza, who constantly wrote to her from this time onward. Vague promises of a speedy return were expressed to her and also to poor old Madame de Maltzam, but there can be no doubt the Countess was eager to return to Florence, if only to inspect the costly monument to Alfieri that Canova had recently completed in her absence. Together with Fabre, she was glad to settle once more in Casa Alfieri, but in the following year, 1811, she and the painter again spent a whole winter away from Florence, setting out for Rome in October.

* *Le Portefeuille de la Comtesse d'Albany*, pp. 68, 69.

Here the pair remained some months, Fabre busy in inspecting the galleries and buying works of art, whilst the Countess enjoyed seeing the artistic treasures of Rome under the guidance of so able and distinguished a connoisseur. Rome must, however, have been full of ghosts of the past for the portly, comfortable-looking, rather untidy middle-aged lady, for she could scarcely have resisted gazing upon the dingy old Stuart palace in the Piazza Santi Apostoli with its memories of her husband, of Bonstetten, and of all the gay lords and ladies of a Rome that had been clean swept away in the cataclysm of the late French conquests. And the Eternal City itself, with Pius VII. absent as a prisoner of the hated tyrant, and with the austere General Miollis, Alfieri's old opponent, in command of the alien garrison, must have seemed melancholy and unnatural to her eyes, which had seen its unreformed pleasures and splendours under Pius VI.

Full of haunting memories also must have appeared the tall mansion of the Cancellaria, her former abode as the guest of the easy-going, easily-deceived royal Cardinal; also the Villa Strozzi with recollections yet sweeter and more alluring, when she thought of its occupant in the far-off days of her second residence in this delightful but now deserted and despoiled city. One day the Countess spent at Frascati, and one morning she paid a visit to the tombs of her husband, his brother and their father in the *Grotte Vaticane*, or crypt of St. Peter's. Both these incidents she mentions in a dull journal she kept during this winter in Rome, but she makes no comment whatever upon her own bare statements. The rest of this work is filled merely with accounts or criticisms of various pictures, which are largely due to the remarks addressed to her by Fabre in the course of their wanderings in the churches, palaces and galleries of the city.*

* L. G. Pélissier, *Lettres et Écrits divers de la Comtesse d'Albany. Souvenirs de Voyage en Italie.*

272

From Rome the pair proceeded early in February to Naples, where the Countess' second sister, the Princess Castelfranco, was now living.* Travelling with them were the French writer, Paul-Louis Courier, and the English antiquary, Mr. James Millingen. Here, settled in a villa in the western suburb of Posilipo, above the waters of the Bay of Naples, the Countess rested for several weeks in order to be near her sister.

This villa is somewhat celebrated as the picturesque scene of Courier's dialogue entitled "Conversation chez la Comtesse d'Albany," which consists of a series of discussions, partly actual and partly imaginary, between the Countess, Courier and Fabre upon the relative superiority and value of the artist and the warrior. This keen but friendly controversy is sustained with great ardour for some hours, and is finally only ended by the approach of the dinner hour. "The Countess was on the point of replying to my last argument," relates Courier, "when a footman entered to announce dinner. 'It comes at an opportune moment for you,' said she to Fabre, 'since I fancy you are come to the end of your resources!' 'On my honour, not at all!' was the reply, 'I have not mentioned a fourth part of my arguments as yet, nor my best ones either. See now, Signora, in fairness, how I can retort.' 'No, no,' she interrupted, 'I admit myself beaten, and am ready to grant everything, provided we can go in to dinner!'† So we sate down, and during the course of the meal the Countess continued to twit Fabre concerning both his argumentative efforts and his late panegyric of the arts. *Apropos* to the arts, we also spoke of Lady Hamilton, who long before had inhabited this very house; and from Lady Hamilton our talk drifted to Nelson, whom the Countess had known and considered rather like Canova in appear-

---

* Her first husband, the Duke of Berwick, had died in 1787, and she had since been married to Prince Castelfranco of Naples.

† Reumont, vol. ii. pp. 413-444. Strange to relate, not one of the many detractors of the Countess of Albany has seized on this remark to prove her lack of real literary interest or her esesntially vulgar nature!

ance. After the meal, she and Fabre went out driving, whilst I returned to my lodging and composed these pages."

From Naples the Countess and Fabre returned in the early spring to Florence, where they again settled down to the usual life of painting, reading, entertaining and daily exercise which made up the sum-total of Madame d'Albany's daily existence during these latter years.

CHAPTER XIV

"QUEEN OF FLORENCE"

In the *salon* of the Casa Alfieri (for after his death thus was the
Palazzo Gianfigliazzi called), Châteaubriand was wont to read his
Martyres ; Lamartine his early poems ; Canova meditated on his
Graces ; Sismondi, the historian of the Italian Republics, spoke
vehemently of German philosophy ; Lord Byron told marvellous
tales of adventures and of *amours ;* Roscoe alluded to his discoveries
among the archives of Italy ; Rogers rhapsodised on the art of
poetry ; Cardinal Consalvi produced the costly snuff-boxes given
him by the sovereigns of Europe. Finally, Madame d'Albany
was wont to read aloud herself the letters of Foscolo to her most
intimate circle, or even those of Madame de Stael, in those days
a real power, and the only power that had been known to oppose
Napoleon I. without bayonets or cannon.

> E. DEL CERRO, *Epistolario di Ugo Foscolo*, p. 24

" I SHUT my eyes," writes the Italian statesman, Massimo
d'Azeglio in his *Ricordi*, " and I behold, as though it were
yesterday, the Countess' *salon* with the chimney-piece
facing the windows, and close beside it, sitting in a low
chair, the Countess of Albany with her inevitable *fichu
à la Marie Antoinette* crossed over her bosom. I see the
two familiar paintings by Fabre on the walls ; one of them
representing Saul with the Witch of Endor, and the other
some part of the ruins of Pompeii. I see the round-
arched windows over-looking the Lung' Arno with their
three steps below, whereon I am myself seated as a small
boy enjoying an ice with two cakes, which was the Countess' fixed allowance for myself and my childish com-
panions. I see my father discussing politics with Monsieur Lagenswerd, the Swedish Minister, with Carletti
and with Libri. Underneath the pictures I see the two
ponderous sofas of gold and white wood-work upholstered

275

with crimson damask ; I see them so clearly that I almost fancy I can touch them. . . .

"Again I mark the ample proportions of that celebrity, the Countess of Albany, dressed all in white with her large old-fashioned shawl, slowly mount a chair, so as to place her hand upon the box of sugar-plums that reposed on the book-shelf overhead." *

These childish impressions of d'Azeglio's certainly serve to bring before us the exact aspect of that *salon* in the Casa Alfieri where, in the first quarter of the past century, and especially in the years succeeding the fall of Napoleon, the whole of Florentine society and the whole mass of distinguished travellers of every nationality that at once poured into Italy with the definite return of peace, were wont to assemble.—" The great magic lantern of Europe passes ever under your eyes, and perhaps your own *salon*, Madame, can be considered as the best spot whence to observe the spectacle " ; so writes Sismondi to the Countess, when she complains to him of her utter weariness and indifference to passing events, and merely regards herself as a spectator of the international magic lantern, or else as an onlooker from a window, whence she observes with amusement but without vital interest the never-ending stream of persons as they pursue their way. A princess of wealth and culture living in a fine house in so central a city as Florence could easily attract the cream of travelling Europe in these years of feverish movement ; and a personage with so romantic a past as Madame d'Albany's was naturally reckoned one of the chief social powers of the Tuscan capital. Her receptions were thronged, and their vogue was immense, yet it is not difficult to conceive them as being a little tedious and stiff. In the *salon* that d'Azeglio has described for us so vividly, the Countess was wont to receive of an evening, in the same old-fashioned sombre dress and ever esconced in the same seat, whilst in front of her two semi-circular rows of chairs were filled by the ladies present, the men standing

* *I Miei Ricordi*, vol. i. pp. 81–83.

CASA ALFIERI, THE RESIDENCE OF THE COUNTESS OF ALBANY

Alinari

behind them. Politics and literature were usually discussed, yet somehow these receptions lacked the spontaneous mirth and vivacity of the *salon* of a Madame de Stael or a Madame Récamier. Cultured and affable as was the mistress of Casa Alfieri, yet many persons were wont to complain of the dullness and formality of her nightly parties, for which, however, all strove only too anxiously to obtain an invitation. Sometimes the Countess was wont, as Foscolo christened it, to "alfierise," or tell anecdotes of her dead-and-gone poet, which proved highly acceptable to Foscolo himself and to such as were blind admirers of that departed hero, but probably sounded trivial enough to the chance visitor. Nevertheless, the Florentine *salon* of the "Reine d'Angleterre" was all the fashion, so that a list of the names alone of the distinguished persons who at one time or another frequented her assemblies would fill several pages; indeed, there is hardly a celebrity of this period who visited Florence without paying his or her respects at Casa Alfieri. Conspicuous amongst her guests were Sismondi, the Swiss historian; Ugo Foscolo, the poet; Canova, the sculptor; Cardinal Consalvi; the learned Duchess of Devonshire; the still lovely Princess Rospigliosi, who many years before had acted in Alfieri's drama of *Antigone* in the Roman palace; Morghen and Jesi, the engravers; Pietro Benvenuti, the fashionable Tuscan painter; the diplomatists, Carletti and Lucchesini; the Florentine Marchese Gino Capponi, who did not love his hostess over-much, but at least did not insult her memory in the vile manner of the ungallant and ungrateful d'Azeglio. English men and women of quality or erudition also swarmed in these rooms, where still could be seen the canopy of a reigning queen and where every piece of plate or china was ostentatiously emblazoned with the royal arms of Britain. Thomas Moore and Lord Byron, the poets; Lord John Russell, the Liberal politician, Sir Humphrey and Lady Davey; the Misses Berry; James Millingen, the antiquary; and old Miss Cornelia

Knight are amongst the hundreds of English visitors who were entertained at various times by the widow of "the Young Pretender."

Having ceased to take an active interest in life, and being content to sit at the window, as she herself expresses her attitude constantly, the Countess of Albany had long since abandoned all care of her personal appearance, so that her dowdy aspect, her squat figure, and the queer but comfortable garments of her choice are commented on severely by several of her guests, whose visits to Casa Alfieri were undertaken from curiosity rather than from pure friendship or respect. Says the critical Châteaubriand in his *Mémoires d'Outre Tombeau*, " I knew Madame d'Albany at Florence. Age had produced in her the opposite effects that it usually brings. Time is wont to ennoble the countenance, and when the subject comes of a generous race, it imprints something of nobility on the face it has marked. But the Countess of Albany with her thick figure and her lack of expression presented a common-place appearance. If the women on Rubens' canvases could have grown old, they would have resembled Madame d'Albany at the age I knew her." *

Bonstetten, who had not set eyes on the Countess since the distant days of her reign as " Queen of Hearts " in the Palazzo Santi Apostoli, was also greatly shocked at the changes Time had wrought in the lovely princess, who had once carried on so sprightly a correspondence with himself. After sentimentalising during his visit to Rome in front of the former Stuart palace (which he declared he never could pass without expecting to see the smiling face of its erstwhile mistress peeping forth from a window), the Swiss writer found her, so he tells us, to his horror, grown an old woman whose voice alone served to recall her past attractions. This was in the spring of 1807, thirty years and more since he had last beheld her, yet this childish old man of talent declares

* St. Beuve, *Nouveaux Lundis*, vol. v. p. 433.

himself amazed at finding her thus altered and aged, and become (in his eyes at least) uninteresting. Some inkling of Bonstetten's disappointment or chagrin must have revealed itself to the shrewd Countess, for she lectures him with some asperity in a letter dated February 9, 1808.

" . . . I am astonished that such a philosopher as yourself should deplore the changes wrought in faces and figures during the passage of thirty years. I am very glad to count myself among the number of those who change thus. I should be truly sorry at fifty-five years of age to look at things with the glasses of twenty, though such an absurdity is common enough in Italy. Please do not regret the one thing that affords me satisfaction. And please do not be under the impression that I need to become *dévote*. My own philosophy supports me, whilst my taste for study occupies my time, which is flying fast. Despite my cynicism, I am not morose in society, and you would never imagine how much I love to be alone and how great is my contempt for men. I live on from day to day, fearing nothing and expecting nothing. However, I gladly seize any opportunity of helping the unhappy, of whom at this moment there is an abundant supply. I could not follow the example of the person you mention, and bury myself amongst the mountains. I do not care for the country, nor have I much interest in what is doing in the world, though I delight in what is published, and I want to have all the books possible. . . .

"Adieu, my dear Monsieur. Forgive me for wearying you with my chatter, and rest assured of my warm esteem. Only my heart is worthy of your esteem, for it is the sole thing about me that distinguishes me from the common crowd." •

That the Countess had lost all trace of her once vaunted beauty is evident enough, whilst she herself assisted the

• L. G. Pélissier, *Lettres et Écrits divers de la Comtesse d'Albany*, pp. 15, 16.

work of " Nature's changing course untrimmed " by dressing solely for comfort, and by neglecting a number of subtle but not unusual contrivances for keeping at bay the demon of old age. Nevertheless, she was not without certain charms. Her hands and arms remained shapely to the last ; her eyes (over the exact hue of which poets and courtiers had once disputed) were still clear and expressive; and her masses of iron-grey hair appeared not unbecoming with their bunches of pale pink ribbands. As she sate in her usual chair of state, " the sole Queen of Florence," as Sismondi once jested, Madame d'Albany still carried a certain dignity which her romantic past invested with an additional interest. The gentle Lamartine, a more indulgent critic than Châteaubriand or Bonstetten, speaks warmly of her bright eyes, her lovely grey hair and well-formed mouth ; whilst he also mentions her intelligent and kindly countenance, in contrast with the verdict of his fellow country-man on this point. Indeed, it is hard to believe that so celebrated a woman, who had seen so much, read so much, suffered so much, and experienced so much, could really be endowed in her old age with a vacant or expressionless face. Perhaps her persistent attitude of cynicism or indifference towards everybody and everything may have nettled certain of the consequential geniuses, who entered her *salon* and peradventure deemed their special claims to notice overlooked by this calm impassive figure, sitting in her old-world garments by the fireside and affecting to live only in the distant past, although keenly following the present with an irritating and contemptuous amusement.

It has been pointed out with truth by her biographers that, whilst the *salon* of Casa Alfieri attracted the great personages of the European social and intellectual worlds, the actual correspondents of the Countess of Albany, a numerous and cosmopolitan band, reckoned but few persons of real eminence amongst their number. The men and women, whose letters to the Countess still survive in hundreds, were mostly mediocrities of their age, who might even have remained wholly unknown to us save for their chance connection with an historical figure, such as Madame d'Albany. Almost every civilised nation is represented in the bulky *Portfolio,** which the industry of Monsieur Pélissier has collected and edited for us, and from a glance at its contents, the reader will be amazed at the variety of her chosen correspondents. Britain is represented by the Duchess of Devonshire,† Lady Davey, Mr. Millingen and Miss Knight ; whilst America can boast of Mr. Everett and Mrs. Derby. The poetess, Frederica Brun, and the diplomatist, Akerblad, belong to the Scandinavian nations ; also many Russian noblemen, including Count Bourtouline, were amongst her acquaintances. The Germans, outside her own family, are few in number, nor are there more than two or three Spaniards ; but naturally Italy and France are well represented. Amongst this mass of friends, a few illustrious names shine forth, but the majority are merely people of fashion filled with the same reactionary ideals as the great lady whom they address. There are a few letters from Madame de Stael, but none of any special interest, in spite of her genuine regard for the Countess.

Of the French correspondents, Madame de Souza, the novelist, is by far the most interesting, and her picturesque, affectionate, warm-hearted letters to the friend with whom she was so intimate in Paris during the Countess' enforced visit there in 1809–1810 will undoubtedly give pleasure. A very long-winded and very dull correspondent is the Spanish officer, the Chevalier de Sobiratz, a true *codino* of the old order of things, who sometimes diversifies his voluminous epistles with long outpourings of original verse. The letters of old Madame de Maltzam at Soissons afford good reading, and serve to throw a little light on that elusive personage, who was so closely associated with all the phases of the married life of the

---

* *Le Portefeuille de la Comtesse d'Albany.*

† Elizabeth, daughter of Frederick-Augustus, Earl of Bristol and Bishop of Derry, wife of the fifth Duke of Devonshire. She died March 1824.

Countess and of her romance with Alfieri. Several of
her letters are included in the *Portefeuille*, the last being
dated December 18, 1810, which must have been shortly
before her death. Although most of her friends are
strong supporters of the old system and intense haters of
Napoleon, yet we find several letters to her from the
liberal Abbé Luigi di Breme, of Milan, and also some
curious appeals from the Neapolitan reformer, Carlo
Poerio, and his wife. Michele Leoni, the Italian translator of the Shakespearean plays; the Florentine historian,
Gino Capponi; and, of course, her special friend, the Abbé
di Caluso figure amidst the Italian correspondents.
But, generally speaking, the *Portefeuille* of the Countess
does not afford either amusing or instructive reading,
since most of the letters included therein are unnecessarily
deferential in tone to the " Reine D'Angleterre," whom
her distant correspondents seem over-anxious to please.

Of those persons not in the front rank of celebrity,
Madame de Souza will undoubtedly be found by far the
most attractive by the reader. This lady, whom the
Countess had formerly known as the Comtesse de
Flahault during her first residence in Paris, had already
lost her first husband during the Reign of Terror,
and she had since been married to a Portuguese
diplomatist and man of letters, Monsieur de Souza, who
was deeply interested in producing a fine edition of the
works of his national poet, Camoens. Her son, young
Charles de Flahault, the " Néné " of his mother's letters,
later rose to become an *aide-de-camp* to Napoleon and a
distinguished general; a circumstance that did not tend
to endear either mother or son to the embittered heart of
Madame d'Albany, with her unmeasured hatred of the
French Emperor and her readiness to quarrel with all
who admired or defended his acts. Her present displeasure must evidently have been pretty forcibly
expressed in her own letters to Madame de Souza, for
the sympathetic little Frenchwoman complains woefully
of her adored friend, " her elder sister," the Countess of

Albany, for quarrelling with her over matters she could not possibly help at the time of the fall of the Empire, when all Paris was seething with excitement and the old party feelings were running high. At this juncture Madame d'Albany had addressed to her friend in Paris *une grande lettre*, concerning the iniquities of Buonaparte and his rule, to which Adèle de Souza was already pledged owing to the attitude of her son, Néné, about whose conduct the Countess indulged in some most sharp and personal comments.

" If anything could make me angry with you, my dear Friend, it is the letter that I have just received. How could you, with your knowledge of me, tell me that I approved of Napoleon's conquests, because I only saw therein chance of success and of money for my son ? Thank Heaven, so vile a sentiment has never crossed my mind ! And as to money, the invasion of Portugal has deprived us of more wealth than Charles is ever likely to acquire in his campaigns—those hateful campaigns which took him away from my side and caused me such sorrow and anxiety. I tell you, I did not expect to find such a remark in any letter of yours. It has wounded and disturbed me, but I feel sure you will be sorry for having written thus. . . .

" I shall neither argue nor dispute with you on any political matter. They have slandered me, but slander will pass ; and if it does not pass, then I myself shall pass. On the judgment day, the one thing that counts is to be guiltless of causing pain to anybody, and that I can freely say to the Almighty who sees into all hearts.

" Néné is no longer with your *ex-passion*. . . ." •

The last allusion here is to Hortense de Beauharnais, once Queen of Holland, and the mother of the future Emperor Napoleon III., with whom Charles de Flahault was very intimate, being indeed her acknowledged lover.

• *Le Portefeuille*, pp. 228, 229. The date is only " 26," but is probably January 26, 1815.

The Countess had formerly during her visit to Paris expressed such admiration for Hortense, that Madame de Souza used playfully to allude to the queen as her *passion*, an epithet which had always met with Madame d'Albany's approval—at least until the fall of the Buonapartes. The differences between the pair of friends were eventually settled, and later the Countess seems even to have roused herself, for his mother's sake, to forgive Néné for having once more embraced the cause of his master during the episode of the Hundred Days, when General Charles de Flahault was found amongst his old officers who welcomed the returning Emperor. Escaping from France after Waterloo, Flahault retired to England, where he was fortunate enough to win the hand of a Scottish heiress, Miss Margaret Mercer Elphinstone, a former friend of the Princess Charlotte, and his betrothal to this lady urged Flahault to demand grace from his mother's old friend in the following letter.

"DRUMMOND CASTLE, *June* 30, 1817.

"MADAME,—You have always treated me with such kindness since my childhood, and even last year you have afforded me a proof that this old kindly feeling still remains, despite all circumstances, that I venture to hope that you will receive the news of my marriage with Miss Mercy (*sic*) Elphinstone, daughter of Lord Keith, with interest and pleasure. Although her birth and dowry entitled her to expect a match with a leading Englishman, yet she has preferred a stranger and a beggar to her own countrymen.* Her relations have regarded our marriage with disfavour ; a fact which will not astonish you, when you think of my political views and career, and of the English prejudice against foreigners. But I shall do my utmost to remove all their dislike to me, and to prove to

* Monsieur Pélissier very pertinently points out here that the *étranger malheureux* was a peer of France, a Count and General of the Empire, and the acknowledged lover of a Queen !

284

them that my nation, in spite of its sad reputation, can also bring forth model husbands.

"I am addressing you, Madame, from Drummond Castle, where the name of Albany and the traditions of loyalty still linger. My wife's family has itself suffered for its devotion to the Stuarts. I hope, Madame, that will count as a reason for you to receive her with kindness, perhaps in a year or so hence, at Florence. I shall always remember that, in spite of his cockade, you once received your favourite Néné in Florence, an exceptional favour that made Néné proud and the Duc de Feltre, then General Clark, jealous!

"Accept, my dear excellent Lady, the homage of the sincere and unchanging respect of your devoted

"Charles de Flahault." *

It will perhaps be of sufficient interest to relate here that this distinguished young friend of Madame d'Albany's lived to the ripe age of eighty-five, dying in 1870, three years after his wife, who on her father's death had become Baroness Keith in her own right. After the Revolution of July 1830, the Comte de Flahault recovered his peerage and rank of general in France; served the government of King Louis Philippe as ambassador at Vienna, and rose to still higher favour under the Second Empire, wherein his natural son by Queen Hortense, the Duc de Morny, appeared so prominent a figure at the Imperial Court of his half-brother. In 1860, Flahault was appointed ambassador of the French Empire at St. James'; and in 1864, Napoleon III. marked his sincere appreciation of his services by naming him Grand Chancellor of the Legion of Honour, an appointment which served to

---

* *Le Portefeuille*, p. 323. The marriage between the Comte de Flahault and Miss Elphinstone, daughter and heiress of Sir George Keith Elphinstone, Baron and Viscount Keith, took place in July, 1817, a few weeks after the despatch of the above letter, which seems a little premature in its allusion to a "marriage."—*See also* Monsieur F. Lolliée, *Un Frère d'Empereur*. (Paris: Emile Paul, 1909.)

associate the Second Empire with the most illustrious survivor of the reign of the first Napoleon.

Did space permit, it would be pleasant to quote freely from the letters of Madame de Souza during the pregnant years 1810 to 1815, for they contain a number of interesting details about interesting people; whilst they present us with a charming and accurate picture of the daily life of her household, her *Casa*, as she calls it. Her gentle unassuming nature, her shrewdness, her dignified attitude whilst placed in a position of great difficulty owing to her martial son's behaviour, all combine to make of Adèle de Souza a most sympathetic and agreeable personality, so that it is with reluctance that we turn from this cultivated Parisian hostess with her cheerful house, her tiny pleasaunce full of roses, her collection of pictures , and her steadfast devotion to Madame d'Albany, which was proof even against her ungenerous and spiteful remarks at a time of great anxiety.

Amongst the male correspondents of the Countess of Albany, we note at once two men who tower head and shoulders above the smaller fry—the wandering English *dilettanti*, the querulous officials such as Sobiratz, the half-forgotten French or Italian diplomatists and cardinals, the obscure Russian noblemen—and these are Ugo Foscolo, the poet, and Sismondi, the historian of the mediæval republics of Italy. Of her intimacy with the former we intend to speak at length in the ensuing chapter, after a brief account of the friendship and correspondence between the Countess of Albany and Sismondi.

Born in 1773, the son of a pastor of Geneva, though the descendant of an ancient Italian family from Pisa, Jean-Charles-Léonard-Simonde de Sismondi was a witness in his youth of the excesses of the revolutionary party in Geneva, and even suffered imprisonment together with his father. These early experiences not unnaturally gave the young man a deep hatred and horror of the

French Republic, which he nursed whilst living on a small estate near the little cathedral-town of Pescia, in Tuscany, where his mother and himself had sought an asylum from the blind violence of their fellow-citizens. In spite of the claims upon his time that were caused by his property at Pescia, the young Sismondi became an indefatigable student in the great libraries of the neighbouring cities of Florence, Pisa and Lucca ; and to such good purpose were his researches undertaken, that in 1807 he gave to the light the first two volumes of his chief work, *The History of the Italian Republics*, which after a lapse of a century still retains its high reputation as an important contribution to Italian mediæval history. This achievement at once raised the young writer to fame, so that his society was eagerly courted by the Countess of Albany, by Madame de Stael and by other men and women celebrated in the world of letters. In his first published letter to Madame d'Albany, which relates his gift to her of these two recently published volumes, he speaks as though his acquaintance with her were very slight and recent, recommending himself to her favour as a most zealous admirer of the late Vittorio Alfieri.

"PESCIA, *June* 18, 1807.

" . . . I think that the Friend of Alfieri, who henceforth is consecrating her life to render homage to the memory of this grand man, will regard with favour a work from one of his most fervent admirers ; a work wherein she will recognise many of the conceptions and ideals that Alfieri has himself produced with so much of earnest eloquence. Before the close of this summer, I expect to visit Florence to pay you my respects and to hear from your own lips, Madame, your verdict on my *Républiques Italiennes.*" *

This quotation is drawn from the first of a series of letters which forms a continuous correspondence with the

* Taillandier, *Lettres Inédites de J C. L. de Sismondi*, &c., pp. 67, 68.

Countess from this date until the fall of the French Empire. A very large proportion, if not the whole, of Sismondi's letters to the Countess has been preserved intact at Montpellier, but unfortunately the replies of Madame d'Albany still remain to be discovered. During these seven years, a literary intimacy of a most interesting type existed between the elderly Countess and the young Swiss historian, who in the beginning usually found themselves in full agreement upon all current political problems. Sismondi occasionally spends some time in Florence, and on all these brief visits he appears as a welcome guest in Casa Alfieri, where he was wont to hold long conversations with his hostess, whom in one of his letters with apparent sincerity he styles his " greatest source of pride" (*son plus grand titre d'orgeuil*). Although courteous to the last degree towards this great lady, who aspired to be thought the social and intellectual queen of Florence, Sismondi, never shows himself obsequious or flattering; always upright and honest, he never concedes any point from a mere desire to please the important lady whom he holds in such esteem and veneration. His eulogy of her own ability and her singular gift of drawing forth the powers of her guests is therefore all the more valuable; and certainly Sismondi's frank tribute to the Countess' intellectual force ought never to be omitted in any account of her.

" I have brought home to my mother," so Sismondi writes from Pescia on June 23, 1812, "a head and a heart full of all I have seen, all I have heard, all I have attempted in Florence. I have lived more fully, I have thought more deeply, during those three days than I could ever have done in three weeks at Pescia. But it is you yourself, Madame, that have opened out this new life to me, and roused this energy of mine, which is not habitual with me, I assure you. Sometimes I reproach myself for having talked so much, so that I dread your possible accusation of chattering. But then again it was yourself that supplied me with my words, and roused my anima-

288

tion by making me feel in our conversations a certain
satisfaction to which I had long been a stranger. So,
after all, I flatter myself you cannot well blame me for a
fault whereof you were the principal cause! On the
contrary, I should like to begin all over again. I long and
hope to pass many hours of the future in your delightful
company, and here in Pescia I try to feed on such recollections of your conversation as still flit through my
mind." *

After a visit to Paris, however, where amongst others
he was warmly welcomed by the kind Madame de Souza,
Sismondi began slowly but definitely to shed his deep-
rooted prejudices and his distrust of the French emperor
and his policy, and this change in his opinions was regarded
with growing indignation by the Countess of Albany,
Against her accusations, often couched in sharp language,
the historian sought to defend and justify his conduct in
open but courteous terms, begging the Countess to
remember their points of agreement rather than their
new-sprung differences. With the fall of Napoleon in
the spring of 1814 this literary duel came to a head, and
Sismondi thus defends himself against the bitter charges
of his correspondent in Florence.—" I admit without
restriction all you say about Buonaparte; so why should
not you admit all I say, or even think about the Allies?
It is only that you always look back upon the past, whilst
I am ever watching the future. Each of us thinks the
devil plays a great part in all we see before us, and it is
likely enough that we are both in the right." † And
again in a letter from Geneva, his native town, written on
October 6, 1814, Sismondi returns to the charge.

" In your last letter you were still all-triumphant over
the recent changes, full of hope for the future and full of
horror for the past. My opinion is very different, for I
am full of a kindly feeling for the power that has fallen

* *Lettres de Sismondi*, p. 149.   † *Ibidem.*

and is no longer to be feared, and full of distrust of what is now being brought forth. I am much afraid that, as so often happens in such a case, we hold our separate opinions with hard determination. I perceive with a growing concern what is now proceeding all over Europe, with the sole exception of France. I can understand the hatred felt towards a monarch of boundless ambition, but such hatred is not equal to the intensity of my contempt for the silly sovereigns, and I do not know whether I feel the more disgust or indignation, when I behold so many princes and so many governments being re-established solely on account of their folly and utter incapacity. I strongly doubt whether this restoration, to-day so universal and so acclaimed, can long serve to satisfy the nations ; whilst I fancy this reaction towards despotism seems to us both the presage of fresh revolutions in the future. Then, possibly, Madame, we shall once more find ourselves in full agreement, though till that day I sincerely trust our disputes will not weaken the friendship wherewith you have deigned to honour me." *

That Sismondi was correct in his prophecy that the Countess would ere long declaim against the imbecility and blindness of the restored princes can easily be confirmed from a letter of hers to Foscolo, which is included in the following chapter. In a letter dated a few days before the momentous escape of Napoleon from Elba, the historian again enlarges on the theme of the differences between himself and the Countess, the reason for which he seeks to find in the more personal, and therefore more vouthful, outlook of the lady upon the world of individual men rather than of political ideals—a curious contrast in masculine and feminine reasoning in a clever man and a clever woman.

" Our failure to agree results from the circumstance that you attach yourself to *persons* and I to *principles*. Each of us is faithful to the original object of our devotion

* *Ibidem*, p. 259.

or our hate ; I to things, you to individuals.   For myself
I always profess the same approval of liberal ideas, the
same horror of despotism, the same love of civil and
religious liberty, the same contempt and the same loathing of intolerance and the doctrine of passive obedience.
Whereas, Madame, you keep the same attitude towards
persons, in whatsoever situation you may find them.
Those whom you have pitied and admired in misfortune,
you also admire in prosperity ; and those whom you
execrated during their day of tyranny, you still execrate in
their fall.   You keep for the Pope on his throne the
respect he gained whilst a prisoner ; you remain equally
faithful to the ejected kings, to the refugees, and to the
priests, although they demand your pity no longer.   On
the other hand, you are just as bitter against the Emperor
as when, with the sole exception of yourself, the whole
world cringed at his feet.   In comparing these two varieties
of political faith, yours to persons and mine to principles,
I shall observe, despite any protest on your part, that
your view is far more passionate, far more youthful than
mine ; and that notwithstanding all your efforts to keep
calm by means of the study of philosophy and a lengthy
retirement, you still own a warmer heart and more fiery
sentiments than the man whom you sometimes in your
letters accuse of youth and immaturity ! " *

One can imagine the feelings of horror wherewith the
Countess must have heard the news, a few weeks later,
that the wavering Sismondi had actually decided to
support the returning Emperor, by whom he had been
most graciously received in Paris in the opening week of
May 1815.   Would that we could see with our own eyes
the letter the enraged lady indited to this new convert
to Napoleonic despotism !   She herself tells us in a letter
to Foscolo that she had spoken pretty plainly to the
erring Sismondi, so we can only imagine an exceedingly
severe lecture.   Such conduct naturally helped to

* *Ibidem*, p. 270.

weaken the valued bonds of friendship, yet even for such
heinous behaviour as his recognition of Napoleon during
the Hundred Days, the historian was eventually forgiven.
Within a year of this incident Sismondi presented to the
Countess, "as an offering in hope of forgiveness," the
three recently published volumes of his *Italian Republics*,
and presumably the gift was graciously accepted, for he
writes again ten days later to express his intention of
calling ere long at Casa Alfieri. More letters follow,
and with many details of interest concerning Madame de
Stael—Sismondi may almost be described as forming an
intellectual link between the *salons* of Madame de Stael
and of Madame d'Albany—Bonstetten, Lord Byron,
and other persons of interest ; the last communication between this pair of correspondents being dated
November 2, 1823, within three months of the death of
the Countess.

Sismondi had already announced to his old patroness
his marriage with Miss Jessie Allen, the daughter of Mr.
Allen of Cresselly, a Pembrokeshire squire, on April 19,
1819, whom he had met whilst she was travelling in Italy
with her sister, Lady Mackintosh. He hopes that his
old friend will receive Madame Sismondi when they
arrive in Florence, especially since it appears the lady
had already been presented to the Countess. Sismondi
himself died at Geneva in 1842, whilst his widow survived
her husband many years, settling at Tenby in South
Wales, where a few persons still living can recall her as an
agreeable and clever old lady, who had seen and
experienced much in the intellectual world whereof we
have just been speaking.

CHAPTER XV

UGO FOSCOLO *

"It is some eight or ten years since I last saw Monsieur Foscolo. He was then quite a youth, but he had a magnificent face, melancholy and passionate in its expression, and closely resembling one's idea of his own hero, Jacopo Ortis. At the same time he showed a quickness, a flow of subjects, an eagerness in his conversation which made him a most agreeable person to meet. . . . Is it ambition, or is it dissipation that has turned him off that path of glory, which he seemed so anxious to pursue? I can only hope that neither one nor the other was the cause, and that in the midst of the general upheaval his ideals remained as pure as of old." — *Letter of* SISMONDI *to the* COUNTESS OF ALBANY, *of October* 12, 1812

THE correspondence of the Countess of Albany with Ugo Foscolo ranks as second in importance only to that with Teresa Mocenni, and we therefore offer no apology for inserting here some portion of the thirty-nine letters, which she addressed to the Italian patriot-poet between 1813–1816, the last-named year being the date of his departure for England, where he finally died in 1827. The letters, or portions of letters, quoted ought to speak for themselves, so that we leave the reader confidently to draw therefrom the same conclusion as our own; namely, that whatever prejudiced Italian writers may aver to the contrary on this subject, the relations between Foscolo and the Countess were strictly those of a great lady of sixty, who strove (vainly as it will be seen) to exercise a benevolent and on the whole a judicious influence over a hasty and unscrupulous man of letters,

* The quotations contained in this chapter are taken (unless otherwise stated) from Signore Antona-Traversi's work, *Lettere Inedite di Luigia di Stolberg, Comtessa d'Albany, a Ugo Foscolo.* (Roma, 1887.)

293

nearly a quarter of a century her junior. Her strong
affection for Foscolo is never once disguised ; her advice
to him is always sound and practical, even if somewhat
cynically material—and the Countess was truly, as Gino
Capponi once affirmed, *un po' materiolotta*—whilst her
open interest in his love intrigues with his " Graces,"
if not a wholesome sentiment, goes at least to prove as
genuine her constantly recurring statement that for her
own part she infinitely preferred the poet as a friend
than as a lover : a statement which some of the Italian
critics stoutly deny, for the sole reason that they appear
to regard such an attitude in any woman towards any
man as utterly inconceivable. Yet whatever else Madame
d'Albany may have been, she was no mere elderly
coquette. Her flagrant disregard of the fashion of the
day, her dowdy appearance, her studious and retired
life, her early hours, all serve to exhibit her what she
described herself ; a great lady who had enjoyed her
share of love, of rivalry and of pleasure, and was now
content to sit at the window and gaze with mingled
amusement and contempt at the magic-lantern show
of the passing years. She was a mature Lady of Shalott
watching in her enchanted mirror the events of the
outside world, but a Lady whose Sir Launcelot had long
since come and gone, and who neither expected nor
desired a second knight. There is not a scrap of evidence
to be found in these letters for the spiteful comments
and deductions concerning this friendship with Foscolo,
that may be said to find their full expression in the
following outrageous remarks, which we quote as a
specimen of modern Italian vituperation against the
" Donna Amata " of Alfieri.

" The Countess of Albany, thanks to the blessing of
her sixty years, being prevented from according her heart
to the author of the *Sepolcri*, tendered him her special
and powerful protection ; a protection which Quirina
Mocenni-Magiotti, writing to Foscolo, ironically named
maternal ; but which the Countess would gladly have
called by a more amorous name, if Foscolo, with regard

to women, had owned the same taste as the painter
Fabre. However, in the bottom of her heart, she never
knew how to forgive the Poet for having preferred the
smile of Isabella Roncioni, or the graceful figure of the
Nencini, or the cultured mind of Quirina Mocenni to
her own very mature attractions. For such neglect
she avenged herself—as old flames know how—by saying
every possible vile thing of her youthful rivals."*

From such unfair abuse as this the actual contents of
her correspondence with Foscolo will prove Madame
d'Albany's best protection, and we feel we can safely
leave her character in the hands of the reader.

Ugo Foscolo, the son of a Venetian father and a Greek
mother, was born in 1776, at Zante, one of the Ionian
Islands. Full of vague but patriotic fervour and of
poetic ideas as yet unmatured, he had visited Florence
so early as the close of the past century ; but he does
not on this occasion seem to have ventured to introduce
himself to the notice of the great Alfieri, of whose verses,
aspirations and ideals he had always been a blind admirer.
Still a very young man at the date of this first visit, he
had, however, secretly and at a distance, pursued the
footsteps of his idol, following the gloomy and self-
absorbed poet of Asti in his wanderings through the
historic churches of Santa Croce and Santa Maria
Novella, enriched with the tombs of the illustrious dead
or else had dogged his footsteps, as Alfieri strode fiercely
and blindly along the mouldering ring of the mediæval
walls of Florence, or beside the reed-beds fringing the
deserted banks of the Arno. In the inimitably beautiful
language of his famous poem, the *Sepolcri*, Foscolo has preserved his romantic picture of Alfieri as he first appeared
to the young disciple's warm imagination and worshipping
eyes at this period.

> . . . *a questi marmi*
> *Venne spesso Vittorio ad ispirarsi.*
> *Irato a patri numi, errava muto*
> *Ove Arno è piu deserto.*

---

* Emilio del Cerro, *Epistolario . . . di Ugo Foscolo.*

A dozen years later Foscolo revisited Florence at the age of thirty-six, surrounded by the glamour of his *Sepolcri* and the *Last Letters of Jacopo Ortis*, that morbid romance which may be accounted an Italian version of Goethe's *Sorrows of Werther*. Naturally, he received a warm, even an enthusiastic welcome in the Tuscan capital, then under the easy rule of Élise Buonaparte. His literary fame and his past career with its varied adventures appealed strongly to all, for one who was at once "poet, soldier, philosopher, novelist, patriot and untamed rover," cannot have appeared otherwise than as a romantic personage. Moreover, his sad reputation for gallantry must have acted as an additional attraction to the frivolous ladies of Florentine society, of whom Madame d'Albany's pen has left us so unpleasant but apparently so veracious a picture. To the Countess herself this fascinating disciple of her dead Friend naturally appealed with a special force. Foscolo's poetic imagination, his marked ability, his agreeable conversation, his good looks (whose type recalled those of Alfieri), his extreme deference to herself as the widow of a king, as the "Degno Amore" of his idol, as a woman of unusual talents and experience, all combined, and very naturally so, to invest him in her eyes with a deep and peculiar interest. Again, we appeal to the reader to discover for himself how far that peculiar interest extended, what was its exact nature, and to what extent she helped this brilliant but erratic genius with her social influence, her counsel, and also, be it added, with her purse.

Very soon after his arrival in Florence, Foscolo became an habitual visitor at Casa Alfieri and an intimate friend both of the Countess and of Fabre, who at Madame d'Albany's request began to paint a portrait of the handsome poet. "On the evenings," so he writes, "when I do not wander forth to commune with the river, the trees and the clouds, or do not require solitude in my own chamber, I go to pass a short hour with the Countess of Albany. And I go there because I am lodging hard by, because she herself retires early at ten o'clock, and because she often talks about Alfieri." Many and long were the discussions on politics and literature between Foscolo and his hostess in the *salon* overlooking the Lung' Arno; that same room which some years later received the impressionable Lamartine, who describes his ecstasy in watching from its windows the moonbeams sparkling on the Arno and in meditating on the departed Alfieri. These intellectual conversations in Casa Alfieri revealed, as the Countess well knew, only one side of the poet's mind, for intrigue occupied a large portion of his leisure, and it was against this perpetual waste of his time, his health, and his scanty means on such employment, that the Countess was for ever cautioning him. Possibly her advice and lectures were not wholly disinterested; but who can deny that the time spent by Foscolo in her *salon* was not more profitable than the long hours wasted on his Florentine " Graces," who in Madame d'Albany's own bitter words were wholly averse to sharing the lover with his Muse ?

The first of these letters following is directed to the poet at the picturesque Villa dell' Ombrellino, on the beautiful hill of Bellosguardo above Florence, where he had lately taken up his abode.

" Monday, April 19th, 1813.

" MY DEAR UGO,—. . . I did not know you had been ill, and I am very sorry for it. But I am not surprised, for it is too great a strain on your constitution, this running backwards and forwards twice daily between Florence and Bellosguardo. You make the mistake of thinking your physical strength equal to your mental powers, and in your warm imagination you picture yourself as a Hercules. Have a care, I beg you ! Health is the only substantial blessing in this world, and it is something more than a necessity to one like yourself, who offers prayer and sacrifice to the God of Love in addition to the vows he has already made to Apollo.

297

" I miss your presence, for I had grown only too much accustomed to enjoy your agreeable and instructive conversation, which it would be difficult to match. When I received your letter last evening, your former Graces seemed anxious as to your state of health, and in particular the R . . . and Isabella (Roncioni) eagerly asked me for news of you. Your attention to our sex has made you the spoiled darling of the ladies. As to myself, I fancy I appreciate your high moral gifts, for I consider you both good and talented, and I am ready to work warmly and sincerely on your behalf. Make any possible use therefore you like of me, and rely on my interest and affection. Descend from your hill [of Bellosguardo] to be nursed and to be nearer us. I await your coming with pleasure.

" Drink some milk boiled with sugar for your digestion, and try to extinguish the mischief in your breast with which you ought not to trifle."

A letter from Leghorn three months later, dated July 15, bids farewell to Foscolo, who, although still in indifferent health, was on the point of rejoining the army at Milan.

" I am very sorry, my dear Monsieur, for what you tell me in your letter to-day. I fear you are inclined to burn the candle at both ends. When you work so much with your head, you must be moderate in other things. . . . The Muses demand continence, so the change to Milan will benefit you.

" Life is a sea of worries and contradictions, besides the enemies we have to guard against. Monsieur Fabre sends you his compliments. He is kept to his bed by the gout, which he strives in vain to cure. I nurse him as best I can, for it is in sickness that friends are most essential. I hope your friends, of either sex, do not abandon you to solitude at Bellosguardo. Return as soon as possible to Florence for the sake of those who

love your art and for the sake of your Graces. Tell
me your news and all your adventures; from one brief
hint I can guess the rest. Keep well; take care of yourself; and remember we all have but one life to live,
and also that if we wish to leave a great name behind us,
there is need of all our faculties to attain that end. I
have filled my paper. *Comptez sur ma discretion.*"

From the contents of the following letter, dated
August 5, it becomes evident that the crafty Foscolo
had addressed his distinguished correspondent in terms
that were certainly amatory, or at least likely to become
so, if the Countess were willing to accept his professions in good faith. The shrewd sense of Madame
d'Albany was, however, fully proof against the wiles of
the patriot-poet, whom she was anxious to please but
not to serve.

"My dear Ugo, . . . I thank you for your very kind
recollection of me, which I value greatly. If I had
more self-esteem and less experience of the world, I
should be deeply flattered by your remarks, but I lay
all eulogy at the feet of One who, for only too brief a
space, occupied the house that you sometimes visit and
that always receives you with pleasure, because, apart
from your fine qualities of mind, your native goodness
of heart attracts me. I can assure you that I miss your
presence every evening, and I tell my friends frankly of
my loss. But I realise your better worth as a friend than
as a lover; however, at my age and in my circumstances
you suit me admirably.
". . . The first of your Graces, La Nencini, is consoling herself for your departure with a handsome Frenchman, but then they tell me you had already grown cold
to her before you left Florence. You take love like a
philosopher, enjoying all the fruit you can get and avoiding the thorns. Very good! Fortunately, Italian
women are like yourself; whilst I could never be of their

299

opinion, for I always intended to surrender myself absolutely to a first and solitary passion.

" You do not tell me if my dear *Ricciarda* * is to be put on the stage, but of course you will tell me how it succeeds. It ought to win approval, for it is graceful and pleasant, and full of a passion, whereof your Graces are wholly incapable, luckily for yourself ! With regard to your Graces, you must be more moderate, otherwise you will die young. Keep all your power for the Muses, and only spare a trifle of it for the Graces. One a week is sufficient.

" That poor bankrupt Molini, the book-seller, has not sent me your translation of Sterne ; first he tried to deny your gift to me, and then declared the volumes had not yet been sent from Pisa. I am anxious to read them, as I am to read anything of yours, for all your work carries a spice of originality with it. The Abbé di Caluso is here, but is just leaving. Monsieur Fabre, gouty as ever, sends you messages. I keep very well, and await with impatience your company and conversation at my round table, no longer garnished with knights. Keep your friendly feelings towards me, since I deserve them in return for my friendship to yourself. I have nothing to recommend me, except that I am a good woman very devoted to her friends and making no claims upon them. Return quickly hither to sacrifice to your Graces, and to bestow on me the boon of your cheerful, agreeable and instructive society."

" FLORENCE, *August* 15th, 1813.

" . . . You observe that in Florence we hardly think of great passing events, with such trifles are the Florentine occupied. We shall discuss that question on your return hither. As to love, of necessity you regard it as a writer of tragedies, who has not yet bestowed his heart seriously and still wants to play the butterfly. I agree with your first Tuscan Flame (the Roncioni) in preferring you as

* The play of that name, which Ugo Foscolo dedicated to Lord John Russell.

a friend rather than as a lover ; and I am glad of it, for one can count on your friendship, whilst you can rely on its return on my part. I know the fundamental goodness of your heart, apart from the qualities which attract and amuse society here. I eagerly await your return. Monsieur Sismondi writes me that he too will be in Florence in October. I want you to make his acquaintance, for he unites solid worth with agreeable manners, an unusual combination in original minds, which are often morose and haughty.

" Monsieur Fabre, who is still a martyr to the gout, thanks you for your kind remembrances. He has almost finished restoring a superb picture by Raphael in his early manner, that has recently come to light."

The next letter, dated Friday, November 19, refers to Foscolo's mistress, Madame Maddalena Bignami, at Milan, and also foreshadows the beginning of the writer's break with Sismondi, whom she has only lately so belauded to Foscolo.

" My dear Ugo,—I have only just received your letter of Monday from Bologna. Please accept my warmest thanks for sending me your news. I am still more anxiously expecting your letter from Milan, to tell me you have escaped capture by the brigands, of whom I stand in great dread. I trust Tuesday will find you safe and sound beside your excellent friend (Madame Bignami), whom I should like to meet, since she is so devoted to you. Return her all her affection in full. To be loved is the perfect gift of this world, as well as the power of relying on an honest heart in a person worthy of esteem.

" I miss you, and the more so because on better acquaintance I admire you. I can tell you without fear that I love you, for at my age love for one who deserves love becomes a pure sentiment, for which I have no need to blush. You have spoiled me, so that I shall find it hard now to perceive merit in others. I have been deeply disappointed in observing the author of the

Républiques Italiennes grown less capable and more precise. He seems to have parted with some of his good qualities in Paris. Weak-minded persons going into that wretched country easily pick up French notions, and become fascinated by French grimaces. He has also assimilated some German ideas on *perfectibilité*. He is swayed not a little by the chimæras of other people. He is still here, and I see him daily. I shall give him your message. He is a warm admirer of your genius, and if he knew your other qualities, he would like you, for you are good and sensitive. I do not regret having known you, but I do regret that we did not inhabit the same city.

" What you tell me of your craving to see your idol of Italian independence surprises me. I myself only imagine the new scheme* to be a ruse of Napoleon's for his own ends. God grant yourself and others it may be for the best. But it really matters nothing whether Peter or Paul be master in Italy. . . .

" Your portrait is making good progress and is almost completed. Your friend, Madame Bignami, will be delighted to see it and possess it. I enjoin prudence for you—you understand me ?—otherwise you will come to utter grief. Keep calm, and do not allow too free a rein to your fancy.

" We have had fine weather and a hard frost the last two days. I am only too glad to sit alone of an evening, for the Florentines bore me, and I love my books a thousand times better than any gossip of theirs. I lament your absence with my whole heart, and I regret the events that have separated us.

" Take care of your health, and remember you have a friend in Florence who loves you. Monsieur Fabre has finished your picture, and sends you messages. . . . Did you get, before leaving, my note and the copy of Homer, which belonged once to *Someone* you admire ? "

* The erection of Italy into a kingdom under the vice-royalty of Eugène de Beauharnais.

The letters of the Countess grow more affectionate in tone, as the poet writes from time to time. " Do not think I can forget you," she writes on December 10, " for my friendship for you is based on your good qualities, and I shall carry my affection for you to the grave. I should like to live in the same town with you, in which case you might consecrate to myself such hours as you could spare from your friend Madame Bignami. . . .

" Some day you will be fortunate enough to gain a sure Friend, ready to share in your inmost feelings. So long as we are young, we want to play the butterfly, but in mature years we long to give the heart and mind full repose on the bosom of some Friend, on whom we can rely. That is the only real boon the world can grant. One grows weary of all women that are unworthy of esteem, because, when once desire is satisfied, there remains nothing ; it is only the deep devotion of the heart that survives and lasts. If inquisitive eyes were to peep into this letter, how edified they would be at the morality contained herein ! . . ."

" Florence, *February* 2, 1814.

" My dear Ugo, . . . I cannot imagine who it is that finds amusement in waylaying our correspondence, which can interest nobody but ourselves ! I observe by your last letter that you are happier, which is as I predicted ; nevertheless, you could not come on a visit to Florence at this moment. Yesterday [Murat's] Neapolitan troops left us, and the G[rand] D[uchess Élise] is gone. The officials and the garrison remain. We hear no news. God grant us the peace whereof we stand in such need. As for myself, I advise you to put some water in your wine, in a moral and not a material sense, for you do not drink wine. It is useless to rack yourself on behalf of others. Very few persons merit the smallest sacrifice, and this is still more true of the multitude at large. In the midst of a corrupt nation one must be noted for loftiness of morals and high culture. If you will but abandon yourself wholly to literature, you will gain more fame thereby than by conquering the world, particularly if you surrender yourself entirely to the Muses and do not flit from one subject to another, for I consider you change your direction too often. Your mind is as fickle as your heart. You pursue an evanescent glory. You waste too much of your time over women. When study is your first thought, you must not take love too seriously, but must regard it merely as an evening's distraction in moderation. Better still, you should cultivate an attachment to some person that can share your tastes and ideals, though it is a difficult task to find such an one in Italy, where the women decline to share the lover with his Muse, and do not care a doit for his fame. . . ."

The break with Madame Bignami, the Milanese " Grace," was of course inevitable, and the poet at once wrote of the matter to the Countess in Florence, who had doubtless foreseen what was coming, and was not in the least sorry to learn that Foscolo's susceptible and fickle heart was once again free. Her letter on this occasion contains much good advice but only a modicum of genuine sympathy.

" I have received from Turin, my dear Ugo," she writes on February 2, " within the last two or three days your missing letters of last month. I believe you really forget to post them ! Well, anyhow I have got them, and have deciphered their contents with infinite labour. I clearly perceive that you are enthralled by your own imagination, and I pity you with all my heart. Unhappily you have no remedy. All poets are the same. Of course it is sad and tiresome to be deprived of the society of a woman you love, but surely you must remember she belongs to another, who objects to your presence in his house. So you must make up your mind to resign her, and to limit your claims to those of mere friendship.

You surely have not forgotten that here in Florence you were guilty of a score of intrigues ? If you had been dominated by a *grande passion*, you would never have become so greedy for fresh conquests. Only desire had a share in them, for your flames have plainly shown that it was *men* they wanted. . . .

"To hark back to your literary career. You must start by putting your finances in order, and by trying to realise the folly of flinging your money about without rhyme or reason. You must become sensible (which you are not), and you must take care of your health, for it appears to me to be much shattered. It would have made a good excuse for you to leave the army. How funny you are about your honour ! Surely you must realise there is sham honour and real honour, and that to defend what is valueless is sheer folly. Your last letter is full of nonsensical ideas. You want somebody to keep you in the path of common-sense, from which you so constantly stray. You require some talks at my round table. You confide in my common-sense, my sole quality of worth, for I do not pretend to be a genius. I only pride myself, and rightly so, on my good sense and good judgment. I have been making trial of these two qualities the last few days, when everybody was in wild alarm, and I caused my friends annoyance by my placid attitude, because I saw things as they really were. You know how cowardly the Florentines are.

"Take care of your health, and we shall yet find the opportunity to talk, dispute, and smile over human folly. You have not yet attained the age, when the world appears only as a magic-lantern, bright or sombre according to the objects presented.

"Always count on my friendship and my warm interest. Monsieur Fabre exhorts you to grow reasonable. I scold him too sometimes. Love me ever, and tell me all possible news of yourself."

In the following letter Madame d'Albany returns

to the same subject, and also lectures Foscolo on what she considers his Quixotic attachment to the vague growing movement on behalf of Italian unity, an alleged weakness with which she had already twitted him in a previous epistle.

" . . . I could wish the present icy weather would cool your volcanic temperament, which seems to have been in constant eruption ever since you quitted my round table ! You want a steadying hand to keep you in the path of common-sense, and also somebody to make you see things as they really are, and not as they loom before your poet's eye.

" I believe you are sincerely attached to your friend, Madame Bignami, but your late behaviour here has proved you can have had no real love for her. When one is truly in love, all women seem alike, except the one adored object. It is true, however, that men have a different standard of love from ours. Your imagination finds incessant need of occupation, no matter for what purpose.

" You will do wisely to renounce the Other Dame (Italy), believe me. She deserves nothing. Her sons are too corrupt and feeble to fly on their own wings. One would like to see their strength restored ; but the doctor appointed (the Viceroy Prince Eugène) is not wise enough to inspire confidence.

" For myself, I lead my usual existence. I sit at the window, and watch the scenes of the magic-lantern pass and find them sufficiently amusing.

" Guard your health. Come back here, when you can, sound in body and mind, ready for work, for fame, and for the true enjoyment of life. It is wiser to produce good books than to seek to conquer the world.

" Keep your affection for me, and rely on mine in return for it. Monsieur Fabre salutes you. He is solely occupied with *his* Dame, Painting ! "

In a subsequent letter, of May 19, the Countess continues to warn Foscolo against wrecking his future prospects by joining too ardently in the new-born move-ment for Italian independence and unity, then attracting so many adherents in Milan.

" . . . Believe me, neither the world at large nor individual men are worth the trouble of embroiling yourself on their behalf. You are sure to emerge from the coming struggle injured both in mind and body. Your beloved fellow-countrymen [in Milan] do not know what they want, any more than they do elsewhere in Italy. They consider the whole world ought to exert itself on their behalf, yet they would not sacrifice a life, or even a penny-piece, to obtain any government whatsoever. Besides, they are, and always will be, the prey of any man who cares to hold them by a *force majeure*.

" It is the common fate of all lands that have become corrupt and selfish, where the citizens are the slaves of idle pleasures or of monkish bigotry, and where education has been neglected. If our modern Attila [Napoleon] had been able to tyrannise over Europe for another decade, possibly Italy might have acquired a little energy, but at present she is fallen into a condition of apathy, and her inhabitants have sunk afresh into the worship of the Madonna, equally of Heaven and of earth."

The mention of " the modern Attila " in this letter reminds us of the Countess' undying antipathy to Napoleon, whose recent fall and removal to Elba, unpleasantly near the Tuscan coast, are at various times commented on with a bitterness which is extended to Sismondi and to any of her friends who had shown sympathy with the Emperor in his downfall.

On May 20, the Countess writes of Napoleon's arrival in Elba.

" . . . King of his island, he has found a rascally priest there, who is ready to thank Heaven for sending so great a man to so insignificant a spot. He is going to build a palace, a school, a theatre, a poor-house and a hospital. Elba will become the Fortunate Island! How I wish another world had been favoured with his presence. He admits himself that his career is not yet closed. Tuscany is quiet, and only demands its Grand-Duke Ferdinand's return.

" . . . You will accuse me of contradicting my own remarks, but I cannot think of the expression ' sublime ' in connection with the Sovereign of the Isle of Elba. I do certainly allow him to be one of those gigantic beings, a veritable Cyclops, who has spread consternation throughout the world. But I hold him, as I have always declared, merely an adventurer. All his great schemes had no solid foundation, and when once united resistance was made to them, they have crumbled to nothing The Allies, thanks to his wife the Empress Marie-Louise, have been too lenient, and have inflicted him upon us as a dangerous neighbour. Since his arrival at Elba, he has already shown himself more vain than high-minded. He stayed twelve hours on board ship, so as to arrange the ceremonial of his entry and reception, and now he has set up a court with two chamberlains and four pages. It is a paltry Mock Majesty, and his subjects are even more contemptible than he. The French will for many a day to come be lamenting their quarter of a century of so-called glory, which I call infamy. They made a resolution to obtain liberty, so they got tyrants to decimate France. To escape anarchy they then threw themselves into the clutches of a monstre like Napoleon, and now the Allies have had to save them from the consequences of their own folly, after they have made the name of Frenchman loathed for generations to come.

" They will be weeping over their national honour, stained by their own fault. Monsieur Sismondi, who calls himself French merely because he writes and speaks that language,* is one of those creatures who would have welcomed a continuation of this tyranny. . . .

* Ducrest, vol. i. p. 95. " M. Sismondi retained the Genevese accent in all its purity ! "

308

" At present we are having a course of Church ceremonies and chantings of the *Te Deum* here, and truly
we are justified in returning thanks in song to Providence
for having delivered us from an abominable *Monstre*,
who is making absurd changes in his island.   I was never
mistaken in my estimate of him.   Do you recollect our
arguments, in which, solely out of politeness, you would
not tell me flatly I was talking nonsense ?   Now time
has proved me in the right.   I pity the King of France,
his successor, who finds a kingdom in ruins, an empty
treasury and a nation utterly demoralised.

" . . . It seems that the returning monarchs, with
the exception of Louis XVIII., are making great mistakes.
The *Monstre*, whose island I can see from my window
here in Leghorn, has put us all back a century, for fear
of imitating his example.   For the ' revenants ' have
not assimilated a single new idea for the last fifteen years.
They have been fast asleep, and have now awakened
at the exact point where slumber overtook them.   I
really think the world is composed of slaves from its
endurance of past and present rulers."

" FLORENCE, *September 2nd*, 1814.

" MY DEAR UGO,—The 20 *francesconi* have arrived
safe.   After paying out 18, I spent the remainder yesterday.   Since you have sent no remittance to your servant,
I shall continue to pay the customary *zecchino* a month
to his mother. . . .

" Excuse me, but the Italians in general are poor-
spirited, know nothing of glory, and are incapable of
making the smallest sacrifice.   The country, too, is very
rich, nor has it suffered sufficiently to make its citizens
despair.   *Basta la dessus.* . . . The picture you draw
of your own city of Milan is somewhat similar to that
of Florence.   I believe the people have gained, and the
returning royalties have lost, fifteen years, so the two
are bound to fall out and disagree.   The priests expect
to regain their old power, and are jeered at, yet the

Government upholds them. When our Grand-Duke condescends to return to his capital, many at present in command and under priestly influence will be dismissed. As to myself, I laugh at it all . . . for the world is amusing enough to one like myself who has no need of it, and it now affords me a constant comedy, particularly since the principal actor in the late tragedy is shut up in an island.

" Tell me of your health, and of your intentions. What about your return to Florence ? At what are you working now ?

" Monsieur Fabre salutes you. He is engaged upon a splendid picture for my party, *The Death of Narcissus*,* in a lovely landscape. Your Belle (la Nencini) has just returned from Naples, where her friend, the General, has been nominated governor. There is a Tuscan officer here of the Anglo-Sicilian army, as enthusiastic as yourself for the glory of Italy, now engaged in courting the Belle, who happens to be an old flame of his. I often wished you two could find yourselves together in my *salon*, for the four walls could never have held the pair of you ! . . ."

" FLORENCE, *January* 7, 1815.

" I thank you, my dear Ugo, for your good wishes for the New Year just begun. I trust it will not draw to a close without your presence here. I flatter myself that when the big-wigs have finished (at the Congress of Vienna) you will contrive to take up a more reasonable and safer attitude in politics. I wish you could have admired the Graces the other evening at my party, Graces very different from those *you* are wont to sing ! It was a collection of virginal charms with beautiful features, rivalling the Muse of Canova. Such exquisite figures, plump but not too fat. It is many a long day since I have seen so many pretty faces. Your beauty of the Porta San Gallo (La Nencini), would sink even in your eyes by comparison. Where are you, my dear

* This picture was bequeathed by the Countess to the Florentine gallery.

310

Ugo ? Why are you not here ? Your poetic fire would be rekindled and would burn up all your melancholy. I deplore your absence every day for myself, and on Saturdays (when I have my parties) for your own sake. . . ."

The next letter, dated August 13, 1815, and directed " à Monsieur Ugo Foscolo dans l'île d'Ouffenau, Canton de Schwyz, près Zurich," expresses the writer's displeasure at Foscolo's refusal to take the required oath of allegiance to the newly-established Austrian Government in Milan, and at his action in voluntarily exchanging Italian for Swiss soil, and thereby becoming in fact the first popular patriot of the new-born movement towards Italian unity, known later as the " Risorgimento." It is hard to understand the extreme degree of offence this particular letter has always given to Italian writers and critics of this period. Its tone, though satirical, is far from unkind ; and indeed, the Countess was certainly entitled to give Foscolo a private piece of well-intentioned advice as a friend and well-wisher so many years older than himself. That her remarks proved unpalatable to the conceited poet can easily be understood ; but for critics to argue in these days from the contents of a private letter that the Countess was opposed on principle to the very notion of national independence, and was deliberately in favour of the *ancien régime* in Italy is utterly at variance with the evidence we possess of her acknowledged and open sympathy with the various liberal ideas that were then permeating Italian thought. It is at least certain, for example, that the patriotic Abbé Luigi di Breme regarded Madame d'Albany as one of those who were in accord with the new national aspirations, however cynical or pessimistic may have been her views as to the ultimate success of the movement. Rightly or wrongly, the Countess looked upon Foscolo's refusal to settle quietly in Italy as a mistake due to false sentiment, and she says so plainly ; but to

interpret her remarks as an open expression of hostility
to the cause of Italian unity is both absurd and unfair.

"MY DEAR SIR,—I have received your letter of the
4th. I was told you had been in Paris, and had thence
crossed over to England. If you had consented to behave
like everybody else, you would have stayed on quietly
at Milan, and none would' have concerned themselves
more about you than others ; and I think this the more
likely since a gentleman from Milan tells me that the
taking of the oath [of allegiance] was optional. So it
has seemed good to you to start off into the mountains ;
and if you find such a course amusing, well and good.
As to your lately published *Discourses on the Servitude
of Italy*, you have not taught the people anything new,
for there was nothing left to be said on the subject. It
was the cannons that spoke and acted. For my own
part, I count on a tranquil life, for none will compel
me to change my abode, unless I choose to do so ; towards
all other matters I feel indifferent. And I advise everybody to think of settling down with the least possible
discomfort, and this course I recommend to yourself
in particular. If in the midst of your Swiss crags you
read the newspapers, you will have learnt how Monsieur
Sismondi has written on behalf of Him who has fallen
so ignobly,* but the behaviour of his brother-in-law
(Murat) amazes me no less. Only fools or schemers
ally themselves with these little-great men. I am told
you sympathise with them, but then I am also told you
are changeable, like so many others, despite all your
efforts to attain originality. I cannot conceal the fact
that I disapprove of your conduct. Perhaps if I heard
your own side of the story, you would make me alter my
opinion. In any case, accept the assurance of interest
both from myself and the Painter. I did receive your
former letter, but could not reply at once, for the very
good reason that the spies were active ; and as you had

* Napoleon I.

disappeared so suddenly, I thought it more prudent to hold no communication with you. Keep well. Enjoy the chilly scenery of Switzerland, and feed your imagination thereon, for it will help you to make good poetry, though it will never bring you happiness. But then happiness itself is relative, and its definition varies with the individual.

" Your friend, poor Mr. Rose, has had a stroke at Verona, and is paralyzed on one side. He is now at the baths of Abano with some Venetian woman, whom he has dragged with him all over Italy. Apparently this sort of life was too much for him. He was expecting to travel with you to England, when I told him of your disappearance. Farewell, send me your news. I am glad to hear necessity has taught you to shave yourself, there are so many little luxuries in this life one can well dispense with."

"January 16th, 1816.

" I have received, my dear Ugo, your letter of December 21st. I am sorry I have annoyed you by telling you what I thought of your retirement to Switzerland. But since it suits you and you consider the step necessary, *soit un fou en sait plus chez soi que des sages chez les autres.* Your imagination is satisfied, and it ought to be cooled by the prospect of all the snow that covers your present abode. As a native of Zante, you must have excellent reasons for electing to dwell in such a place. By the bye, your own islands have become free, and are now under British protection. I congratulate you, for you can now go and play at liberty there ! But I fear you crave for something very different. You have lived too long amongst a corrupt and enslaved people to feel satisfied with the severe rule of Liberty. You adore society ; you love to shine in it ; to shake a well-formed leg in it ; to be a social butterfly ; to read aloud and to win praise for your own works of genius. At Zante I expect you would find nothing of that kind, and no social stage big enough for your needs. So, my dear Ugo, you must

313

rest content with our despotism here, and enjoy existence under it. This world is too decadent to deserve real liberty, and this is especially true of Italy. Perhaps the new uprising generation may live to realise our dreams. . . ."

"FLORENCE, *March 22, 1816.*

" MY DEAR UGO,—I have received your letter of the 12th of this month with particular pleasure, as I had heard a report of your having blown out your brains. Not that I gave it credit, for I feel pretty sure you are not sufficiently dissatisfied with life to mean to part with it. To threaten and to act is not the same thing, and your hero Ortis killing himself affords no reason for your doing the same ; indeed, I have felt quite easy about you. You enjoy good living and the amenities of life far too well to renounce life itself. I scarcely thought you would feel happy among the snows of Switzerland, but your imagination was assuaged by the thought that you were a genuine victim in the cause of liberty. I believe, however, you are perfectly free to live quietly at Milan with your books and your papers. I am impatiently awaiting your present [volumes of the *Ortis* and the *Ipercalissi*], that you are sending me, for which I thank you in advance. Since you have not yet visited England, you are quite sure to admire the country, although the English have somewhat declined of late from their high standard of the past. You will meet with a poet of whom the English are very proud, Lord Byron. He has talent, but is said to be *un méchant homme*. I hope you will write to tell me your impressions of a country, which is still the first in Europe, and in which all can live honourably without fear of exile or tyranny. There man has every blessing ; he can write and think as he pleases.

" I do not wish to deprive you of your portrait, and if you want it for purposes of engraving, I am ready to remain content with an impression. So I shall have it packed and sent to you. Madame Magiotti has had it

314

copied with your permission. The poor creature is always ailing, and that chills her *bureau d'esprit*. Do you know Botta's poem, ' The Capture of Veii by the Romans ' ? The subject seems dull enough to me.

" Tell me what you are doing. Do not forget to send me news of your journey the moment you reach London, as I want to charge you with some small commissions there.

" Do you know that Sismondi, who has added three more volumes to his *History of the Italian Republics*, is compromised in the affair of Napoleon's return, and that he has sung his praises in face of all Europe ? He is at Pescia, still writing. I have told him plainly what I think of his behaviour. He intends to come to Florence to see Madame de Stael, who means to remain here the whole of May for the sake of a friend (Monsieur Rocca), who is in the last stage of consumption. Her conversation amuses me, and would delight you. But Florence is not a wide enough field for her, for people cannot discuss matters here ; they only grow rude in argument. Monsieur Fabre sends his compliments, and I beg you never to forget my warm and life-long interest in you. I must warn you that pictures imported into England have to pay a duty of a *louis* for each square foot of canvas."

The casual and disparaging allusion to Quirina Mocenni-Magiotti that occurs in this letter just quoted is apparently the sole mention to Foscolo of the child of her beloved Teresa Mocenni, that the Countess of Albany makes in this correspondence. And yet she cannot have been unaware of the little tragi-comedy of those very years 1812–1813, when the poet was residing in Florence and won the heart for ever of Quirina, his " Donna Gentile," the only member of that numerous band of his Graces, who could aspire to any real worth of heart or mind. For, whilst Foscolo was bent on obtaining all the advantage and prestige that was possible

out of his close friendship with the Countess of Albany,
he was also carrying on an amorous intrigue (concurrently
with half a dozen others) with the obscure, unhappy,
and misunderstood wife of the semi-imbecile Ferdinando
Magiotti, to whom, as she herself admits in one of her
letters, she was bound by her hand and by no other tie.
At the time of Foscolo's arrival in Florence, in the full
flush of his literary success and in the full beauty of his
vigorous manhood, Quirina Mocenni-Magiotti was thirty-
three years old, and it was at this somewhat mature age
that the cultured daughter of the passionate Teresa
Mocenni met at last with the *beau-ideal* of her wistful
dreams in the handsome but unscrupulous author of
the *Sepolcri* and the *Letters of Jacopo Ortis*. Before
their formal introduction to one another in the house
of Leopoldo Cicognara, the sculptor, Ugo and Quirina
had already met by chance and fallen into mutual love,
without need of speech, as they passed one day in the busy
Via Por Santa Maria, that leads from the New Market
to the historic Ponte Vecchio, at which spot Foscolo
made an immediate and lasting conquest not only of
poor Quirina's heart, but also, as it were, of her very
reason. Madame Magiotti, who was then living in the
narrow Via dei Servi, between the Duomo and the
Piazza dell' Annunziata, soon gave way before her ardent
lover's fierce protestations of undying devotion ; she
admitted him to every meeting he demanded ; she
nursed him tenderly during a dangerous fever in the
Villa dell' Ombrellino, at Bellosguardo ; and later she
put her slender purse at his disposal, whereof in after
years her lover shamelessly availed himself ; a circumstance which alone would make such a personage as Ugo
Foscolo contemptible and repulsive in the eyes of most
people, though it does not seem to have detracted much
from the honour wherein he is still held by his own
countrymen. But can we wonder at Madame d'Albany's
sharp reminder to her favourite Ugo of the difference
between false and real honour, when the patriot-poet

316

prated theatrically to her in his letters of that particular virtue ? Louise of Albany with her long experience of men was able to distinguish the good from the bad in Foscolo, and to deal with him accordingly ; but the poor, infatuated, fascinated Quirina remained head over ears in love both with the disreputable man and with his undisputed genius ; blindly condoning his extravagant life for which she stinted herself to pay, his constant gallantries, and even his abominable acts of treachery. She only saw his fame through a golden haze of devoted attachment. Even in Florence she must have known his professed love for herself was being extended to various other women, to whom he wrote amorous notes in terms of undying affection, such as the following specimens addressed to herself.

" *Signora mia !* This evening I shall be with you. If you do not go to the theatre, I shall remain a long time with you. If you do go to the theatre, I shall quickly depart. If you refuse to open your door to me, I shall kiss the very doorstep amidst my tears."

Or this sprightly message, written apparently during his long illness in the villa at Bellosguardo.

" *Buon giorno, Quirina, Buon giorno !* Pray to God for me, for this bitter weather indeed affects my health, and freezes my soul and body, so that I shall soon have my very heart frozen too, unless I can have yourself ever beside me to keep it warm. . . ."

Truly, real love such as Quirina's is blind, or else is purposely kept blindfolded !

Deprived of her adored Ugo's presence in the summer of 1813, Quirina found her sole remaining pleasure in dwelling on the memory and genius of her absent lover, though she must have been aware that Foscolo was busying himself in Milan with the conquest of a fresh Grace, in the person of Maddalena Bignami. But somehow Quirina's adoration, or infatuation, was proof

against all evil reports, and even against the clearest
evidence of her lover's worthlessness and infidelity;
she was not even sickened or disheartened by a horrible
piece of vulgar vengeance, which he wreaked on one of
her own sex at Zurich, in the days of his voluntary Swiss
exile.   For it seems that in this town Foscolo, according
to his immutable custom, must needs go philandering
after a certain Madame Pestalozzi, wife of a doctor in
Zurich, and because this silly woman preferred the
blandishments of an elderly Italian tutor to his own,
Foscolo—such infamy seems almost incredible—in his
jealousy and wounded pride actually informed the
husband of his wife's intrigue, and then triumphantly
told the whole story of this escapade to the unhappy
" Donna Gentile " in Florence ! *   Yet in spite of this
brutality of conduct to another; in spite of his cold-
blooded indifference to herself; in spite of the fact that
he was a borrower from women and never repaid his
debts, Quirina never once flinched in her devotion
towards one who was, notwithstanding so many acknowledged blemishes, still first of poets and first of Italian
patriots in her eyes; she saw the clay feet indeed of her
idol, but this discovery, however painful, seems to have
increased rather than diminished the original ardour,
wherewith she had chosen to worship him ever since
their first meeting in the streets of Florence.   Her steady
attachment to his genius for so many years, and her continued exertions to keep his name before the public have
undoubtedly operated to win eventually for Foscolo
that deathless fame which the Countess of Albany was
always vainly urging him to attain; and it is largely
due to Quirina's unreasoning, unselfish love that this
man of genius, the story of whose career must ever arouse
our contempt and abhorrence, was finally honoured
with a place of burial in the nave of Santa Croce, the
Pantheon of Florence, close to the tombs of Alfieri and
Machiavelli.   Quirina herself, who worshipped so stub-

* Quirina calls Foscolo's letter containing this admission *una letteraccia.*

318

bornly and so blindly, survived her lover for twenty years, dying in July 1847, and being buried in the Green Cloister of Santa Maria Novella, the great Dominican church in Florence, where her simple monument can be seen to-day. She died in a cold sunless old house in the neighbouring gloomy Via Melarancio, whereon pious hands have placed a marble tablet to one whose memory is far more worthy to be perpetuated than that of the erratic and contemptible genius, whose bones were specially brought from their humble resting-place in Chiswick churchyard to be interred with civic honours within the hallowed precincts of Santa Croce.

With regard to this particular allusion to the poor "Donna Gentile," in Madame d'Albany's last quoted letter, the Countess (to whom Foscolo already owed fifty *louis* besides other trifling sums) had been specially asked by the poet, who was an adept in tactful dissimulation, to allow poor love-sick Quirina to obtain a copy (of course at her own expense) of his portrait, which Fabre had painted in the autumn of 1812. By various cunning ruses, he had contrived to extort this favour on behalf of Madame Magiotti from the not over-willing Countess, and hence the brief, half-pitying, half-contemptuous remark in the letter quoted. In any case, the desired end was attained; so that the humble Quirina, a nominal friend although a conscious or unconscious rival of the high-born Countess of Albany, secured her coveted copy of the picture. Madame d'Albany's slighting allusion to the daughter of her beloved Teresa is not pleasant to read, yet somehow one can scarcely marvel at her mingled pity and contempt when we read the half-crazy rhapsody of the love-lorn "Donna Gentile" over the picture of her absent and neglectful paramour.

"I have got it! I have got it! I hold thee! I see thee! And I seem to see thee as I did that very day we met between the Ponte Vecchio and the Mercato

Nuovo, and thou didst make my heart beat so violently !
I did not know thee then, but my heart spoke to me
before my head, and even now those same thrills make
my pen tremble so that I can barely guide my fingers.
Yearning, hope, fear, sorrow, all overwhelm me at once,
whilst thy haughty countenance speaks to me of a separation from thee, a prolonged and perhaps an eternal one.
Yet here in front of me stands thy counterfeit as real
as life ; and, believe me, I do not dare approach my lips
near it, for there is more soul than body upon that canvas,
and to kiss it would seem a profanation to me."

Certainly the " maternal interest " (as Quirina herself
ironically calls the Countess' relations with Foscolo)
was infinitely to be preferred to this unwholesome
vapouring for an unworthy and fickle adventurer.
Certainly from every point of view the " Donna Amata "
of Vittorio Alfieri had every cause for self-congratulation,
seeing the miserable and ignominious treatment of the
love-sick " Donna Gentile " of Ugo Foscolo.

CHAPTER XVI

LAST DAYS OF THE STUART QUEEN

Quoique Reine, elle est Femme. Il faut que l'art de plaire,
Prêtant à ses vertus un aspect moins austère,
     La dédommage largement
Des superbes ennuis que le trône procure !
                                        CHEVALIER DE SOBIRATZ

THE last twelve years spent in Casa Alfieri were essentially
years of peace, almost of stagnation. Every day the
Countess led the same existence, walking each morning
clad in an old-fashioned cloak and bonnet along the
Lung' Arno towards the wooded lawns of the Cascinè,
dining on her return, spending the hours of the afternoon
in reading and writing (and how indefatigable a correspondent she had grown it is easy to realise from the
extant masses of letters addressed to her from every kind
of person and from all quarters !) and passing her
evenings in the reception of the same company, seated in
the same chair, in the same room. Her reputation for
past romance as the widow of Prince Charles Stuart and
the adored lady of the great Alfieri, and the vogue of her
salon naturally invested the rapidly ageing woman with
a deep amount of interest or curiosity on the part of those
persons in a humbler station who visited Florence,
tourists as we should call them in these days. The
short sturdy figure of the " Reine d'Angleterre " plodding;
rain or shine, along the banks of the Arno at the same
hour and in the same queer garments, became a familiar
and a popular spectacle for such persons, who constantly
watched for a glimpse of this little old lady who preserved scarcely a trace of her once vaunted beauty and
attraction. She was openly saluted with respect by the

officials or loungers of the city, but certain irreverent persons were wont secretly to make game of this living relic of a bygone age and fashion. A cruel epigram of the period expresses this idea, in poking fun at the gaping strangers, who each morning waited, probably at the instigation of a guide, to stare at the former Queen of Hearts taking her daily exercise.

> *Lung Arn' ammiravano i fuorestieri*
> *Una reliquia del Cont' Alfieri ;*
> *Si crede il fodero del pugnale*
> *Secondo i fisici è l'orinale !*

(On the banks of our Arno the strangers regard
A relic of Count Alfieri the bard ;
But so old and so altered the lady appears,
Her framework alone has survived the past years ! *)

The physical condition of the Countess seemed indeed to defy the passing years, in strong contrast with her younger companion Fabre, who had long been a martyr to chronic gout, throughout which he was nursed by her with great patience and devotion, as the unkindly d'Azeglio himself admits, when in after years he occasionally visited at Casa Alfieri " in grateful remembrance of the sweetmeats given in his boyhood." † Already soured and depressed by political adversities, the Countess grew more and more cynical and self-centred as time advanced, and took away one by one the surviving friends of herself and Alfieri. A few weeks before Waterloo, the death of the virtuous and learned Abbé di Caluso broke the chief link of her old life with Alfieri, for Caluso was the last surviving intimate friend of the poet, and had spent much time with the Countess after his death. With him perished her oldest and most valued correspondent, and though many of their letters still remain, yet they were by the Abbé's expressed wish so mutilated or defaced, that a large part of their contents, and that probably the

* E. Del Cerro, *V. Alfieri e la Comtessa d'Albany.*
† *J. Miei Ricordi*, vol. i. p. 85.

most interesting part, is undecipherable to-day.* On Caluso's death, the Dante ring, that had been bequeathed him by Alfieri was doubtless returned to the Countess, for it has eventually found its way into the Musée Fabre at Montpellier. There can be no reason to suppose, as an Italian writer has hinted, that the Abbé never received this historic trinket, and that Madame d'Albany withheld it in order to bestow it on Fabre, for it would probably be restored, either freely or on request, after the Abbé's death to the Countess, for whom alone of all living persons would it possess any special significance ; whilst after her death it naturally and very properly devolved with other precious relics of Alfieri upon the French painter.

A year or so later the Countess lost another friend of a humbler kind, but one whose loss was keenly felt both by herself and by her companion. This was Dr. Edouard Fabre, who has often been mentioned in the course of this book, and whose death in the summer of 1816 Sismondi deplores.

" The death of Doctor Fabre," he writes, " will undoubtedly have caused you grief, Madame, if only for the sorrow it will have brought to your friend. Up till now he has had the good fortune to possess a near relation in a foreign land. It was for him like standing on a plot of French soil, for in the midst of Italians he had a man sharing his views, his prejudices, and recalling all the scenes of his infancy. So long as his brother survived, he scarcely inhabited an alien land." †

A curious little side-light into the daily existence of this lonely pair—if any pair of congenial persons can in reality be accounted lonely !—appears in a scarce and forgotten little French book of memoirs, the *Souvenirs de Soixante Années*, of Étienne de Lécluze. The passage is worth quoting as presenting us with a clear picture of

* G. Mazzatinti, *Le Carte Alfieriane*. (*Giornale Storico*, vol. iii. p. 30.)

† *Lettres Inédites de Sismondi*, p. 290. Madame Fabre, the mother, had already died in 1809.

the grey calm evening of life, which was now the portion
of the Countess and also of the invalid painter, still
absorbed in their mutual worship of Alfieri and still
debating over the destination of the precious contents of
Casa Alfieri, after the death of the mistress of the house and
the death also (which could not be very far distant) of
Fabre himself, who was seemingly in a deplorable state
of ill-health. For some time past, the Countess had
surrendered to Fabre's wish to bestow the whole of these
valuable relics on the town of Montpellier, and though
she had originally thought of giving them either to Asti,
to Florence, to Turin or to Milan, she had ultimately accepted Fabre's plan, whereby the three libraries of herself,
of Alfieri and of Fabre, together with the valuable collections of paintings and engravings of the latter, might for
ever be kept intact in one place. This decision does not
seem very unnatural when all the attendant circumstances are taken into consideration, although to this
day Italian scholars profess to feel sore and aggrieved
at the transfer of so many relics of the great Italian poet
to a French provincial town. The following little account
throws some light on this point, in addition to supplying
us with a pathetic sketch of the aged Countess and her
invalid friend.

" When Étienne saw Fabre at Florence, the latter was
suffering cruelly from the gout,'and every day the Countess
of Albany was wont to spend three or four hours of the
morning with him. Fabre owned a valuable collection
of paintings formed by himself, also a great part of the
library of Alfieri, which the poet had bequeathed to
him.* A friendship of long duration had existed between these three persons during Alfieri's lifetime ; and
after his death, this tie, becoming simplified, gave greater
force to the regard between the two survivors.
" When Étienne made the acquaintance of this pair,
Alfieri had been dead more than thirteen years, and

* This is evidently a mistake on the narrator's part.

Fabre was nearly sixty, whilst the Countess of Albany had reached the age wherein the change of features in women leaves not a vestige of the beauty or charm of youth. Clever and especially endowed with that ease of manner which only belongs to the great world, she then gave one the impression of wishing to attract by the goodness of her disposition rather than by her shining mental gifts.

"When the state of the gouty artist so permitted, he supped at table, after which Madame d'Albany and Étienne usually passed into the library, full of volumes that had once belonged to Alfieri. Étienne eagerly set to examining them, and the Countess lost no opportunity of fingering them herself and remarking upon their beauty. Those volumes of the writings of the great poet, which she had herself edited and bound, seemed the objects of a species of worship to her. . .

"The real interest that Étienne displayed in visiting this library, precious in itself and yet more precious in its memories of its former owner, seemed to touch the Countess, so that one day, whilst examining these books, she said to him, ' I should very much like you to carry away a memento of our great poet.' Then taking two volumes from the shelves, she went with Étienne to Fabre's room, where the artist was sitting in a great arm-chair by his bedside. ' I think you will approve of my intention,' she remarked. ' Here are two works of our Alfieri's in duplicate. Will you make a present of this set to Étienne ? He will be very grateful to you, I am sure.' Fabre then examined the two volumes, read their titles and returned them with a smile to Madame d'Albany, who placed them in Étienne's hands.

"This little action was not perhaps wholly disinterested. In fact, some days later, Fabre, feeling better, himself showed all his pictures to Étienne, and in the Countess' presence observed to him : ' Having no relations, my intention is to devise this valuable collection to my native town of Montpellier.' Madame d'Albany gave a sign

325

of approval, and both of them begged Étienne to make known this important bequest by means of the *Journal des Débats.*" *

Another, but a less pleasing glimpse of the Countess is afforded us by Lady Morgan, who in imitation of Madame de Stael and great ladies such as the Duchess of Devonshire, was wont to speak openly of Madame d'Albany as "her dear Queen." The following anecdote certainly does not present us with a very flattering account of her reputation for natural kindliness, but it is interesting nevertheless as proving to us the exclusive attitude combined with occasional outbursts of familiarity which formed the usual pose assumed by the royal widow of Charles Stuart.

"It happened that my countryman, Mr. Moore (Thomas Moore the poet); my husband, and myself were seated on a sofa in our old palace in the Borgo Santa Croce looking at the cloud-capt Apennines, which seemed walking in at the windows, and talking of Lord Byron, from whose villa on the Brenta, Mr. Moore had just arrived, when our Italian servant, Pasquale, announced "The Countess of Albany!" Here was an honour which none but a Florentine could appreciate! (for all personal consequence is so local!) Madame d'Albany never paid visits to private individuals, never left her palace on the Lung' Arno, except for the English ambassador's or the Grand-Duke's. I had just time to whisper Mr. Moore, 'The widow of the Pretender! Your legitimate Queen, and the love of your brother-poet Alfieri!' and then came my turn to present my celebrated compatriot, with all his much more durable titles of illustration; so down we all sate and 'fell to discourse.'" *

* *Souvenirs de Soixante Années.* The article announcing the donation was inserted in the *Journal des Débats*, August 9, 1824.
* Lady Morgan, *Book of the Boudoir.* Also Reumont, *Appendix*, pp. 385–387.

The presence of so eminent a poet as Tom Moore was sufficient of itself to render the Countess affable on this occasion, but Lady Morgan comments severely on Madame d'Albany's capricious behaviour at other times.

" The Countess of Albany could be the most agreeable woman in the world, and upon the occasion of this flattering visit she was so. She could also be the most disagreeable, for like most great ladies, her temper was uncertain, and her natural hauteur, when not subdued by her brilliant bursts of good humour, was occasionally extremely revolting. Still, she loved what is vulgarly called fun, and no wit or sally of humour could offend her." *

On another occasion Lady Morgan, in order to curry favour with this capricious Stuart queen, actually made an absurd scene on the occasion of George III's death, in January 1820, when suddenly striking a theatrical pose she greeted the Countess with two extemporary lines in French.

> *Grande Princesse, dont les torts tout un peuple déplore,*
> *Je viens vous annoncèr, l'Usurpateur est mort !*

" What usurper ? " was the not unnatural reply of the mystified Countess who, however, was certainly flattered at this novel (and to speak the truth exceedingly objectionable) mode of announcing poor old King George's demise ; although she herself was indebted for half her income to his late Majesty and even possessed a picture of the Prince Regent, which she affected to value highly.

In this monotonous but far from unpleasant existence, the last years were spent. With the exception of a visit to France, undertaken with the   ' object of seeing Fabre's native town of Montpe   , a the summer of 1822, the Countess rarely left the palace on the Lung' Arno. Universally distinguished, if not actually beloved,

* *Ibidem.*

327

she lived on at Florence, a privileged great lady in the city of her adoption, growing ever more cynical and pessimistic, yet conscientiously fulfilling her social duties to the last. For some months after her return from France, her health, always so far excellent thanks to her frugal diet and healthy mode of life, began to show signs of a break-down, in spite of the care spent in striving to prolong an existence, which ever since Alfieri's death she had always described as irksome. Symptoms of dropsy made their appearance in the closing months of 1823, whilst in the January of the following year her condition became so grave, that finally Fabre warned her of the suspected fatal nature of her malady. She then prepared to meet her end with calmness and resignation, though suffering much at the last, especially from an incessant thirst. Even so late as January 24 she still owned sufficient strength to write to her favourite sister Gustavine, who was now living with the old Princess-Mother at Frankfort. Terribly alarmed and saddened by the bad news from Florence, poor Gustavine had for some time been sending anxious inquiries and offers of assistance, so that the concluding pages of the *Portefeuille de la Comtesse d'Albany* are filled with the pathetic letters of her absent sister.

On January 19, she writes thus on receiving a bad account of her eldest sister, whom she constantly speaks of as her true mother, though Louise and Gustavine must of necessity have seen comparatively little of one another during their life-time.

" . . . My dear, good sister, I have just received your letter of the 10th. It makes me wretched. My God! Take jelly if you cannot eat solid food, for that ought to support you. I also implore Monsieur Fabre to write to me, if writing tires you. He will gain my warmest gratitude thereby. But, O God, what does the doctor really say? Why does he not resort to every possible means for you to overcome this weakness? Think over my offer to you. I shall come only too gladly to stay with you until you are well again, my excellent sister, my real mother. I embrace you, and I am terribly unhappy at feeling myself so far removed from you."

After sending an imploring letter direct to Fabre, Gustavine again writes to the dying Countess on January 26.

" Whilst waiting, my dearest sister, for the letter I expect to arrive to-day, and in the hope of diminishing my anxiety, if possible, I begin my usual letter to you.

" I have been most unhappy all this week owing to the bad account of your health. The thought of your illness was almost more than I could endure. I saw you sad and suffering, and I felt sorrow and pain at the thought of the long distance between us. Again, I implore you, my most beloved sister, to send for me to nurse you. Never mind about the winter weather. When you have quite recovered, then I can quit yourself, my true mother, and return home, where all is well. . . . Alas, my darling sister, I have just got your letter of the 17th. Would that you could know with what anguish I awaited it, and what a week of misery I have passed ! You must have realised my unhappiness, for you have made the effort to write to me, despite all your suffering. I thank you from the bottom of my heart. Well-meaning friends try to console me, but I tell them, ' She is more than a sister, she is a most tender parent, and my true mother.' I must tell you that, fearing lest you would be unable to write from excess of weakness, I asked Monsieur Fabre to give me news of you. . . . I am very grateful for your letter, but then nobody loves you as I do, both as daughter and sister. Again, I beg you send for me, if I can be of service. I am ready to start, day or night."

Gustavine's last letter is dated February 2, four days after the beloved sister's death. She had just received a sad letter, the last she was fated ever to obtain, from the

329

Countess, which the latter had contrived to write on January 24.—" My dear Sister," so the heart-broken Gustavine hastens to reply, " I have your letter of the 24th. It wrings my heart to a degree I cannot express. Nevertheless, I thank you for your affection in writing thus, and have only the time to send you my love." *

There is pathos to be found in these concluding letters from various persons in the *Portefeuille*, many of which deal with trivial matters and ask advice or sympathy from a dying, and even a dead woman, for at a quarter past seven on the morning of January 29, there passed peacefully away Louise of Stolberg-Gedern, widow of Prince Charles-Edward Stuart, and the surviving " Donna Amata " of the great poet Vittorio Alfieri. A consistent if not a very devout Catholic, she departed from this life fortified duly by the full rites of the Church; whilst by a special decree of the Grand-Duke Ferdinand III. her body was interred in Santa Croce.

The stilted notice of the deceased lady, published in the official *Gazzetta di Firenze* of February 7, is perhaps worth quoting here.

" The Imperial and Royal Grand Duke Ferdinand constantly honoured the Countess of Albany with open signs of approval and esteem, since he regarded her as a choice ornament of his Capital, and sincerely hoped that the rising generation of Florence would find an edifying example in the true majesty of her upright and loyal manner of life. This enlightened Prince, after feeling deep anxiety during the course of her fatal illness and an intense regret at her demise, has permitted by his sovereign will that her body should repose in the Church of Santa Croce.

" The high esteem, wherein She was held by the Imperial and Royal Arch-duke Leopold,† was amply proved by the many opportunities he had sought for intimate con-

---

* *Le Portefeuille*, pp. 647–651.
† Afterwards Leopold II. of Tuscany, who abdicated in 1859

versations with Her. Her death has also been a severe blow to the August Princesses, who have lamented in death the virtues they have admired in life.

"Every human being secretly nurtures the germ of his own destruction. The Countess of Albany was naturally inclined to dropsy, and certain symptoms had for many years past caused her some degree of ill-health. But four years before her death, very grave symptoms had appeared, whilst finally she was attacked by a feverish catarrh, causing an intolerable thirst, constant accessions of high fever, a weakness of the pulse, lack of appetite and other distressing signs of illness. Still, she suffered no acute pain, and never thought her end was near. At last, however, she was warned by faithful friends that her malady was gaining on her, and that her life was threatened, whereupon She fortified herself with those aids that pious Mother Church offers to her own children at their last moments on earth. And thus in the full possession of all her faculties, by turns praying and comforting her grief-stricken friends, She passed away on the twenty-ninth day of January 1824, at a quarter past seven in the morning, to the grief of the City which she had selected for her residence." *

Although the Countess of Albany lived to the considerable age of seventy-one years and four months, yet she was the first to expire of the four Stolberg sisters; Princess Castelfranco (formerly Duchess of Berwick) dying in 1829, the Comtesse d'Arberg in 1836, and the unmarried Gustavine so late as 1837. The old Princess-Mother, who was living with her youngest daughter at Frankfort, and was still even in spite of her advanced age absolutely devoted to dress and amusement, survived the Countess by two years, dying in 1826. The famous English historian, Earl Stanhope, was once introduced to her at Frankfort, where he " found her in extreme old age still lively and agreeable. It is singular," he com-

* Reumont, *Appendix*, pp. 396, 397.

ments, " that a man, born eighty-five years after the Chevalier, should have seen his mother-in-law ! " * Only in the month previous to the death of the Countess, the dissatisfied and critical Gustavine had told her eldest sister that " our Mother is very well. She is very much excited about her winter gowns. She has purchased a white one, which she made me inspect to her delight yesterday, whilst I kept on thinking how much better employed she would be in busying herself with what is good and serious, instead of taking pleasure in such follies as have occupied her mind, so it seems to me, during her whole ninety years of existence."

Of the various eulogies and expressions of condolence received by Fabre on this sad loss of a friend, who in his own words " had made his life a pleasant one for thirty years," the following letter from the warm-hearted and generous Adèle de Souza must suffice here.

"[Paris]. *February 9th,* 1824.

" How I pity you, Monsieur, and how deeply I feel your loss, the loss that we have all sustained ! Where can one find again, so good, so indulgent, so sympathetic a friend ? I shall lament her all my life, for I loved her with my whole heart. I don't believe that in the whole course of her life she ever did a thing or said a word to hurt anybody.†

" I should like to know if my poor friend suffered much ; if her last moment was hidden from her, that terrible moment abhorred of our natural weakness, despite all the courage and moral reflections wherewith we have armed ourselves against it during life. Ah, Monsieur, if you are not equal to writing to me, dictate a line to someone at hand—in any case, tell me of her, for my heart craves for news. Also tell me of yourself. What a long and happy intimacy broken at last, and for ever. You must

* *History of England*, vol. iii. p. 558, *note* 2.

† Madame de Souza must have generously forgotten or forgiven the extremely disagreeable letter sent to her by the Countess in 1814 !

feel as though your days, your hours, your very life had stopped ;—ah, how well I understand it. Be well assured, Monsieur, that the friend of my good and dear friend will always find me interested and sympathetic, and that you must send me your news as though I could pass it on to her. So I am waiting impatiently for a word from you, for I really believe I am the sole person who can properly estimate your sufferings.

"I had written to her for the New Year, to send my greeting and wishes for her good health and good fortune. Alas, in my letter, I spoke of her return to Paris, for I was very, very far from imagining I should never, never see her again.

"Did she ever receive my letter ?

"But I shall make an end, Monsieur, since I do not wish to add to your grief by dwelling on my own. Tell me your news, speak to me of my poor darling friend, and accept my most sincere sympathy.

"A. DE SOUZA." *

By her will, carefully drawn up and attested on March 29, 1817, the Countess made a variety of bequests. To her two married sisters, the Princess Castelfranco and the Comtesse d'Arberg, she left mementoes in the form of silver and costly china, whilst to her favourite Gustavine she bequeathed the sum of 15,000 *scudi*, presumably the bulk of her savings out of her not very large income, which, as we have already shown, ceased abruptly at her death. Other specific bequests are not without interest.

To her nephew, the Duke of Berwick, head of the illegitimate branch of the Royal Stuarts on the Continent, she left a cameo portrait of the Pretender and also a tortoise-shell box, inset with miniatures of Mary Queen of Scots and of the Cardinal of York. To the Florentine galleries she devised the two celebrated portraits by Fabre of herself, and of Alfieri, which to-day adorn the

* *Le Portefeuille*, p. 655.

French Room of the Uffizi, and also the picture of *The Death of Narcissus* by the same artist. The portrait by Fabre of her valued friend the Abbé di Caluso, she left to the head of his family; whilst to the patriotic Abbé Luigi di Breme she bequeathed a likeness of Alfieri from her own hand, on the back of which the poet had inscribed a sonnet. To her old friend, Cardinal Consalvi, " the Siren of Rome " (who died within a few days of the Countess herself), she named another work by Fabre, a half-length painting of St. Jerome. She also commanded her general heir to pay annuities to her two servants, Luigi Biondi and Gaetano Masi, who had spent over twenty years in her service. Her heir-general, as might have been expected, was none other than François-Xavier-Pascal Fabre, son of the late Monsieur Joseph Fabre, a painter by profession, born at Montpellier, in the department of the Hérault, dwelling in Florence at No. 2320, Via de' Mori *—" I have decided to nominate him as my Universal Heir so as to prove my gratitude for the attachment he has ever borne me, in which I have never been deceived during twenty-four years, and upon the continuance of which I can with certainty rely."

One very important provision in this will, composed nearly seven years before her death, was subsequently invalidated by a donation during life, doubtless at the instigation of Fabre. This was the bequest to the Library of the Brera, at Milan, of practically the whole of Alfieri's books and manuscripts, together with a marble bust of their former owner, the Abbé Luigi di Breme being entrusted with the execution of this bequest. But with the object of keeping intact the valuable possessions of Casa Alfieri—the books and manuscripts of Alfieri, her own library and a large collection of pictures owned by herself and Fabre—the Countess made a complete donation of the whole of the contents of the palace on the

---

* Apparently the narrow Via del Moro, that runs from the Ponte alla Carraja towards the piazza of Santa Maria Novella.

Lung' Arno to her Universal Heir, who subsequently surrendered nearly all the Alfieri manuscripts to the city of Florence; whilst, as we shall presently show, he removed the libraries and works of art into his native land of France. To one who is not an Italian, this decision seems fair and reasonable enough. Fabre's anxiety to obtain possession of the belongings of the Countess was certainly not prompted by any base or mercenary motive, when he proposed to her his scheme for placing all these valuable and historic objects in one museum in his natal town of Montpellier; in any case, his arguments seem to have overcome any objection on the part of the Countess, whose former bitterness against France had quite disappeared since the fall of the French empire and the restoration of the Bourbons.

Throughout this biographical sketch of the Countess of Albany we have endeavoured to use strict impartiality. From what has been written therefore, the reader will probably carry away the general impression that Louise de Stolberg, Countess of Albany, was neither good nor bad, but merely very human, and with the usual mixture of human virtues and failings. For she was very far removed from being the prodigy of duplicity and ingratitude that Signore Bertana and some other critics seek to prove her; nor was she a species of aristocratic Magdalen or Marguerite, such as her French biographer, M. Taillandier, portrays her. For our own part, we have described her career and character without favour or prejudice, and as a result we find no reason to agree with Signore Bertana, when he calls her " a sceptical, mocking, gossiping, utilitarian, evil-speaking woman, who denounced patriotism as imposture, valour as folly, justice as a myth, and slavery as the eternal destiny of whole nations . . . and whose only gifts were her superficial powers as a *reine de salon*, a consummate mastery of the art of conversation, and a disposition at once morbid and serene." * On the other hand, she cannot assuredly be

* Bertana, pp. 277–279.

deemed a blameless and romantic princess, whose only
fault lay in her deep attachment to a man who was never
her husband, for her life from the first was very far from
being free from deceit, selfishness and ingratitude. Her
perfidious conduct towards the Cardinal of York would
of itself always remain a dark stain upon her character;
nor have we attempted to excuse it; indeed, its sole
palliation can be sought in the fact that it was Alfieri
himself who largely dictated to her this dishonourable
course. That she was absolutely devoted, body and soul,
to Vittorio Alfieri we firmly believe, and we likewise hold
that the belated attempts to accuse her of infidelity or
ingratitude towards her Friend are not only false, but
also malevolent. One thing, however, is certain in
connection with the Alfieri episode; and that is the
circumstance that it would have been far better for the
present-day esteem and reputation of the Countess, had
she followed her lover to the grave at no great distance of
time, instead of living on for twenty years of a comfortable
and rather prosaic existence; what she gained in her
long life, she has lost in the eyes of posterity. The ease
and stagnation of her latter years undoubtedly helped
to make her character deteriorate; she grew hard and
cynical, whilst yet acquiring a love of gossip which sometimes proved mischievous. Some of her later views on
morality moreover, as addressed to Foscolo, albeit
shrewd and amusing, appear far from edifying in an
elderly woman. It is in truth this long spell of a Florentine residence after Alfieri's death, that has done more
than aught else to root up the fair flowers of romance
which were plentiful enough in her youth, when she was
the Queen of Hearts of Roman society, the ill-treated
but brave and struggling consort of the Stuart king, the
woman beloved and worshipped as a semi-divine creature
by the tragic poet of Piedmont. Indeed, the Countess
of Albany may almost be said to have lived down a sympathetic and poetical reputation; for she survived her
own generation, whilst the rising generation in Florence

only beheld in her a quaint, conceited, satirical, rather spiteful and pessimistic old lady, "*una reliquia del Conte Alfieri*," whose authenticity seemed almost doubtful, such ages ago had her poet expired and the society wherein she had moved and been admired had passed away. Says Professor Callegaris with some degree of truth; "The Countess was an old Legitimist, dragged across the whirl-pool of the French Revolution, ever absorbed in the contemplation of a world that had collapsed, and scarcely able to understand the new era that was dawning." *

But such a statement merely brings us back to our original remark, that Louise, Countess of Albany, was neither good nor bad, but only very human, with a character chequered over with the lights and shadows of faults and virtues, so that it lies with the reader to apportion the exact amount of praise or blame after the perusal of this unbiased biography. We shall, therefore, only sum up one or two salient points that we have decided for ourselves. (1) That the Countess of Albany was fully justified in deserting her husband. (2) That she acted throughout with low cunning and base ingratitude towards her brother-in-law, the Cardinal of York. (3) That her devotion to Alfieri, however much open to censure, was sincere, unselfish and imperishable. (4) That her relations with François-Xavier Fabre were merely those of natural and simple friendship. (5) That in many matters her character, though far from perfect, has been most unjustifiably maligned by certain modern critics.

.   .   .   .

With the death of Madame d'Albany and with the recent restoration of the Bourbon dynasty in France, there no longer remained any obstacle to Fabre's departure from Florence, in order to settle once more in the fatherland to which he had been almost a stranger for over thirty years. The painter indeed, despite his age and his con-

* *Di un Carteggio della Comtessa d'Albany. Op. cit.*

stant ill-health, seems to have been imbued with a strong desire to return to France so as to spend the evening of his life at Montpellier, wherein few persons living could now recall their humble fellow-citizen, who had risen to the highest rank in his profession. But first of all, he made the necessary arrangements to erect the required monument in the Chapel of the Sacrament in Santa Croce to the princess, to whom he owed so much, and who, as he himself simply states, made his life a pleasant one for thirty years. This monument, with its mourning cherubs and classical altar-tomb, was originally designed by Fabre's friend, Perçier, the French architect of the Arc de Triomphe ; whilst its minor details were carried out by the Florentine sculptors Emilio Santarelli and Ottavio Giovannozzi.*

It presents a tolerable appearance considering the soulless epoch of its erection, for some of its ornamentation is evidently intended to imitate the graceful designs of the early Renaissance, in which the beautiful church is so rich. In the tympanum above, appear the shields of Britain and of Stolberg-Gedern, surmounted by a regal crown and supported by the familiar Lion and Unicorn of the British royal arms. As will be noticed from the accompanying illustration, the memorial itself is declared on its pedestal to be the outcome of a grateful heart and of a sincere reverence, which seems to denote accurately the spirit wherein Fabre raised it to the Countess ; but the striking epitaph composed originally by Alfieri is wholly absent from the inscription.†

Having paid this last tribute to the memory of the Countess of Albany, and having carried out various instructions received from her, Fabre prepared to quit Florence, taking with him, by special permission of the Tuscan

* Reumont, vol. ii. pp. 154–156. Vernon Lee, p. 222.

† *A Vittorio Alfierio ultra res omnes dilecta et quasi mortale numen ab ipso constanter habita et observata.* (Loved above all things by Vittorio Alfieri, and ever held and venerated by him as a semi-divine creature.)

MONUMENT TO LOUISE, COUNTESS OF
ALBANY, IN SANTA CROCE, FLORENCE

Government, the greater portion of the contents of Casa Alfieri, all of which had now become his property. First, however, he sorted out the manuscripts of Alfieri from the rest, and these he formally presented to the famous Laurentian Library, that magnificent monument of Medicean patronage, where they are still preserved. For this gift to the city of Florence, which may or may not have been made *con amore*, Fabre was named a Chevalier of the Tuscan Order of San Stefano, by the Grand-Duke, who at any rate thereby proved himself satisfied with his conduct in the matter. After selling the furniture and other domestic objects in Casa Alfieri, the painter now announced his intention to the Mayor of Montpellier of presenting the whole of this valuable and interesting collection to his native town upon certain conditions.

On January 5, 1825, within a year of the Countess' death, Fabre writes thus to the Mayor respecting his decision.

" I own in Italy a very large number of pictures old and modern, books, engravings, sketches, and other objects, which I purpose offering as a gift to the town of Montpellier, my birth-place. My own library in particular includes all important publications on the arts, ancient buildings, museums, public and private galleries, travels of artistic interest, &c. A donation in my favour made during her life-time by Madame la Comtesse d'Albany, born Princess of Stolberg, has rendered me absolute owner of her own library as well as that of the celebrated Count Vittorio Alfieri of Asti. This last includes everything of value in Greek, Latin and Italian literature ; whilst that of the Countess is chiefly composed of the best books in French, English and German." *

This munificent gift to a French provincial town was in fact composed of the three libraries of Alfieri, of the

* Mazzatinti, *Le Carte Alfieriane di Montpellier. Op. cit.* p. 28.

Countess, and of Fabre himself ; whilst in addition there were pictures of varying degrees of excellence to the number of two hundred and twenty-four, besides a quantity of sketches, engravings, bronzes and other objects of art. All this mass of precious books, manuscripts, paintings and other effects was eventually removed out of Italy and arranged in the building of the " Musée Fabre," at Montpellier, where the citizens expressed their sense of gratitude by causing a gold medal to be struck, bearing on one side a figure of Minerva with the words *Musée Fabre*, and on the reverse the inscription : *A. F.-X. Fabre de Montpellier La Ville Reconnaissante*, 1828 ; the year wherein this new collection was opened to the public. The painter, who now assumed the modest title of " Conservateur de la Musée Fabre," was also made the recipient of a barony, and the ribband of the Legion of Honour from King Charles X., in March 1830, shortly before the Revolution of July and the final expulsion of the Legitimist Bourbons. Fabre, who never ceased to suffer acutely from his old enemy the gout, lived on a confirmed invalid at Montpellier, though he undertook occasional visits to Paris, where in the spring of 1835 he was honoured with a public banquet by his admirers. He finally expired at Montpellier, on March 15, 1837, at the age of seventy, having survived the Countess of Albany a little over thirteen years.

His death was made the theme of a public eulogy pronounced by the artist, Garnier, at the *Institut Royale de France*, on March 25, of the same year. In his address the speaker lamented the passing away of yet another distinguished pupil of the great painter David, for his old colleagues Girodet, Gros and Gérard were already dead. Fabre, so Garnier declared in his speech, had had the fortune and honour of an early presentation to the late Countess of Albany, whose influential friendship had undoubtedly proved of especial service to his career.— " His particular talents are marked by extreme purity of design, by rich colouring, and by careful finish, whilst he

340

was greatly attracted by landscape painting. By his long residence at Florence he lost many opportunities for producing grand historical compositions, but found in that city many subjects for portraiture." *

* *Funerailles de l'Institut Royale de France. Pièces Diverses. Notice sur Mr. F. X. Fabre par Mr. Garnier* (1837–1838).

APPENDIX

THE ensuing seven letters from the Countess of Albany to Signora Teresa Mocenni and the Arch-priest Luti are preserved in *Fascicolo A*, 146, 538, at the Biblioteca Marucelliana in Florence. They are not included in Monsieur Pélissier's collection, *Les Lettres Inédites de la Comtesse d'Albany à ses Amis de Sienne*, to which I have often made allusion in the course of this work, nor have they as yet been published, so far as I am aware. Since they help to fill certain gaps in the lengthy correspondence so ably edited by Monsieur Pélissier, I have ventured to include them in this Appendix for the convenience or pleasure of the reader, who may take the opportunity to study the Albany-Mocenni letters, as already given to the public by him in the above-mentioned work.

Illegible and dubious words are frequent throughout these seven letters, and the sense is occasionally obscure, but they undoubtedly form, even in this unsatisfactory state, an interesting addition to Monsieur Pélissier's valuable collection. The dates of month and year have in most cases been filled in by a later hand, apparently that of Quirina Mocenni-Magiotti.

I   "*22 Fevrier* (1800)

" J'ai reçu, ma chère Thérèse, votre engagement avec le Poète que je lui ai remis d'abord. Il attendra pour faire faire son chocolat que les drogues sont à meilleures marchés d'autant plus qu'elles sont déjà baissés de beaucoup. Le sucre et le cacao ne sont pas plus chers que il n'etait il y a deux ans, et alors il a payé son chocolat quatre paules et demie. Pour ce prix on en a du très bon à

342

Florence. Si je ne faite pas assez vite mon marché de livres, je vous renvoyerai votre argent. Je vous dois 42 paules. J'ai à faire à un Jeuf qui veut vendre ses livres comme neuf, et moi je ne veux pas les payer que pour ce qu'ils vallent. Cela fait que je ne cede pas, parce que de les avoir un mois plutôt ou plus tard m'est égale. J'ai reçu le livre sur la France, il y a du bon dans cet ouvrage, mais c'est un livre de parti, comme tout ce qu'on écrit à present. Il a une grande reputation, et il a été écrit pour plaire au Roi de Sardaigne qui est dévote.

"J'espère toujours que votre mari échappera la prison, si la gouvernement s'interesse à lui, car ici on ne peut rien faire pour lui, à ce que m'a dit le Senateur Protecteur. Le carnaval est très triste, l'argent est rare, le pain est cher, tout cela ne rejoui personne. Le tems est aussi si mauvais, il ne peut pas se remettre a beau.—Je salue l'Archipretre. On dit que les Russes restiront de nouveau qu'ils marchent vers le Rhin cette versalité (?) perpetuelle est bien ridicule. Il est vrai qu'ils avoient raison de se plaindre de la capitulation d'Ancone (?). Je crois qu'il y a des gens payés pour brouiller les deux cours. La France y a un grand interêt. Dans peu de jours nous entendrons dire qu'il y aura encore une nouvelle cause de tracasseries. Dieu veuille que nous ne soyons pas la victime de tantes des dissensions, car c'est toujoirs nous qui payons les pot cassés. J'aurais autant aimé que ce Buonaparte soit resté en Egypte avec ses Mamelukes, c'est une tête ardente et active qui fait aller les hommes, et les Francais suivent eux qui les font marcher avec le bâton, et avec des coups de pieds. Il est incroyable que les Français ayont souffert dix ans tous les malheurs possible pour avoir un Roi Corse. Je ne connais rien de plus humiliant. Adieu, ma chère Thérèse. Aimez moi, et comptez à jamais sur ma tendre amitié pour la vie.

"Mille choses à Vittorio.

"(AL SIGNOR ARCIPRETE LUTI, Provveditore degli Studi dell Universita di Siena, a Siena)."

II   15 *Mars à midi* (1800)

" J'avais oublié, ma chere Thérèse, de vous dire que nous avions reçu la Misogallo. Je vous écris donc ces deux lignes pour vous en accuser la reception, et vous renvoyez votre engagement. Mille complimens du Poète. Je vous embrasse de tout mon coeur. Ayez soin de vous, promenez vous, et jouissez de votre liberté."

III   9 *Aout* (1800)

" Je conçois, ma Thérèse, que vous regretterez votre campagne où vous êtes tranquille loin de votre Brontolone, mais votre devoir vous appelle à Sienne et votre plaisir doit y ceder, puisque vous retirez votre fille du couvent. J'avoue que je ne conçois pas pourquoi, car en Italie les filles ne sont bien que renfermées. J'en ai vue de tristes exemples ici dans mes yeux, et je me suis convaincue que les filles doivent rester en couvent jusqu' a la mariage. Leurs sens parlent trop tot dans ce pays ici, elles ne sont pas comme nous qui sommes froides, et puis dans mon pays les etouderies d'une fille ne signifient rien, on est plus sévère pour les femmes. Basta, vous aurez vos raisons pour agir comme vous faites, car vous ne faites jamais rien à la legère, ou on vous force à ne pas faire très bien. J'espère que après votre retraite de tant de tems vous reviendrez dans le monde plus indulgente pour les hommes qui sont comme leur permet la nature qui les a formés de chair et d'os. Il y a quelques êtres priviligiés qui sçavent faire dominer le morale sur la physique. Soyez donc de ce nombre et voyez les pour ce qu'ils sont. Apprennez à les voir comme une lanterne magique, et à ne vous arretter que aux objets ridicules pour en rire. Je suis parvenue à ce point. J'entends les commerages que le soir et je le prends comme une comédie. Apprenez encore a sçavoir vous recuillir au milieu du monde, et quand il n'est pas nécessaire de parler de vous accoutumer à penser. Il est inutile, ma Thérèse, de lire et de réflechir, si vous ne sçavez pas vous en servir pour élever votre âme, mais je ne crois pas le moitié de ce que vous me dites. Nous ne pouvons pas nous empêcher de préferer une chose à l'autre, mais d'abord (?) que nous sacrificons notre plaisir à notre devoir, nous en avons plus de mérite.

"Je suis fachée de ce que vous m'avez dit de vostre figliastre, l'envie difficilement se guérit, il se cache mais ne se deracine guere, il annonce toujours une âme vile. Il est possible que la physique de ce jeune homme soit la cause que son morale soit inquiet. Vittorio est heureusement né, c'est un excellent jeune homme, pourvu qu'il ne se gâte pas. Il a une grande qualite—c'est de vouloir se distinguer. L'amour de la gloire annonce une âme noble et grande. Quel dommage qu'il ne puisse pas faire une carrière brillante, quoique cependant il sera plus heureux dans son état.

"A propos de carrière, Mgr. Consalvi est Cardinal Sécretaire d'Etat. Il la mérite par une conduite noble et ferme, c'est un homme qui a de l'esprit et de l'activite, il travaille pour quatre (*illegible*) et mange très peu.

"Mr. Cicciaporci désire de faire votre connaissance, ma Thérèse, il sera content de vous. Je ne donnerai aucunes nouvelles à l'Archiprêtre, parce que Cicciaporci le lui donnera.

"Le fou de Bristol est encore couru à Sienne. Il va faire faire un tableau plus grand du premier à Fabre. Son argent est bon, et il le depense, ce qui est un bonheur pour les artistes dans ce moment. Adieu, ma Thérèse. Je vous embrasse de t(ou)t mon cœur mille fois. Aimez moi et comptez à jamais sur ma tendre amitié. Je n'ai pas entendu parler des presens de Buonaparte au Pape. Il peut lui donner des Calices, car il doit en avoir la quantité à sa disposition en ayant volé beaucoup. Avez vous déjà le nouveau Gouverneur ? Où est on plus content que du précédent ?

Il G (ran) D (uca) l'a fatto pulito, l'ha sostenuto contro la moltitudine e poi a contentato chi non lo voleva quando a piacciuto a lui—chi piacce quando le case vanno in regola. Il poeta li saluta tutti caramente.

Fabre lavora molto, e li presenti i suoi respetti. Il fratello medico guarisce per lo piu, e non ha ancora mandate nessuno nel paese di lei. Egli e prudente e buon medico e conosce perfettamente il male Gal..., lo guarisce radicalmente, non e poco. Addio, amatemi."

(There follows a long Postscript in Alfieri's handwriting, concerning the proposed epitaph for Gori, which is included in *Lettere Inedite*, p. 261. No address given.)

IV

18 *viii bre* (1800)

" Vous avez été, ma chère Thérèse, aussi étonnée que moi des évenemens. On ne sait à quoi les atribuer, qui assure que c'est une convention entre les deux puissances, qui dit que c'est une infraction d'armistice,—pour moi je ne sais que dire, je laisse chacun raisonner à sa guise. Il faut baisser la tête et se resigner. On n'entend plus rien à la politique, ni à rien dans ce monde, la bonne foi des traités, rien n'est plus sauve, on ne pense qu'à prendre à qui convient, et au cela convient.

"Tout Florence est allé à la campagne. La ville est deserte. On ne voit que du peuple dans les rues, peu de soldats, la force principale est allée vers Avorio, on dit qu'ils vont à Naples. C'est une tache d'huile qui s'étend a l'infini. On n'y concoit rien. Toutes les personnes qui avaient abandonné leur pays avec les Francais sont rentrées, et jusqu'à present elles sont tres tranquilles. Tout le monde l'est. Et l'entrée des Francais en ville paraissait une pompe funèbre, tout le monde pleurait, et pas une personne n'applaudissait.

"Je salue l'Archiprêtre et je le prie de ne pas perdre courage, mais de brûler tous ces livres de politique.

"Mille choses al Signor Cicciaproci, et dites lui que je lui recommande de se saigner, non pas en se faisant saigner mais en étant très sobre, buvant peu de vin.

"Je ne lui reponds pas, parce que je n'ai pas la force d'écrire beaucoup, la lettre est pour tous les amis. Mille remercimens à notre Vittorio. Je suis charmée que St.

Thérèse lui plait. Je lui recommande de se conduire comme il a toujours fait.

"Le poëte vous salue. Il se porte bien malgré tous les chagrins qu'il'a. Fabre vous presente ses hommages, il est charmé que vous êtes contente de la Sainte. Il y a travaillé beaucoup pour qu'elle soit mieux et plus belle pour votre oratoire. J'ai un grand plaisir que vous en soyez contente, c'est une vraie jouissance pour moi. Prenez garde à votre Danois, s'il plait, cela pouvait vous procurer des desagrémens. Il est vrai que les abitans du Nord respectent les jeunes personnes. Adieu. Aimez moi toujours, comme je vous aime. Je vous embrasse de tout mon coeur.

"(*Address.* AL SIGNOR ARCIPRETE LUTI, Provveditore di degli Studi di Siena, a Siena.)"

V

Le 29 (October 1800)

"Vous sçavez, ma chère Thérèse, que le gouvernement provisoire a donné sa démission et qu'il a été remplacé par Chiaventi ci-devant Médecin, Speroni noble de Cortona, et Gover (?) dont j'ignore le ci-devant état. L'avocat Leoni est Président de la Police, il a remplacé Vacca qui a été l'acteur à Pisa. Tous ces messieurs sont revenus avec l'invasion des Français. Nous ignorons si nous avons la paix ni la guerre ou meme l'armistice. Nous vivons dans l'obscurité, au jour la journée, et passons le tems avec l'epaule (?) qui est bien long et bien triste. car il pleut averse tous les jours.

"Je vous prie, ma très chère, de ne me pas confondre avec les gens de la ville qui ne prennent pas l'air, car je sort par tous les tems, meme quand il pleut à sceau, je prends mon parapluie et galoppe comme s'il faisait beau tems et je m'en trouve très bien. Je crois cependant que une situation humide comme Piano et où la brouillard domine et les eaux sont mauvaises n'est pas un endroit saine pour personne. Ayez soin de vous, pour vos en-

347

fants et pour vos amis. Je Vous envoie deux petits volumes à l'addresse de l'Archiprête, que je vous prie d'accepter et de ne montrer à personne, en les lisant vous en verrez la conséquence, et si même vous en entendez parler n'avouez jamais que je vous les ai donnés. Je me fie a votre parole que je connais aussi sacrée que la mienne.

" Le Poète vous salue, il ne fait plus qu'étudier le grec et a renoncé a poetura. D'ailleurs il est trop mélancholique pour avoir le courage de faire des vers.

" Mille complimens al Signor Antonio. Je ne sais aucunes nouvelles à lui écrire, nous vivons dans l'obscurité. On dit que le Comte de Cobenzl est allé à Lunéville avec Joseph Buonaparte à ce que disent les gazettes que je ne lis guère, mais qu'on me raconte. J'ecris peu et pour cause. J'aime à parler franchement, et la franchise n'est pas à l'ordre du jour. Tout le monde veut faire le mal, mais ne veut pas qu'en leur disse sotto il muso (?). Adieu. Tiriamo avanti alla meglio, après la pluie vient le bon tems. Il n'y a rien de durable dans ce monde. Pope dit que tantes les operations humaines sont fondées sur le sable.

" J'embrasse ma Thérèse et salue Vittorio. Je prie l'aimable Triumvirat de ne pas m'oublier et de m'aimer, parceque je le mérite leur étant très attachés. Mardi j'ecrirai al Signor Antonio, forse ci sara qualche nuove.

" (*Address.* AL SIGNOR ARCIPRETE LUTI, &c.).

VI   6 *Decembre* (1800)

" Je suis charmée, ma chère Thérèse, que vous pensez sérieusement à vous guerir de cette incommodité qui étant prolongée peut devenir très nuisible à votre santé. Ayez soin de vous, je vous en prie. Nous avons un tems abominable, il pleut jour et nuit, c'est un terrible hiver.

" Je tache m'occuper le plusque je puis pour agreer (?) le tems passe plus vite, mais il s'en va à pas de tortues, ainsi que d'autres que je connais, mais qui arriveront cependant. J'exhorte l'Archiprêtre a se faire courage,

348

"apres la pluye vient le bon tems," et mon Baromètre annonce que la Tempête passera. Il doit se ressouvenir que mon Baromètre est excellent, qu'il a ete fait par un Professeur de Pavia. Toutes les choses excessives ne peuvent pas durer, par consequent il ne peut pas grêler éternellement. Je vous prie de dire la même chose al Signor Antonio. Il est affreux d'avoir un hiver aussi rigide avec tous nos autres meaux. Je suis charmé que notre Vittorio soit si raisonnable que de mériter d'etre admis dans la société des Dames Cicciaporci, cela doit lui donner de l'emulation pour se conduire toujours mieux.

"Nous ne savons plus rien des nouvelles politiques, on ne parle ni de paix ni de guerre. Il parait qu'on traite (?) à Luneville puisque Mr. de Cobenzel y est. Dieu veuille nous rendre le repos et la tranquillité tant desirée et tant attendue. Dites al Signor Antonio (pour ne pas multiplier les lettres) que mon beau-frere traite (?) directement avec le sien pour l'affaire en question, et qu'il n'a jamais pense à revendiquer l'ancienne dette.

"Le Poète se porte bien et vous salue tous, il est impossible de lui (*illegible*) pour la Thérèse, car il ne fait plus rien que de lire du Grec, ainsi excepté des paroles de cette langue il n'écrit plus dans aucune autre pour le moment. Vous sçavez que lorsqu il entreprend une chose *le vuol spuntare.*

"Je ne puis pas envoyer les livres promis et pour cause. J'exhorte l'Archiprêtre à se calmer la tête et a s'occuper de ses Tusculans (?) et de tous les ouvrages de Ciceron qui s'est trouvé dans ce mauvais momens.

"Adieu, ma chère Thérèse, ayez soin de votre santé. Aimez moi autant que je vous aime. Je salue l'aimable Triumvirat et la lettre servira pour tous les trois. J'espère que vous y *devinerez* les sentimens que m'animent pour Vous—Vous avez entendu parler de la colère du Baron de Falkenstein de ce que Mr. Theodore s'etait emparé de sa titre (?) et avait mis le (*illegible*) dessus, il veut le

349

revoir plutot ou (*illegible*) un procés très sérieux—Dites moi si vous sçavez cette affaire ?

"(*Address*. AL SIGNOR ARCIPRETE, &c.).

VII

"Je remercie notre Quirina, ma chère Thérèse, de m'avoir donné de vos nouvelles pendant que vous étiez à soigner votre mari qui probablement sera guéri à présent pour se mettre en route Mercredi. Vous souffrirez terriblement de la chaleur. L'époux attend l'épouse avec beaucoup d'ardeur, comme l'époux du Cantique des Cantiques, et on dit dans un grand orgasme, on distrait son ardeur charnel en lui donnant des pepins de melons a pialler peur en faire de l'argent (?). Cette première nuit sera curieuse, et la Quirina sera obligée de le conduire, et s'il prend gout il la faire mentira. C'est absolumment comme un Asne, car la tête (?) n'y sera pour rien.

"Nous étouffons al solito, et il pouvait que le chaleur ne veut pas diminuer. Vous trouverez Fabre un peu déconcerté. Son père, qui était Hydropiaque, a en Mardi une attaque d'apoplexie dont il a un coté tout perdu et ne peut pas parler. Il vit, mais comme hier au soir il était plus mal, il est possible que ce matin il sera mort, ce qui serait bien heureux pour lui et pour eux, car un être dans cet état est trop malheureux, et rend tout le monde tel. La femme est au desespoir, car c'était sa seule société, ne connaissant personne ici, et les femmes ne sont pas capable de lui tenir compagnie sur tout le soir. Adieu, ma chère Thérèse, au plaisir de vous revoir. Portez vous bien. Mille choses à la Quirina.

"P.S. Je salue l'Archiprêtre qui a béni cet extra-ordinaire mariage.

"(*Address*. AL SIGNOR ARCIPRETE, &c.)." *

* This letter is most carelessly written and most difficult to decipher in many places. *See also* chapter xi. of this present volume.

INDEX

351

z

Printed by
BALLANTYNE & COMPANY LTD
Tavistock Street Covent Garden London

Lightning Source UK Ltd.
Milton Keynes UK
UKHW050641150421
382040UK00008B/613